FREEDOM
FROM
WITHIN

A Gift of Love

Teresa Alexander

BALBOA.
PRESS

A DIVISION OF HAY HOUSE

Balboa Press books may be ordered through booksellers or by contacting:

Balboa Press
A Division of Hay House
1663 Liberty Drive
Bloomington, IN 47403
www.balboapress.com.au
1-(877) 407-4847

ISBN: 978-1-4525-0180-2 (sc)
ISBN: 978-1-4525-0181-9 (e)

Printed in the United States of America

Balboa Press rev. date: 04/17/2012

FOREWORD

My late husband and I first met Teresa in 1997 when she came to live in Port Stephens and from all conversations with her, both inside and outside our church, we soon came to realise and appreciate her special qualities and many gifts which she shared with us and others.

Our friendship grew as we became aware of her sincerity, her love of God for people, the love and care of her late father, together with her family and friends and her willingness to help others in any way she can.

Teresa is able to express herself through her counselling and ability to all who come to her for help with their problems, her oneness with God and nature and her inspirational poems and writings as witnessed in her 'Poems from the Heart House' published in 2003, and many treasured words she has written for me and others which continue to comfort and inspire.

Life hasn't always been easy for Teresa but her dedication to God has made her what she is today, sincere and courageous - a blessing to all who have the privilege to call her 'Friend'.

Having read with interest Teresa's book 'Freedom from within' I believe her writings will help both young and old who need them. They offer opportunities for growth within, and their growth will be for the world's benefit.

Being now in my mid-nineties I have naturally experienced highs and lows along the way which relate to some of Teresa's experiences, questioning how I dealt with happenings in my life which are foremost in my mind. Her writings are interesting and challenging and will certainly influence my travel into the future, and with God's help and those of my family and friends my journey will be filled with love, joy and hope.

♥ Maisie Sparrow

WHY I WROTE THIS BOOK.

Three days after major surgery, still on the drip, my spirit left my Body! I floated above; clearly seeing it was my body lying in the bed. Hearing nurses speaking, my thoughts of them immediately had me travelling through the wall to the nurses in their room.

I heard them say, "We don't know what is wrong with her." I had all of my Faculties accept the ability to physically touch. I was aware of other dimensions. My deceased mother and grandmother were telling me by thought form to return to my body. My response was "No, I don't want to go back." Several times I refused in thought until finally my mother or grandmother sent the thought "Well if you don't want your body one of us will have it." The moment I thought "No" I was back into my body with a jolt.

If I could return to the physical form there were answers to so many questions I needed to understand. Death wasn't the end if one could come back to the physical form.

I had experienced and learned of the beauty and the fear of other dimensions. The realm of higher intelligence is not the place to experiment. There can be manipulation by living and deceased thought forms of others. The need for understanding and protection for yourself in this life and from others manipulation that is not love based. Understanding of life's forces is essential. This is particularly important where you can be open to outside spiritual forces that may attempt to use fear thoughts to put you off balance. The majority of people do not understand death, don't discuss it and probably fear it. By reading and finding your own truth may the beauty of life give you freedom, understanding, trust, no fear and accept

the wholeness of love that is. My love for the future and the well being of all has prompted me to share my journey.

Is there a purpose for life? That was in 1984. Since then I have observed myself to become aware what brings me inner peace, lack of love, confrontations or reaction. I have watched my self in relationships and observed others in theirs. In 1990 I commenced writing this book. Freedom from within has brought me to the depths of inner love to sustain me in peace throughout my journey. Freedom from within is written to assist you to bring the love, joy and inner peace back into your life. When we are born we are free, somewhere the joy is lost.

May the reading of this book from higher intelligence give you the support and the understanding to live in the joy and love of the moment where time doesn't exist?

In the totality of love, love is. It is only with fragmentation that negative forces are created to take you away from love. Peace and stillness as you grow and enjoy the journey to your inner freedom. "Know thyself."

INTRODUCTION

The journey to freedom is one of patience. Studying these few pages for your understanding takes time. They will certainly widen your vision. Many people tell me that they want more information around a statement I make. This means you need to seek your personal understanding to find your own reality. It has taken you many years to decide on this quest. There is much healing to be done within. Your years of accumulation of non-loving thoughts used by the Ego can be changed to supportive loving thoughts. Your life will be filled with joy as you commence achieving your hearts dreams to be true to self in total love. Allow yourself the time to be still and aim to complete your understanding of yourself and your journey. The depth of the writing requires understanding, completion of each sentence for your own truth. The following pages take attitudes; examine them that the information contributes to healing within. Your reward freedom, love and fulfilment on your journey to maximise the opportunity in living the life we were born to live. If this book helps you to love your self, when you have always been there for others but not yourself your journey is just beginning. This takes courage, honesty, vulnerability, trust, intimacy, sharing, and caring, respect and total faith.

DEDICATION

Dedicated to my father Richard Lachlan Alexander 1909-2005. My father had a passion to become free by understanding the human mind. He was singular in his journey believing that to obtain freedom for one could free the world.

Misunderstood by some he journeyed for the most part of his life in isolation.

The following poem written by our father is authorised by him to go in this book that he knew was to have my dedication to him.

OUR FATHERS GIFT

GOD IS A MYSTERY, BUT THIS WE KNOW
HE CREATED US ALL AND ALLOWED US TO GO
WALKING THROUGH EDEN, THE CHOICE WAS OURS
THE TREE OF LIFE, OR KNOWLEDGE, BAD HOURS

WE ALL BLAME THE PAST AND DAD AND MUM
AND DON'T HAVE THE GUT'S TO GET OFF OUR BUM.
FOR GOD IS STILL LIVING AND SO IS HIS SON
WHO CAME HERE TO TEACH US, NOT FOR FUN.

THE LESSON IS THERE FOR ALL TO SHARE
THAT THE CHOICE IS OURS, IF ONLY WE CARE.
DON'T REACT TO THE PAST, TO RITUAL AND ROT.
CAST OUT ALL THE JUNK — INTO THE POT.

CHRIST LEFT INSTRUCTIONS AND BUDDHA LIKEWISE.
A WHOLE HOST OF OTHERS AS WELL, WHO WERE WISE

AND THE LESSONS IS THIS, IT'S EASY TO DO
IF YOUR KEEN ON LIVING AND NOT IN A ZOO.

LET YOUR MIND GO QUIET WHEN TROUBLES APPEAR
DON'T WORRY, DON'T QUESTION, JUST STAND THERE, NO FEAR,
AND THEN FROM WITHIN YOU, NEW POWER WILL ARRIVE,
WHICH IS NOT OF THE MIND, BUT THE THING TO SURVIVE.
THIS NEW THING WILL FUNCTION, RESOLVE ALL YOUR DOUBTS,
DESPITE ALL THE CONFLICTS, OR TROUBLES OR SHOUTS

'TIS NOT FOR THE FEW, JUST THE PRIESTS OR THE OLD.
FOR CHRIST'S INJUNCTION WAS EVER SO BOLD.
KEEP THE MIND OF A CHILD, DO NOT GET COMPLEX.
SEE THINGS AS THEY ARE, KNOW WHAT TO DO NEXT.

DOWN THROUGH THE AGES THIS WEAPON HAS BEEN
THE STRENGTH OF THE MEEK, THE POWER OF THE KEEN.
NOT THOSE KEEN TO HAVE MONEY, AUTHORITY, LIES,
BUT THOSE WHO LOVE ALL AND LIVES SATISFIED.

R. L Alexander 1968

CONTENTS

The Golden Grail, the quest for understanding self. Why the journey, why life? 1

Do we live a life of inner joy and freedom? 9

What is the Soul? 13

Suicide 18

An instrument of light 22

Death, Dying or Living 28

Which path? 32

Sensitivity 35

Friend or foe 38

Being true to our self 41

Self image 46

Work 50

Confidence/Fear 57

Feeling Unloved 61

Energies affecting others and one's self 66

Seeking Direction 71

Meditation 76

Categorize 81

Environment 86

Higher Intelligence 94

We are one with the universe 101

Marriage 104

Numerology 109

Miracles of Love 113

Time 121

God, I am. 126

The leaf of life 134

Do it your way 135

Life is for living 136

Our healing park 138

My guide 139

No expectations	140
Play the game	141
Observation	142
The challenge	143
Tradition	144
New chapters	145
Smile on the day	146
Be still	147
Friendships like a river	148
Courage	150
For today	151
Christmas	152
Birthday beginnings	153
Thank you for today	154
Our tree	155
Loss, the joy of having	157
Mothers gift	158
Fathers gift	159
Self observe	161
Opening your heart	162
This moment	163
The road to success	164
All things pass	165
Life is good	166
Count your blessings	167
Birthday celebrations	168
The joy of the years	170
Little boy	171
There is a room in the heart	172
Oneness	173
Life's destiny	175
Natures bounty	176
Beauty to enjoy	177
A special friend	178
Once in a while	179
Beauty is around	180

Open pathways	181
Enchantment in the moment	182
Put out your hand	183
Gentle time	184
I love you as you are	185
Honest living	186
Feeling new	187
Home is where the heart is	188
United	189
Love comes	190
A mother's world	191
A special person	192
Forever there	193
What is a friend	194
The rose	195
My troubled friend	196
True love	197
Greetings my friend	198
Greetings brother	200
My brother	201
Loves declaration	202
Reaching out	203
In my heart	204
Family love	205
In the garden	206
The joy of sharing	207
Come my friend	208
In this life together	209
Your inner child	210
Birthday remembrance	211
Write your dreams	212
The proposal	213
Sharing for the moment	214
Graces Christmas	215
Family Christmas	217
Courage my friend	218

A time of parting	219
My big sister	220
Life times shared	221
Life times shared cont	222
The key	223
Destiny	224
Quiet times	225
Smile as you learn	226
Live	227
Another chapter	228
The realization	229
Meditation day	231
The awakening	232
Love in focus	233
The state of grace	235
A day of learning	236
Birthday reflections	237
The secret of the poem	238
Which path	239
The airport	240
Self growth	241
Lighten up the heart	243
A Christmas prayer from a child's heart	244
Merry Christmas	245
Faith, goodness, grace	246
Love is power	247
Never give up	248
Opening new doors	249
Christmas reflections	250
Birthdays journey	251
Open up your day	252
Music of the voices	253
Complete your journey	254
The mirror of the soul	256
The power of thoughts	257
Love is trusting	258

Breathe softly · · · · · · · · · · · · · · · · 259
Life is change · · · · · · · · · · · · · · · · 260
A shared world · · · · · · · · · · · · · · · · 262
Letting go · · · · · · · · · · · · · · · · 263
Support · · · · · · · · · · · · · · · · 264
The path of learning · · · · · · · · · · · · · · · · 265
My future · · · · · · · · · · · · · · · · 266
Until death do us part · · · · · · · · · · · · · · · · 267
Hullo my friend · · · · · · · · · · · · · · · · 269
Claiming today · · · · · · · · · · · · · · · · 271
Communications gift · · · · · · · · · · · · · · · · 272
Beauty in Creation · · · · · · · · · · · · · · · · 273
With you · · · · · · · · · · · · · · · · 274
Surgery of joy · · · · · · · · · · · · · · · · 275
To serve · · · · · · · · · · · · · · · · 276
Looking for the beauty · · · · · · · · · · · · · · · · 277
Moving forward · · · · · · · · · · · · · · · · 278
Treat me gentle · · · · · · · · · · · · · · · · 279
Inner searching · · · · · · · · · · · · · · · · 281
Throw away the can of worms · · · · · · · · · · · · · · · · 282
Life is a wonder · · · · · · · · · · · · · · · · 283
Kind wishes · · · · · · · · · · · · · · · · 284
Healing in the process · · · · · · · · · · · · · · · · 285
The ego · · · · · · · · · · · · · · · · 286
Atonement · · · · · · · · · · · · · · · · 287
Sunshine after rain · · · · · · · · · · · · · · · · 288
On a song · · · · · · · · · · · · · · · · 289
Seeing our self · · · · · · · · · · · · · · · · 290
Healing –the release from fear · · · · · · · · · · · · · · · · 291
A better world · · · · · · · · · · · · · · · · 292
America Think Big · · · · · · · · · · · · · · · · 294
Take the first step · · · · · · · · · · · · · · · · 296
Grace, gratitude and gladness · · · · · · · · · · · · · · · · 297
The child within · · · · · · · · · · · · · · · · 298
A day at a time · · · · · · · · · · · · · · · · 299
Quiet times · · · · · · · · · · · · · · · · 300

Stillness in the moment   301
The heart of the garden   302
Laughter from the heart.   303
New beginnings   304
Freedom waits   305
Life's journey   306
Brighten up your day   307
Faith in your growth to beauty   308
Dignity   309
Reach for the Stars   311
the highest tower   312
Mothers' care   313
Meet the day   314
Here to Learn   315
Family Ties   316
Welcome Aboard Australia   317
The Five Cent Coin   319
A Song For Australia   322
Skippy   323
This Sustains Me   324
Reflections   325
The Birth of the Messenger   326
The Box of Toys   327
What is love   328
Insight leads to love   329
My secret garden   331
Life's celebration   332
The courage to try   333
It is safe to say goodbye   334
Enjoy the day   335
The journey of life   336
Let your best friend be yourself   337
Recognition comes   338
Focus on the beauty   339
Life is a gift   340
Don't shoot the messenger   341

Dearest dreams	342
Sweet song	343
On loves terms	344
The first step	345
Poetry in motion	346
God bless the child within	347
Opening the heart	348
Turning hurts and pain to glory	349
The path of the heart	350
The journey ever onward	351
Birthright	353
Start to sow what you want	354
The front of the queue	355
Enjoy the experience	356
Life isn't a risk life is an opportunity	358

HERE TO LEARN

IF LOVE IS THE REASON
WE COME INTO THE WORLD.
NOT MATERIALISTIC GREED, WEALTH,
OR THE FOCUS ON JUST OURSELF.
OUR FOCUS MUST BE TO LEARN
TO GIVE OF THAT SPECIAL LOVE.
BY OBSERVING SELF WITH WHAT WE SAY,
ALLOWING STILLNESS FOR GUIDANCE FROM ABOVE

EACH ONE TO SELF OBSERVE,
TO REALLY BE AWARE.
ALLOWS EACH TO MAKE THEIR CHANGES
IN THE TIME THAT WE ARE HERE.
WHEN EACH ONE ALLOWS A MIRROR IMAGE
TO REFLECT WHAT THEY HEAR AND SAY.
THEN EACH ONE CAN SEE THE PICTURE
OF WHERE THEY DECIDE TO CHANGE.

LOVE ISN'T FULL OF SELF
WITH ANGER, PRIDE OR FEAR.
IN FACT THE EMOTIONS OF JEALOUSY,
TOLERANCE OR SELFISHNESS DO NOT APPEAR.
LOVE CONTAINS NOTHING BUT LOVE THAT COMES STRAIGHT
FROM THE HEART.
THE ONE TRUE LOVE OF GOD THAT TELLS US WE WILL NEVER
BE APART.
EACH ONE MUST FOCUS ON THEIR JOURNEY
WHILE THEY ARE HERE WITHOUT CONCERN
EACH DAY GIVES US OPPORTUNITY TO BECOME THAT WE CHOOSE
TO LEARN.

LIFE IS FOR LIVING

So you have a challenge,
A further chance for growth.
Just how to go about it
To ensure you gain the most.
Stay at the top of where you are
With your spiritual insight.
Follow your faith to focus there
To turn darkness into light.

For doubt or judgement brings you down
When you focus on your plight.
Energies are passing; so be your faith,
Stay up in the positive white light.
Know that learning comes from
Courage in believing who you are.
Continually working upward.
A happy sparkling star.

Pick your gifts to help you.
Faith, courage, love.
Know you are a winner when you
Engage the higher energies from above.
For happy is the moment
When we take our self in hand.
Happy is the moment when
At last we understand.

THE GOLDEN GRAIL, THE QUEST FOR UNDERSTANDING SELF. WHY THE JOURNEY, WHY LIFE?

So you want to learn, I wanted to teach. Now I understand that all learning comes from self-realisation. One becomes the words. As you teach you should observe the words and from this observation can come your learning.

The majority of people accept another person's concept as their belief, religion, and behaviour pattern because it appears to be in line with the majority of people's beliefs. It is easier.

Now ask yourself the question; does this make the belief right? Years ago it was claimed the world was not round. Aeroplanes were not possible. Fortunately change is possible – if one has an enquiring mind and does not accept imposed limitations. A mind that does not accept imposed limitations has the opportunity to recognise and create something new.

A theory, an object, an emotion of energy. Is it necessary to look for something new or have we the essence within us now? Possibly repeat the patterns and follow the same path of our parents with an expected heavy load.

A job. It sustains us for security for food, shelter, family support and all the materialistic embellishments that humanity has created an assumed need for.

In the expectation of the struggle for these things is created that energy output from the individual that is multiplied many times in the world. Despair, grief, low self-esteem and many other negative thoughts. As others absorb this energy it begins to dominate many other lives. Few rise above this energy: most do not. Another name for it is stress or fear.

Man has tried to develop a conscience over the centuries justified from imposing their will on others in the name of education and criticism of other beliefs, customs and laws the very essence that is theirs. What gives another the right to impose their will on another? Do I hear you say there

would be chaos without it! There is war now with it. There is fear, jealousy, hate, poverty, rape, vandalism loneliness and we wonder why people finally think or say "What is life for or about? Or do I want to live?

Do you really want to ask the previous questions and really consider your answer as an observer of yourself? Let it be what you yourself feel, see or think and not that of someone else. It is only then you can identify your own quality of life. The reason for life and what you would like to do. Only the individual can choose to make changes through their free will. It is wrong to inhibit or attempt to manipulate another. Each person has a right to choose their own path, to live their destiny. So let us begin our enquiry to find your own truth.

Is there reincarnation Yes No?
God or death as in final Is the soul or energy force preserved in any way?
 Heaven?
Our birth. Do we have a choice Yes No?
If so, why? Is it for learning or karma?
Birth date Coincidence or important as in Numerology that
 Indicates the planes, strengths, weakness on our
 intellectual, emotional and our physical planes.
Parents Do we choose them, the family type, patterns.
 Behaviour i.e. alcoholic, rich, poor, karma
If rebirth Is it the same soul with the opportunity to
 Accumulate learning? What purpose?

A baby is born dependent, feeling aware and observant. Parents try to support to maturity. Mans support usually falls into the category of conditioning. I.e. Dependence. In order for you to survive you need me, therefore I expect from you: -
You belong to me

You will do this
You will not do that
You will not eat that
This is love
That is not love

In this way we have conditioning. The child already arrives with a deep subconscious list. The acknowledged list of recognised lessons, learning opportunities for this current life' time. To learn, understand the knowledge of cause and effect. Some call this karma.

In the first seven years of life there is an extra protection around a child as they are open to all energy forms around them. A child absorbs parents conditioning, observations of the environment and experiences with others in the community. The child now has a measurement of expectation. Therefore conflict for as long as there is expectation there is dissatisfaction, disappointment, hurt, feeling not loved, anger, jealousy, fear, failure, loss etc. when the expectation is not met. Where the expectation is met there is happiness, love, a feeling of being loved, joy, sharing, success, confidence, and self-esteem. I am a winner, etc.

We have experiences of monetary, intellectual learning, sexual nature, and relationships, practical learning with the hands, emotions, feeling, and knowing. There is opportunity for soul growth from both negative and positive experiences. To maximise these experiences we must be observing to learn, to change, be focussed. To be very clear where we wish to move foreword too. We also need to know exactly what the total meaning is to achieve our chosen destiny? If it is love then love cannot be fragmented. Love is total love. Any thought, vocalisation, action that is with total love needs to be recognised giving opportunity for free will to become the action of love. Self-awareness is the key to life, the opportunity to follow our heart. Age does not necessarily give wisdom. If one believes

the purpose is to accumulate and become the energy of love opportunity through inner seeking is there to create joy daily.

Some souls will never question to go forward, to go beyond basic man made principals of materialistic greed and power for others or for themselves. We are all responsible for our own journey. In health we are what we eat and think. Crunch time comes and we think. I am not happy. None of my expectations have been met. What is life about? Who am I? Where is the beginning? What am I here for? Therefore what do I have to achieve?

Let us share the journey together.

We know that no matter what the discussion it returns to cause and effect.

The world is full of dissatisfaction, anger, ill health, material wants. Someone else created these. Yet we have marvellous words for many centuries with the answers so why is it we are not applying them?

Yes you are what you think and eat. What about the power of positive action? When you self observe would you want to manifest the thoughts you are thinking now? Thought creates hope, love, despair, hate. Most people think about someone else's actions. Is it because they do not believe their own action creates change for it is the silent approval to allow what is happening to continue? Until we can accept that all thought creates energy that shows itself; we will remain ignorant of the greatest influence to our lives.

Ever changing, a special moment of richness, then it is gone. We try to recapture it in so many ways. We hope for the same again and in the comparison we lose the presence of the now. The moment of stillness, experiencing nature, maybe a taste or perfume. It is called expectation. A measurement. When we expect or measure and the comparison isn't there we feel loss, loneliness, unloved, all the negative emotions that lower self worth, self-esteem. So why do we measure? Generally speaking for all the 'so called' new discoveries in the material world man is a creature of habit. Relying on others to set the stereotype framework of their life. Where does

this acceptance that other people make the decisions to run our lives come from? Has man given up the quest for self? What does he think it is? It isn't measurement of material success for at all levels of acquisition of wealth, business success, fame, family life, this has failed to appease.

The difference in people's life styles, religions, has created wars, envy, resentment; the need to possess and still it has not worked.

So why or should we say why not look to see and apply the common bond of the base of the religions, the lifestyle? Yes! It has been done before, but it has only been words. We must not assume a common thread. Knowledge of love must be applied. Best results come from one to one teaching, small groups, classes, until when there is a gathering locally, worldwide, TV. Etc we broadcast the words and each one accepts, rejects, perceives it their way or ignores it. So if it matters or is important enough to us we listen, we discuss, decide on our change and become it. Freedom then becomes the action: it is not fragmented in any way. Freedom just is, the individual is responsible for their own change either deliberately or by being exposed to the environment and being conditioned. Until there is responsibility for the individual's own purpose of what life is about, not lip service, there will be no purpose. After all, how many people really question life? They accept what is handed to them. Man has always scorned anyone that dares to be different without substantiating facts. Yet so many people previously labelled mad are now called genius; people with insights before the people are ready to accept their truth. Still man desires proof. Well it is there for each individual. Even telescopes or brain scans do not bring in all the thought waves available to us that are now being shown by scopes (dimensions, frequencies) this time the prize is beyond comprehension. It is only when individuals seek their own truth that it becomes their own. Those who have found it are generally scorned by others who have not. Fortunately more awareness comes daily as each person's sensitivity can increase to claim what has always been his or hers. When will we reach a point where the awareness of knowing exceeds that of not knowing

and the opposite force helps all to attain insight, of course you have to want to. Choice is what life is about. Listening is the key. In that stillness is the message. What you do with the message will always be up to the individual.

BE STILL

LET THE SILENCE ENTER THAT LITTLE
CHAMBER FILLED WITH LOVE AND LIGHT

THAT IN THE SPACE ONE MAY SEE
AND BE GIVEN MORE INSIGHT.

A HEART OF JOY IS FILLED WITH GOLD,
COURAGE AND STRENGTH FOR A FIRM FOOTHOLD.

SO REMEMBER THE PEACE FROM WITHIN
WHEN YOU WERE STILL.

STILLNESS IN THE MOMENT

THIS MORNING I HEARD THE BIRDS;
IT SEEMED THAT TIME STOOD STILL.
THEN I CAME TO REALISE IT WAS MY MIND;
SO QUIET AND STILL.
EACH SANG THEIR JOYFUL CHORUS
AS THEY CALLED IN THE NEW DAY.
BE STILL AND BE AT PEACE,
IT IS THE ONLY WAY.
WHEN OUR MIND IS FULL OF THOUGHTS
THAT CHATTER DAY AND NIGHT.
THEY DO NOT LEAVE THE SPACE
WHICH ALLOWS US OUR INSIGHT.
THE VERY SPECIAL GUIDANCE
WHICH REACHES TO OUR HEART.
THE MESSAGE WHICH GIVES US HOPE
AND SHOWS US HOW TO START.

Do we live a life of inner joy and freedom?

How much of life do we actually live? Of course, we are here. We go through the motions of living. Yes people think that what happens has to be, it is normal, a pattern. A child lives each moment anew. There is no measurement of expectation. It is written that unless we become like the mind of a child we will not pass through the eye of the needle. There is an approach that all things are possible. That everything is there for us. Conditioning replaces all things are possible with possible, maybe, never, why bother.

It is recognised we have a left and a right side to the brain. The right using the gifts of intuition and a knowing from within, while the left works on the linear physical plain. Both balance us. The intuition side is often shut down. Constant noise, voices, internal thoughts, all of these can contribute. Even other people in our space, their thoughts and activities can distract us.
One needs stillness.
Intuition, at times referred to as clairvoyance or clairaudience is available to everyone.
The balance of left and right brain activity allows maximum development of intellect and our higher intelligence that is very beautiful. The mental plane may become very materialistic without the connection to higher intelligence.
 Monopoly forces hardship that makes people form attitudes of resentful, bitter, insecurities that if the world is fortunate will make them question the real purpose of life. Now the capitalist system is the drive for control more people are questioning what is important. Due to this more people are finding spiritual guidance as they seek for the pathway to happiness. In time acceptance will seek to retain these gifts in the children. Many negative traits will be reduced, particularly materialistic and sexual ones. Spirituality should not be a control either. The individual must live to true

values, self worth and to ever alter what they deem necessary to become enriched for living love, of self and others moment to moment.

Self-observation is essential to identify and to clear the shadows of past pain, regrets etc from the subconsciousness to allow for new blossoms of love through self worth. How wonderful that each individual can become that which they choose to be. There always is a choice. We should all want to love and to be loved. Doesn't everyone want to be loved and to share love with others. If we all strive toward love the world will have an increased vibration towards love that benefits everyone and allows each person to feel. Knowing what real love is commences the beginning of each ones quest to freedom. There is a saying: you can lead a horse to water but you cannot make it drink Love leaves the other free to accomplish growth. The choice is theirs to make them theirs if you show them by the example you set or discuss with others and they choose to let this become their reality. We loose nothing in giving, in fact we gain everything if the other equips them selves and becomes self-sufficient. There is nothing to be gained if you do it for them.

So what is life? Do we make the most of our opportunities? Do we question? After all, if earth is one of the worlds for learning what is it that we learn? If one listens to the questions asked of very elderly citizens it is; "what do you put down to your great age and health"? In other words is there something you can say that will help us to live longer. Is it an attitude that changes the outcome, the food we eat or physical exercise and movement we take? Knowing what you know now, would you do it differently given the opportunity to live from a young age again. Often the answer is "I wish I knew many years ago what I know now." So we do want to live forever; or do we?

Is it fear of death, or the unknown? Many cultures have different religions but there is a common thread- good karma, bad karma. Soul, heaven, hell, reincarnation, life ended, learning, reward, evil, punishment, that God is Love.

Let us consider one of these possibilities.

Your inner child

The needs of your inner child
Are buried deep within.

So be still and recognize them
So your real life can begin.

For years of pleasing others
At the expense of your self;

Stops you being real
To live with your true wealth.

So enjoy your solitude,
Do not feel alone.

For the dreams will surface;
At last you feel at home.

Be kind to this inner child,
Do not deny the self.

God bless and keep you
As you discover your true wealth.

Faith in your growth to beauty

Under the ground in the fertile earth are the bulbs
awaiting their full creation.
Maybe forgotten, maybe you know.
They wait for suitable conditions .
Nature lifts the temperature
As they quietly begin to grow.
In the dark, unseen,
You may not even know.

Then the green shoots appear
As they grow from the earth.
With the promise of spring time
To fulfil their true worth.
The buds that form
Promise beauty to see.
A scent so soft to
Please us now free.

For the flowers now open
In colour and form.
Remind us our journey
Can suddenly transform
So if you appear blocked and
You are not sure of the way.
Be still, count your blessings,
Your strength for today.

Tomorrow will be brighter and
your heart with a song.
For faith in its beauty
will carry you along.
Your thoughts are your journey
that you create while here.
So be positive and think to sow
Good will and good cheer.

WHAT IS THE SOUL?

The soul, what is the soul? From personal experience of having been outside my physical form, the soul is that which can survive without a vehicle to carry it. The soul is the life force, the energy that has access to all that is, and all that we have ever known and can observe thought, more unrestricted on the other dimensions. Enter and leave its physical body. Be aware of the thought forms of others: either through their speech or thought forms. Many have experienced out of body soul movement but it is only now that people are beginning to share and talk openly about such experiences and to discuss them with others.

Why haven't they wanted to talk about these things? Before many were made to die a cruel death when it was revealed they had insight into spiritual awareness.

Such soul knowledge and spiritual awareness is possible because of an extra perception or power that is available to mankind. It isn't something you can measure, change, tax or easily control. So is it that word control? After all man controls others. Why is this? Is it because not enough people are yet asking the question such as why life? What for? Where do I fit in? What do I want from within myself? Is what we are all doing the purpose of life? How can that be when there is loneliness, poverty, greed, dislike, envy, and materialism with all the fears that go with it when there is not faith and trust in having enough? Man creates what is. All thoughts create an effect to a greater and lesser extent. Individually in a small way, but collectively many thoughts are magnified and can create change. The cause and effect theory is well known, but until each individual sows thoughts of love to create positive outcomes the effect will be the results of the negativity they have asked to come into their life through not being aware of their thoughts. Individually we have the thought power to make a decision about how to live in a better world. Everyone is responsible for his or her own thoughts. There would be no war tomorrow if we all thought

only love. Love is self-perpetuating. To each is given the opportunity to put their internal house in order.

One can live in the now where there is no time. A state of doing! No thought of the past or of tomorrow. Most of us live in a conditioned response to yesterdays conditioning. Time is created by this pattern of desire and expectation.

Do you believe in reincarnation? What if it is the learning ground where you are given the opportunity to learn from your experiences and if you don't learn the experience will be repeated until you do? Then you can move on to other learning for internal growth. Have we looked at all the possibilities or do we believe what we have been conditioned to believe? Not from our heart but a remembered story that we accept without question. If it is right why do we live in fear of death and one could almost say the inability to enjoy the moment in a happy world. So can there be belief where there is fear? One doubts it. Yet the world is filled with fear. So are you marking time in this life time letting it pass you by hoping the life after death gives you all you think you are missing here?

We draw all our learning from different environments, countries, skin colour, riches etc. so you would need many vehicles, wouldn't you?

So death as we call it, the shedding of the physical vehicle is necessary before a new one.

Many cultures, particularly in eastern societies, believe in reincarnation. The west is now adopting the same possibility to an ever-increasing degree. Shouldn't we be open-minded to this possibility, discuss and read about it. Think about it and even be still without thought. In that stillness can come a new awareness that can open each individual to living from his or her heart. Once you have experienced this and identified the joy of just being your life will never be the same again. Make your own decision. Whether you accept or reject, you will have decided yourself. Hopefully you then are left with the decision that self worth is the mainstay of any soul. This

only comes when one is honest and puts their own house in order by daily observing self to make yourself a better loving soul instead of a life time deciding what you think would improve others.

So you accept there is reincarnation. So is there a choice to come back or can your soul stay in or out of body state? From my experience, it can. My life has never been the same since my experience gave me the purpose for life and in that new awareness the journey has purpose. Once you have a clear objective of what you think life is about your purpose is strengthened to motivate you in what are perceived to be difficult times by selecting accumulated knowledge to work through and gain new learning from the experience.

NEVER GIVE UP

COURAGE ISN'T EASY.
IT COMES FROM DEEP WITHIN.
WHEN WE GLIMPSE WITHIN OUR HEART,
WE HAVE THE GUIDE OF WHERE TO START.

EACH DAY GIVES US THE CHANCE TO TRY.
TO STOP OUR GOAL FROM PASSING BY.
LITTLE VICTORIES ALL ADD UP.
SO KEEP ON TRYING, NEVER GIVE UP.

KEEP NOTING THE PROGRESS ALONG THE WAY.
IT SUSTAINS US, GIVES PATIENCE ALONG THE WAY.
COURAGE IS YOURS TO KEEP ON GOING.
YOU HAVE PROGRESSED WITHOUT REALLY KNOWING.

REST IF YOU MUST TO SEE WHERE YOU ARE.
THEN RE FOCUS ON YOUR BRIGHT STAR.
FOR EVERYTHING YOU HAVE EVER WANTED.
CAN BE YOURS IN THE TIME ALLOCATED.

HULLO MY FRIEND

When life becomes hard and
The road seems all up hill.
Your heart feels full of dread.
People are unkind
For reasons of their own.
You wonder if they stay that way
When in their own home.

From observing other people,
We find much to learn.
Even if it is to realise
Their own lessons they must learn.
Life has a purpose
For each and every soul.
For each to seek and follow
To achieve their own goal.

Some will seek out riches
With adornments around their neck.
While others seek out pleasure and
Only look for sex.
Blind to the beauty
The world puts in their way.
No joy in life for them they say,
Unless they drink night and day.

Put aside all these things,
For God has promised more.
The joy, the laughter and the learning
Must be behind another door.
Money cannot buy it,
Not any amount of wealth.
The joy we seek is in our heart,
Deep within our self.

SUICIDE

Perhaps you considered running away from class. Suicide. To suicide is to be without purpose. To not believe any goal is achievable by self. Self worth is nil if you think the soul ends at death this is the state which will hold you at death. Thought power is retained, it is not lost. Full observation remains. You will be held in the darkness or where ever you perceive yourself to be until this thought state changes. However if you believe in reincarnation for soul growth and feel you will do better next time, but have had enough this time consider the greatest gift is the opportunity to manifest soul growth that comes from experiences while in the physical life. To deprive the soul of the physical vehicle is to deprive it of the opportunity for growth towards the white light, becoming total love. There is black light away from love so you wouldn't be considering this option if you understood the purpose of being here and applied the courage to continue. This is a far greater opportunity offered than out of the physical form. For this reason the soul can be deprived from the protection of the white light as the individual surrounds themselves with negative thought patterns blocking positive thoughts from getting through. Until the individual softens to a questioning attitude where there is now not such a barrier for attempts of love to flow through. Then and only then is change possible. The damage from reaction can be sufficient to put the souls progress back several life times. Remember where we have progressed from, there are others wanting the opportunity to continue their life journey. Ignorance is often the cause of hurt as is malicious intent. Both these face the unprotected soul. Do you believe in the path to love? Has it become your path? Now ask yourself the question? Do you want to go back several life times and incur repetition of many of the struggles for learning you have already passed through only to face this fear again, to be able to deal with the issue to move on. Continuing on is the purpose to achieve freedom from your fear. Moving forward, now stronger and wiser. Learn to live in the now,

without yesterday and worries of tomorrow being present to stop us living today. Loving self, giving self in substance to carry you over the difficult time. It is time to look at achievements, re-establishments of goals and the activation of steps to continue forward. The moment you do this, you cross the void. Another path is open. Remember that suicide is not an escape. If one proceeds to suicide they will face the situation again. It will be necessary to pass through birth, childhood to that point in time again and hopefully have the purpose and the strength to go beyond this next time around. All obstacles present opportunities to clear past karma that we may deal with it and with that understanding have no need to experience it again. We then move forward to the next lesson. If we can continue joyfully to handle all situations and rise above all obstacles these obstacles become opportunities for growth. In any lifetime a soul is generally given experiences that can be handled. Obstacles are self-created. We create the negative thoughts that bring loss, poverty, illness and other negative experiences into our life. Having entered into the Ego experience we need to learn to get out of it into the life of freedom in the moment where every thought is one of love for life in total bliss. The Ego being when thought controls instead of using the roll to support the heart. It has been written of great prophets i.e. Jesus, Buddha Mohammed that they never spoke an imperfect word so that their every word or thought was a perfect creation. Yes we are responsible and must rise above our patterns of fear, doubts, to know you are loved and the negative thoughts you have are knifing you! Let your best friend be yourself. Do not isolate the inner child from the wholeness of love that is.

In a world where we cannot claim to know or understand everything we never know just how close we are to a new situation so one should not give in.

THE REALIZATION

THE REALIZATION THAT MY THOUGHTS
FORM WHO I AM.
THEY HAVE ACCUMULATED RIGHT FROM BIRTH,
WHEN LIFE BEGAN.
CONDITIONING BY POSITIVE AND NEGATIVE
MAKE UP MY FORM.
MY ATTITUDES BRING ME SUNSHINE
AS WELL AS MIGHTY STORMS.

THE JOURNEY IS MY MAKING
WITH A CHOICE THE ROAD I TAKE.
CHANGING DIRECTION WHEN MY HEART IS
HEAVY IS THE DECISION FOR ME TO MAKE.
REALIZING I AM A PUZZLE WITH A SUBCONSCIOUSNESS,
BURIED STRINGS.
GIVES ME THE OPPORTUNITY TO CLEANSE THE PAST, FOR MY
HEART TO SING.

THIS LITTLE CHILD AT MY FEET
HAS DREAMS TO COME AND SHARE.
WHEN SHE IS FREE TO BE HER OWN
TRUE SELF LIFE WILL HOLD NO FEAR.
SO LOOK AT THE STORY WHERE THE
JOURNEY HAS COME SO FAR.
SEEK TRULY WHAT YOU REALLY WANT,
BE STILL, SEEK OUT YOUR STAR.

THE KEY

Some one once said that the world
Could be mine.
That everything I wished for
Was possible in time.
Long ago I did not know
Or even understand.
That when the key of life is held
Our heart puts our dreams into out hand.

Courage in the moment
To follow from the heart.
Trusting in the future
To allow me to play my part.
For joyful is the moment
Knowing it is real.
Freedom from within has a joyful,
Happy feel.

Continue on your way,
Knowing you are safe.
Attracting supporting energies that work well with
you in your place.
A joy to share with others.
The quest of life is love.
Supported with higher energies
Available from above.

AN INSTRUMENT OF LIGHT

Those already committed to the path of white light will be given the opportunity to guide others on the path. Growth will then increase in loving energy; it has to, to avoid destruction. Forces of evil already work to try to prevent this from happening. Their efforts will destroy themselves, as eventually they become adversaries of each other. Love cannot be fragmented as its contents are total love, its wholeness would not be love with any other than positive loving attitudes. The moment other thoughts are introduced into the mind the form is not love.

While some of us look forward to contributing to speaking out on increased use of the higher senses of man, others block or attempt to prevent this. Others need to seek their own truth. They must question, seek, and meditate to make it their own. The quest for wholeness is the right of each individual. What is needed comes at the right time for each person but often the opportunities is missed because of insufficient quiet time and the fear that goes with living in yesterday or tomorrow instead of this moment.

Paths vary to such a degree that it is for each soul to identify its own and find as many keys as it can to assist its progress for growth. Food, music, and attitude all increase our growth in awareness. It should be noted that some that are highly evolved appear to go against the practices of food and music that open up awareness. This is because they are so open in their higher chakras that they need assistance to stay grounded in their lower chakras. Ever observed someone that others say is off the planet, or they are obeying the voice they say they hear that is suggesting negative action by them, and forming a control. All chakras need to be balanced for full functioning both spiritually and physically. Personally I find that swimming, leaning against a tree, gardening, or picturing myself firmly standing with my feet in the soil all support me for being grounded. To be grounded one is aware and prepared to take responsibility for their actions.

There are books available that are very informative on the chakras. The main information is that they are energy centres of the body that each have different frequency and therefore spin in the body at different speeds. The principle is similar to radio and television frequencies that enable one to hear and see the program. Our first chakra is at the base of the spine. Our second is at the centre of the gut. The third is located at the stomach. The fourth is at the heart. The fifth is at the throat. The sixth is between our eyebrows and is referred to as the third eye and the seventh is the crown of our head.

The first is our physical centre. This is coloured red and gives energy for sexual activity, anger and physical energy.

The second is our emotional centre. This is coloured orange and controls the emotions.

The third is our intellect centre. This is coloured yellow and as our reasoning centre it controls thought, fear, fight and flight.

The fourth is our heart centre. Coloured green and if we follow it stay on our path instead of following the mental path of the head.

The fifth is our speech centre, this is coloured blue and allows speech as introvert, extrovert. The different tones we use, laughter, anger, speech or silence.

The sixth is our third eye centre Coloured violet and is where we open to psychic insight of clairvoyance, clairaudience, to receive from other dimensions. To receive information that is not available from other senses.

The seventh centre is our crown centre. Where the silver cord is attached to allow us to astral travel. This is where our spirit enters our body and when the cord is severed we experience death from leaving our physical body and do not return. The seventh chakra is where only total love is felt. There is no Ego.

When one serves as a tool for white light toward total love one becomes part of the great plan. You are not the planer. Let God's work be done and not ones own. If you look at what is happening in any country you cannot blame God for this. Certainly it is essential to take in the whole picture. In the matter of starvation there are those that rise above it and there are those who die. To an observer it can appear horrific as their measurement is compared against his or her own comfortable life style. People who are starving know they are hungry, but what do they measure it against? Within the same country the observer will see the greatest display of materialistic wealth. To all things there must be balance. If it is allowed to happen it is possible. Is this then the question for man takes only part of the picture and tries to change the outcome before being aware of the whole? Is what is required to effect change to bring balance being avoided? In fact, all countries have within them the means and ability to heal to wholeness. When will others observe their own country to bring in the potential of each individual living there? Is it harder to work on self? Do we view it as judgement and find ourselves lacking. It is easy to want change in other countries but the pattern has not been changed by outside manipulation. Does it put the observer from another country into one of complacency that stops them working towards their own balance in their country? What is balance? It isn't necessarily materialistic balance. It is attitude. Attitudes from reaction run most lives. Success of life is generally measured in terms of materialistic wealth. If one looks at the growth required for a soul towards the white light- that of total love, there is a way to remove negative emotions of greed, anger, sexual misuse and others. The way is by experiencing them until we observe our own behaviour and the observer is the observed, we are unaware of changes that should and can be made. When the observer can see what change is necessary the pattern can be broken. If greed needs to be understood there must be understanding. With this attitude completely worked through the higher self takes the learning and from there on the knowledge is available for the soul and there is no need to experience it

again. Once one starts working on self there can be rapid progress that will benefit by attracting souls with this growth capacity around you. Each has a different path of learning and the experiences they require for ones growth is there. That is why what appears unjust to the outside observer is not necessarily so. Particularly as the more evolved a soul becomes the heavier the load may become. Once the opportunity or challenge is identified it becomes easier for goals to be set and planned. Before that time the soul is often in a reactionary mode adding negative emotions. As soon as action commences there is movement. You cannot measure a soul's background against its progress. It may be that soul has yet to learn from this environment for their growth. Certainly we ask for our experiences through our thought process. What you see as a failure may appear so because your soul has achieved that learning. You must allow theirs to do so. Covering the obstacle for them will only make it necessary for them to experience it again to give them another opportunity to clear it by gaining the understanding. When one is emotionally involved it is usually termed love. It can be very difficult to watch another under a heavy load, sometimes failure. The ultimate is victory when all rejoice. True loves supports love, communicates and leads to achievement. Ones learning may lead one to stand back and find a way of manifesting the talents one has. Other people need to be receptive. It is important for a teacher to be intuitive to share the vibration of the moment to suit the pupil. They need to give the information accurately. Negative comments should be used productively. If one is ahead of ones time it doesn't mean you need sit back and miss an opportunity to progress further. The opportunity to manifest ones knowledge will come and when it does take it. If only one sentence is given to another there can be opportunity for self-growth. Didn't you confirm your learning from your guide by hearing another? Hard work has got us where we are. Each one is experiencing the journey for their individual growth. Just remember that information very often has to pass us several times to allow consolidation and for us to actively pursue the words to become the action of them.

OPENING NEW DOORS

The end can be the beginning
To open up new doors.
First we must clear our memory
So we can explore.
Deep within our heart
Lies the secret of our dreams.
You are confident, you are strong.
View yourself with high esteem.

Take each day and quietly build.
Everything is yours within this world.
Each step gives you joy
As it opens up your vision.
That you enjoy your journey
For your own sake.
For it no longer matters how
Long the journey takes.

MY FUTURE

MY FUTURE IS MY THOUGHTS
FOR ALL THINGS TO BE.
WATCHED OVER BY MY GUARDIAN ANGEL
WITH KNOWLEDGE FOR ME TO SEE.
LIVING IN THE MOMENT,
WITH KINDNESS FOR ALL.
OBSERVING ALL THE THOUGHTS
NO MATTER HOW SMALL.

REFINED OVER AND OVER
TO ARRIVE AT BEING WHOLE.
A SPIRIT OF LOVE,
AWARE TO COMPLETE ITS ROLE.
REALISATION OF THE JOURNEY
TO MAXIMISE THE MOMENT.
KNOWING THAT EVENTUALLY THE ENDING
OF REACTION IN THOUGHT IS THE OPPONENT.

FOR THINKING EVER FORWARD OR
BACKWARD WITH THE TIME.
PREVENTS THE NEWEST MOMENT
WITH SPACE THE ONLY LINE.
JUST TO BE AT ONE
WITH THE MOMENT AND THE VIBRATION.
FREES THE SOUL TO STILLNESS
WITH NO DREAD OR CELEBRATION.

DEATH, DYING OR LIVING

Do we really mean what we say? We take a person who is near death. The dying person might say, "The suffering is beyond me, why can I not die"? Maybe there is a lack of bodily functions and a feeling of inadequacy for having to depend on others. One might agree with them or more important let them see if they agree with their own words by presenting them back to them. When dealing with choice it is theirs, not yours so present both choices. "You are saying the pain and suffering are so great you want to die, or are you saying the pain is great, when it is there I wish I could die, but if it were to leave me I would wish to live." You do not need an answer. They do. Keep re-presenting their words leaving the choices to them. Let them decide. It doesn't matter if it is today, tomorrow as long as there is meditation on true thought to a decision instead of living in a reactive state where the words are not the true reflection of what is in the heart. When there is calm acceptance of what is to fight to live or to let go to die then there is inner calmness.

They can then put energy behind the decision to let it happen. Every person's right is his or hers decision to create his or hers own outcome. Give them this opportunity to hear themselves. You are not part of the decision making process. People choose their own destiny. Otherwise they accept another's choices as their own. When words do not come it is enough to hold another's hand. The comfort of feeling another is present takes away the isolation. It allows one to sleep, to take courage to face things as they are and to finally let go-to pass on. Death is the subject people least talk about. That is why many feel isolated in their last days, months or years. To face the unknown is fearful for them, not knowing if it is the end or not. When acceptance can come to allow letting go, the person achieves calmness and with this calmness the stillness for loved energy forces in the other dimensions to be in contact and be there with them for support and if accepted, direction. It is wonderful when they feel love on earth and

love beyond; then they are never alone in the experience that strengthens their ability to let go.

When I have been privileged to be with someone that is due to pass they have expressed their fear of the unknown. Explaining their choices of the end, others beyond they have known or loved ones here has appeared to give comfort to let go to pass on.

People close should not attempt to hold others back. Be aware that your emotions weigh on them, so try not to add sorrow, tears etc .to their load. You may need to walk away. Very often people pass soon after a loved one leaves them. Today when many people have experienced out of body experiences as either soul travel during their sleep or near death experiences there is more information available than ever before. There is no need to feel isolated.

THE ROSE

THE ROSE IS A GIFT
WHICH GROWS AND BLOOMS.
WITH FLOWERS SO SOFT
AND FULL OF PERFUME.
WE NOURISH AND PRUNE IT
SO IT FLOWERS EACH YEAR.
A ROSE IN THE ROOM
BRINGS BEAUTY AND CHEER.

SO SOFT ARE THE PETALS
TO LOVE AND TOUCH.
WHEN THEY FINALLY FALL,
THEY HAVE GIVEN SO MUCH.
THEY LIE SO SOFT
AGAINST THE RAIN.
AS WITH A RAINBOW
THE ROSE FLOWERS AGAIN.

THE CYCLE GOES ON
AND THEY GIVE MORE AND MORE.
THOSE ROSES WE LOVE,
ALL OUR FRIENDS DO ADORE.
FROM NOW TO ETERNITY
MAY PEACE BE A ROSE.
LET ITS BEAUTY SPREAD
THROUGH THE WORLD
WHEREVER IT GOES.

THANK YOU ROSE
FOR ALL MANKIND.
MAY YOU BLOOM AND GROW
FOR ALL TIME.
YOUR COLOURS SO MANY ,
SO BRIGHT AND TRUE.
THANK YOU DEAR ROSE;
WE DO LOVE YOU.

WHICH PATH

PATHS CAME TO MEET ME.
NONE WERE REALLY RIGHT.
SO I WALKED AWAY UNTIL
THE RIGHT ONE CAME INTO SIGHT.

NOW MY HEART IS HAPPY.
EACH DAY GIVES ME THE CHANCE.
TO CREATE THE THINGS WHICH GIVE ME JOY.
THEIR BEAUTY TO ENHANCE.

WHICH PATH?

Each moment may be hard work, but when we work from the heart we cease to feel pain or the restraints of time. When we choose our direction with joy and for no other reason, effort becomes satisfaction instead of an uphill struggle. When there is no longer joy in the chosen path it is reasonable to leave it and take another of joy. One should always observe the experience to effect maximum learning and opportunity for growth to avoid having to take the lesson again. It takes courage to strive for joy while it robs us of our energy of the beautiful feeling in our heart to battle with our goal that no longer gives joy. There will always be those who consider they know what is best for others, such people might persuade you to change direction. While they might be right you must remember it is your goal not theirs so even if you change it through discussion it is not only yours, but you live with the action you take. So follow the feeling from your heart and question again. Keep on seeking and if in doubt do nothing. When something has all the components to take you further toward your focused goal you should follow it. There is no such thing as normal. That is what is called "conditioned" response. The path society takes is acceptable. Your soul seeks new experiences. Others may have travelled there but for you there is a challenge, the newness, a reaching out. Recognise when an experience is ended. Then either visualise the next experience you seek or the energy forces you wish to use in achieving it. You might want to lecture, but do not know which position to adopt. Send out your vibrations. If you do not ask you do not get. Destiny exists for all of us but adopting positive thought patterns definitely accelerates the opportunities available to you. When movement does not occur it is important to understand the lesson to learn so we can move forward.

LET YOU BEST FRIEND BE YOURSELF

LOVE STARTS WITH SELF
WHEN YOUR HEART IS OPEN WIDE.
KNOWING WHAT YOU WANT TO DO
IS YOUR REAL GUIDE.

THE SMALL THINGS THAT MATTER
ADD UP TO THE SPLENDOURS ON THIS EARTH.
SMILING, TALKING, TOUCHING
STRIDING ACROSS THE TURF.

SO LOVE THIS LITTLE CHILD WITHIN
STILL THE TEARS, THE FEARS OR WOES.
SET YOUR PATH OF ACTION
FOLLOW EACH STEP ALONG THE PATH UNTIL IT FLOWS.

FOR BELIEVING IN YOURSELF
WITH ENCOURAGEMENT FROM WITHIN
WILL MANIFEST YOUR DREAM TO FRUITION
GO ON, YOU CAN DO IT, BEGIN.

WHEN YOU SEE A SHADOW OF DOUBT
BETWEEN YOU AND YOUR DREAM.
PUT IN AN ATTITUDE OF CONFIDENCE
TO RAISE YOUR SELF ESTEEM.

BELIEVING IN YOURSELF AS YOU
JOURNEY THROUGH LIFE
WILL BRIGHTEN UP EACH DAY
TO WALK WITHOUT THE CONSTANT STRIFE.

SO NOW YOUR HEART DIRECTS
TO WALK TRUE TO SELF
EACH DAY THE OPPORTUNITY
YOU ARE YOUR GREATEST WEALTH.

THE POWER OF THOUGHTS

Writing on the chalk board
Where a duster can wipe it out.
Is the perfect example for clearing our thoughts, for
this is what life is about.

If you thought, that you created
your experiences each day.
By what you send out and
Recognise along the way.

You would send out love
That it came back to you.
In fact it would give healing
For a different point of view.

When your thoughts are negative
Use the duster to let them go.
That the loving energy surrounds you and others that
you know.

Once the world is working
Towards magnifying love.
We will all embrace this loving energy.
The highest source above.

SENSITIVITY

Senses develop. As they do they enable us to perception we might never see that we used to miss. Our hearing develops as we learn to listen instead of waiting for opportunity to speak. Our interpretation from touch can be like Braille. Let us feel what others feel. Give us a story we used to miss. As we become more positive we are in touch with our senses, while when we are negative we often do not see, hear or touch. We put ourselves into darkness.

What about when we become so sensitive that we feel all energy vibrations around us, that joy, anger and so on. Happiness we can take, but what about our reaction to other emotions! Life is a balance, but it is the balance of love, not of all energies, so we do not want to take on less than we have achieved. If one fights anger with anger one is left with more anger. Only love attracts love. Remember to keep the energy of white light around yourself and become the observer when you do not wish to take on the energy. This way you can be there for others without taking on their load. There are people that drain energy from others. Ever been to a shopping centre or met someone new and couldn't wait to get away because you felt uncomfortable, even drained as if there were a sponge absorbing your vital energy. Some of us are so sensitive that we carry the symptoms of others and think it is our health concern. One must learn to stay grounded. That is not to lock onto another's energy but to stay detached and leave others to deal with their concerns instead of carrying their load. Staying detached allows you to give and be more supportive to them. Discard what is less than love, but recognise you are not perfect. It is important not to focus on their concerns and to give them energy for then they become real, yours and others. Love is the key. One must truly turn the other cheek. Then and only then will there be the one true energy of love.

THE BOX OF TOYS

Life is a box of toys
That is wonderful to explore.
With each day to experience
There is so much inside and out of doors.

The journey is ever onward
With so much to see and do!
So many opportunities open before us.
The choice is really up to you!

With many chapters in our destiny
Just like a hand of cards.
How we play is up to us
Where we place each card.

Changing faces in our life
They all have some things to share.
Time gives the understanding to be patient
And to see they care.

Special friends see and love us
For who we really are.
When clouds and storms threaten above
Our friends see us, the little star.

When loneliness tries to beckon
Focus on this love.
True friendship is the love
We will experience when we go above.

For love is the highest
That we can ever go.
Our soul on this journey is forever learning. There is
a need to know.

A SPECIAL PERSON

A FRIEND IS A SPECIAL PERSON
WHO TRUSTS YOU WITH THEIR HEART.
THEY LET YOU TAKE A LOOK INSIDE.
THEIR FEELINGS, THEY DO NOT HIDE.

YOU HAVE THE CHANCE TO HELP THEM
OR PAIN THEM AT THEIR HEART.
THE WAY MUST BE FREE OF RESTRICTIONS
FOR EACH ONE TO GROW STRONG.

TO LEARN THROUGH OBSERVATION
THE SELF SEES NEED TO CHANGE.
THE FRIEND CAN GIVE THE GUIDANCE
IF BOTH CAN SEE THE BALANCE.

BUT BOTH MUST WORK WITH LOVE
FROM WHERE THE OTHER STANDS.
TO GIVE THEM WHAT THE OTHER NEEDS
AND NOT YOUR OWN PLAN.

WE ALL ARE VERY DIFFERENT.
ALLOWANCE MUST BE MADE.
UNTIL THE SOUL IS READY
FOR CHANGES TO BE MADE

FRIEND OR FOE

We attract the people around us that will help us experience the lessons that we have come to learn. They may be in the form of a temptation or desire. One wants for self. It may be to turn away or walk away as we see we have observed the lesson and can comfortably let it pass without fighting it. Often when we observe our friends we note we have several of the same star sign. This is because we attract that which we need. You may be an air sign with several earth signs around you. The air signs may have their vibrations grounded by the earth sign while the earth sign may be lifted in vibrations by the air sign. Hopefully, thus assisting each to aim at balance. By observing others as well as self we get the opportunity to identify a quality that we would like to adopt.

Their example and energy will support us in this. It may occur during the relationship or later, upon reflection. Certainly, there is no loss in changing patterns or ending a relationship if one looks for the learning and achieves further progress on the path or identifies an opportunity to work towards an identified objective.

Our aim is growth for our soul so we must be open to change. Opportunities will open before us as we become prepared to take them on. A rest is by doing what we enjoy doing. It revitalises us before we continue on our journey towards wholeness. Do not blame people around you. Give thanks, for they are there because it is known they will behave in this manner and give you an opportunity to learn from the experience. They are simply the tools. You may have several people giving you the same experience. Look for the lesson. Once you have it new people will come into your life. Observe your attitude for it is only you that can identify and make the changes that can improve your time here. So ask, what am I to learn from this experience?

BIRTHDAY BEGINNINGS

A BIRTHDAY IS THE BEGINNING
OF YOUR OWN PERSONAL YEAR.
AN EXTRA SPECIAL TIME FOR FRIENDS
TO SHOW HOW MUCH THEY CARE.
MY FRIEND I WISH YOU HEALTH AND JOY
ON THIS YOUR SPECIAL DAY.
MAY EVERY DAY THERE AFTER
BE FILLED WITH LOVE AND LAUGHTER.

AN OPPORTUNITY TO BENEFIT FROM THE
GROWTH OF THE PASSING YEAR.
IF WE TAKE THE TIME TO LOOK
IT GIVES STRENGTH AND PURPOSE
FOR THE COMING YEAR.
WISDOM MAKES US YOUNGER
AS WE TEMPER UP THE STEEL.
THOUGH MANY OF US FEEL
IT IS A SPECIAL KIND OF HELL.

IN FACT IF WE ACCEPT THE CHALLENGE
AND FACE IT TO THE END.
WE USUALLY FIND BEFORE TOO LONG
WE FEEL SAFE, AT PEACE AGAIN.
WITH CHANGES COMING AROUND US
AS WE JOURNEY ON OUR PATH.
TAKE TIME TO REFLECT ON ALL THE BEAUTY
OF THIS SPLENDID EARTH.

SMILE AS YOU LEARN

This joy is mine alone,
A love of self and true worth.
The realization of the journey.
The reason for our birth.
Each day is a joyful moment
With blessings from the heart.
To bring happiness to my world
I must live my own part.

Living for the moment
Without fear of concern.
Courage to know the difference
And smile as I learn.
Releasing the past
Each moment of the day.
For then the time is real
And true in every way.

BEING TRUE TO OUR SELF

We grow and as with a newly born baby, we begin to flower in so many ways. Suddenly we can be so sensitive: this sensitivity is reflected in so many ways. We suddenly feel disenchanted with our environment. Often, after many years in this place, people around us. So what is it? There doesn't have to be anything wrong with it. Suddenly we are ready to identify with our own inner needs that we have buried deep in our subconscious and they have become triggered for us to identify a need that is not being met. Instead of reacting we must communicate to identify what it is we need and communicate it to those around us. Without communication it cannot happen and resentment, anger, jealousy, all these and other emotions build up, often affecting us in our general behaviour without us knowing why. When people agree to work towards something it can happen. Otherwise ignorance allows walls to build up created by thought that often leads to the ending of the relationship. The real reason for ending the relationship is seldom identified. Our new sensitivity has us seeking to find something outside our normal pattern. We should question why we are here, the things we take for granted or accept from conditioning. Hopefully we see the path is one leading towards giving to others, self awareness towards love, by thinking before we speak. Halting before we have ill thoughts and not assuming from what we see. We often begin to see ourselves for the first time in our life. Many people feel they are unloved and feel inadequate to cope. This comes from the newness of suddenly being aware. They can retreat or begin to blossom. It is a daily progress. Many just see they do not like what they have. The importance is to identify ones own direction. Then one can begin to make it happen. We all live at different vibrations and. speed of thought. To be in contact with others it is necessary to identify their rate of vibration. If one goes at one hundred miles an hour and they at only thirty miles it is unlikely they will perceive or relate to your communication. It is faster to adjust

and slow to a pace that allows communication for others. Then we have maximum opportunity to listen to each other and identify from where the other person is coming. Running around them at one hundred miles achieves nothing. Adjusting to them allows you feel as they feel. Be in touch so you can relate the benefit of your learning to their needs and therefore maximise their opportunity to receive to adjust and to grow. The guide that channels to you has an amazing vibration rate and also adjusts to lock into the intuitional person. Until vibrations are raised they cannot link in. The link goes from broken interrupted line to an improved connection as the vibrations rise. This happens as a result of meditation, sound tones, food and physical activity. The same is true when it drops. When we can communicate and feel as they feel we can feel compassion to see whence those responses are coming. As they talk we have insight into their past that can afford opportunity to help them identify why they are reacting, thus setting off a chain of events that may be casting them into the darkness of hopelessness, feeling unloved. There is always a door of sunshine among the many dark doors. By identifying and understanding our trigger points we can remove them. When one has the key to meditate and understand the sunshine, doors swing open. When we freely give to others without thought of return we create opportunity to increase our white light area. Selfless giving creates a feeling of wholeness that can fill our life until we cease to become concerned for our own needs. Some people look for opportunity to contribute in all facets of life, while others wait to see if the actions of others will get them what they want. When we wait for others to achieve for us we do just that, wait. They will succeed or fail us. When they succeed we feel part of it for selecting them. If they fail we try to disassociate from them, ignore them or become critical. True growth is realising we take responsibility for our soul. We create and take our own opportunities. We risk being wrong or failing, for unless we do we cannot be ready to move forward and succeed. Are you living each day? Being aware of self and others to become a better person to whom

others are attracted and with whom you feel comfortable. It isn't selfish to seek to take on the qualities of someone you like because this awareness identifies the progress you should acknowledge. You have laughed and cried to achieve this far. Give your new understanding recognition: then identify your next goal by further self-observation. Particularly, in loving relationships it is important to meet ones own needs and not rely on others for them. This is the path to freedom for self, from within - "Your true identity of becoming whole."

SWEET SONG

The seeds have been sown
With care and love
That they will multiply
Throughout the years with love

Peace comes through giving
Without thought of return
Increasing with experience
As we live and learn

The world is for learning
That we may be free
The purpose for being here
Throughout eternity

There is no end
As the energy goes on
When we serve from the heart
With love our own sweet song

HEALING IN THE PROCESS

WHEN FEAR COMES TO THE SURFACE
JUST LET IT PASS AWAY.
FOR HEALING IN THE PROCESS
HAS BEEN THE RELEASE TODAY.

FOCUS ON THE JOY
OF YOUR TREASURES STILL INSIDE.
IT IS TIME TO BLOSSOM WITH THESE GIFTS
SO SMILE, DO NOT HIDE.

THE TEMPERING OF THE STEEL
IS THERE FOR EVERYONE.
ONCE WE KNOW OUR PURPOSE THERE
 IS FREEDOM FOR FOLLOWING GODS SON.

FOR LOVE IS THE WHOLENESS.
THE JOURNEY OF THE HEART.
WHERE EACH ONE RESERVES THE OPPORTUNITY
TO ADD GROWTH; THEIR MISSING PART.

SELF IMAGE

We often limit ourselves by the images we have built of ourself from childhood. A child normally perceives things as they really are. It is wrong to tell them to be quiet. It comes about because they are not listened to in the first place. It leads to a self-image with loss of confidence. They may not project this outwardly. After all, why should they? They were not allowed to be part of the whole before so now they feel outside in many situations. They do not often voice their opinion for fear of rejection. When they do speak it is with disbelief that people will listen so their projection is often lacking. The opposite is also true, voicing their opinion on everything. After all, as a child if they kept on talking surely they would listen. It is hard to remember how it was. Some children block experiences of pain. It isn't that they do not feel. Often the feeling, the loss of that they perceived to have missed stays within them in their subconscious and they try to attract it in their adult life. They do not always realise this is happening to them. Often they repeat their behaviour patterns in an attempt to fulfil their needs that were not met at other times. Their happy times are over emphasised by the subconsciousness attention of the pattern of that time and reward. So in adult life when seeking love, attention or praise, they try to manifest the behaviour pattern. Hoping to feel good by repeating a pattern of the past. If the needs are not met anguish is experienced. It is necessary to observe your expectations of the past for opportunity to let go of expectations. This generally gives critical condemnation of others that justifies our feeling of loss to our self and leaves us with a situation that is unacceptable to us and therefore unresolved. To resolve it we must acknowledge the love of others to allow them to be where they are in growth. To allow that they did the best they knew at the time. If you can accept this, then you set them free from judgement, condemnation and recognise them as another soul on the path. You also recognise that your

soul releases the past, the expectations of that particular pattern and moves forward joyfully to new experiences.

Let us look at the possible inner subconscious dialogue where confidence is lacked and what must be sort after to balance.

I fear rejection	Please accept me
Why bother	confidence
They will not agree	I believe in what I am saying
There are others stating The same point of view	Eventually the message will get through
In serving you give what You have received	I choose to serve

New self image.

I cleanse and let go of the past. My body feels light and free. There is no measurement of past performance. My strength now gives me confidence to speak from the heart and serve.

My voice is heard. My throat is strong. My message is received With each individual on his or her path, I give thanks for the opportunity to serve.

There is acceptance and confidence.

DON'T SHOOT THE MESSENGER

DON'T SHOOT THE MESSENGER
BY BEING FULL OF DOUBT
ACCEPT WITH JOY YOUR JOURNEY
FOR THAT IS WHAT LIFE IS ABOUT
KEEP SHARING LOVE
WITH NO THOUGHT OF RETURN
FOR GOD HAS PROMISED IF YOU SERVE
YOU WILL RECEIVE IN RETURN

FOR FOCUSING ON LOVE TO BRING
IN HOPE, FAITH AND TRUST
SEWS PATIENCE, COURAGE, CONFIDENCE
TO RISE FROM THE DUST
SO DUST YOURSELF OFF
SEE THE SUN OUT TODAY
DECIDE TO SMILE AND ENJOY YOURSELF
WITH EACH STEP ALONG THE WAY

RECOGNISE THE BLESSINGS
THEY ARE THERE EVERY DAY
A SMILE, THE BIRD'S SONG
AS YOU PASS ALONG THE WAY
THIS MOMENT DOESN'T LAST
IT IS FOREVER NEW
WITH LOVE THE CONSTANT FOCUS
YOU WILL REALLY ENJOY THE VIEW

LIFE'S JOURNEY

LOOK FOR THE BEAUTY
TO GIVE THANKS EACH DAY.
TO RENEW YOUR INNER GLOW
AS YOU JOURNEY ALONG YOUR WAY.

THE POWER OF YOUR THOUGHTS
CAN OPEN UP NEW DOORS.
LOOK INSIDE YOUR HEART.
OPEN WIDE YOUR HEART FOR MORE.

CONFIDENCE, STRENGTH,
LAUGHTER FROM WITHIN.
THIS IS WHAT I WISH YOU
FOR YOU WILL GROW AND WIN.

YOUR BEAUTY IS LIKE A FLOWER
WHICH HAS SEASONS TO REST.
FROM STILLNESS COMES INSIGHT,
THEN YOU GROW AND DO YOUR BEST.

MAY THIS NEW PERSONAL YEAR
OPEN MANY GOLDEN OPPORTUNITIES FOR YOU.
WHICH WILL START CREATIVE OUTCOMES
FOR YOUR TALENTS TO SHINE THROUGH.

WORK

Work constitutes a major part of ones life. Most of us work because we have to, not because we want to. This is reflected when the work is chosen from the heart or we just see ourselves meeting the need for an income. So let us look at this because we are each responsible for the survival of the "self". It is right that we should all contribute in our own to the whole. This means supporting our contribution to the many things that have been developed in society today of which we are all a part. The real question is not why do we work but can we find a way to work where we feel beautiful, where we feel comfortable and in which we can put maximum effort. We will possibly change jobs many times in our working lifetime. Those that do not may be happy or feel that what they are doing requires no great effort so they tolerate the repetition, providing security of position. This action reflects insecurity within. The food will always be on their table at the end of the day. Deep within there may be a feeling of fulfilment but lack of achievement. We are not all managers. Some are decisions- makers, some are delegates and some do the actual job. There must be those that decide, delegate or perform the action required. Most people fit into one of these categories.

Let us look at what is most desirable in the work place. We go to work to achieve something. For most of us it means working with other people. It really doesn't matter whether we are giving service over the counter or working within an office or physically producing something. At the end of the day our result with other people gives the collective result required for any business to succeed. It is called unity of action. We are going to talk about unity because when each person works on his or her own, they may or may not achieve. For any given result everyone united in sharing the same goal and working together success is not only quicker, but is more likely to happen. All have to be focused on achieving the same goal. It means that you do not just do your own and walk away. If each can find

a way to share his or her ideas and to ensure that they all share the same goal, then success will be there. Without this fragmentation is inevitable. The result is that some have to be discarded, others altered, while others are perfect.

What is lacking of course is supervision and communication.

Communication comes up time and time again. What we say and what another perceives we are saying can be two different things. This is the importance in the work force that the requirement is repeated back to ascertain clarity of communication that both see the same thing. Then there is one focus behind the project and it will be achieved. Where there are people that disagree with the objective, do not think it is possible, decide to do it their way, then we have fragmentation and are less likely to succeed. We are more likely to want to change our job. If it is through lack of communication we will probably repeat it in the next position. If we look at the pattern of movement we will identify that probably the same reason is given for leaving each position. There is also a possibility that we have not given anyone a chance to discuss it. Where we have tried unsuccessfully to communicate, clearly to grow we need to move on to meet our own needs then our new goal is set. On the other hand, where a soul has grown to a point where they can see through brief attempts at communication or observation that this is not going to be taken up by the other party it may be right to move on for they know what will give their soul balance. They know the job no longer fits against their energy force and is being left behind with souls that have yet to learn communication skills the ones that have yet to focus on one goal and to unite. You have to allow the difference. It is for each to see and create their movement.

It is thought that few follow within their career of choice. This makes it work. We have said what makes a vision, a joy or a task. Let us look at today's frustrations to see what contributes to this. Most work is repetitive and can lead to high competence or boredom of routine. Where is the key to competence through joy in achieving the task? Today the difference in

the work force in attitudes can be many, often resulting to reactions in volatile situations. The key is doing unto others as we would be done by, which in the work place is putting yourself in the other person's position or looking ahead to see the purpose of application of what you create. Where there is a single purpose to achieve and it is reached; acknowledgement gives the signal to strive for the next objective. We must not only share the goal, it is necessary to work together in achieving it. The workplace is one of the opportunities we have to grow from. All aspects of our journey strive to go forward through learning and the work place is a part of this. Unfortunately most associate negative outcomes to the work place as unavoidable situation. The individual's thought creates that. Most of these assumed situations are conditioned responses. Very few break free to enjoy their free time as such from moment to moment. It becomes a circle of repetition, the same as the work place. Repetition of the past keeps them in that energy mode. It we are lucky we get off the roundabout and create a space of silence within. We observe there is no movement. Our life is not interesting. We start to ask questions. If we can isolate what we do not like, we can see what is needed to replace it. Within each of us is the ability to break free of the pattern and create movement to new growth.

WHAT IS LOVE

Love is the energy
That allows another to be whole
Love is the energy
That supports you to meet your goal

For life is the purpose
To grow to your wealth
Life the opportunity
The courage to understand yourself

Acceptance is the key
To joy within your heart
Every moment within each hour
Gives opportunity to play your part
Life's stage is the play
You write for yourself
Judge is the effect
From the cards you dealt yourself

Understanding who you are where you want to be
Opens up each day
To be happy, to be free

For deep inside each one
There is a lovely little spark
That grows and grows to love
The creation of the heart

THE FIVE CENT COIN

ONCE UPON A TIME THERE WAS A FIVE CENT COIN THAT WE WILL CALL LIFE.

LIFE WAS MINTED WITH MANY OTHER FIVE CENT COINS.

THEY WERE ALL SHINY NEW, PACKED IN BAGS READY TO GO OUT IN THE WORLD.

SOME BECAME COLLECTORS COINS IN A SPECIAL BOX!

WHILE OTHERS WENT TO BANKS TO SEE WHERE THEY WOULD GO.

LIFE FELT EXCITED WAITING FOR THE FIRST EXPERIENCE OF BEING IN A HAND.

LIFE WAS TAKEN WITH OTHER MONEY TO MAKE UP COMPANY WAGES.

NOW IN A PURSE IT FELT QUITE SNUG, MADE OF LEATHER IT SMELT WELL TOO.

OTHER COINS WERE GATHERED THERE AS THEY ALL RUBBED TOGETHER.

SOME WERE BIGGER AND TOOK UP THE SPACE

WHILE OTHERS WITH SHARP EDGES COULD PUSH YOU IN THE FACE.

IT WAS DARK INSIDE UNTIL THERE WAS A RING AT A TILL WHEN THE PURSE OPENED WIDE TO PAY THE BILL.

EIGHTEEN NINETY FIVE AND OUT CAME LIFE, HARDLY TIME TO SEE ALL THE GROCERIES ALL AROUND BEFORE BEING DROPPED IN WITH THE OTHER FIVE CENTS WITHOUT A SOUND.

WE ALL SHARED OUR STORIES AND I SAID I WAS NEW, THEY SAID MY WORTH WOULD ALWAYS BE NO MATTER WHAT I DID.

AS PEOPLE USE ME TO SHOP, I WOULD TRAVEL EVERYWHERE.

TIME TO WATCH AND LEARN, NOT ALWAYS JUST THE SAME

LITTLE SCRATCHES ON MY SURFACE SHOW THAT I AM HERE GETTING ALL THE EXPERIENCES.

I'VE BEEN TAKEN TO THE AIRPORT AND OFF IN A PLANE.

EVEN ON THE WATER WHILE THEY FISHED FROM A BOAT ALL DAY.

AND THEN I REALLY PANICKED, FOR AS HE CAME ASHORE, HE CHANGED HIS SHORTS FOR JEANS AND DROPPED ME ON THE SAND.

LUCK WOULD HAVE A METAL DETECTOR HAPPENED TO PASS BY

AND THERE I WAS LIFTED ON TO CONTINUE ON ONCE MORE.

I'VE BEEN ABROAD WHERE THEY COULDN'T SPEND ME.

TO THINK THEY COULD LEAVE ME IN A COUNTRY WITH NO VALUE ANYMORE.

SAFELY BACK HOME IN AUSTRALIA, I WAS RIGHT

THEN DOWN TO BONDI BEACH FOR AN ICE CREAM I WAS SPENT

IN THE TILL AGAIN WITH OTHERS TO SHARE WITH, WE COULDN'T HELP REFLECT

WE HAD BEEN GIVEN A SPECIAL GIFT

FOR WE HAD EXPERIENCED LIFE

AND REALLY SEEN A LOT.

STILL WORTH FIVE CENTS

LIFE MOVED RIGHT ON.

UNTIL ONE DAY FROM A POCKET LIFE ROLLED, ONTO THE STREET WITH LOTS OF CARS CROSSING,

MANY OF THEM GOING OVER HIS TOP.

UNTIL SUDDENLY ALL WAS QUIET AS THE NIGHT DESCENDED OVERHEAD.

THE SUN ROSE FOR ANOTHER DAY

WHEN A LADY SAW THE FIVE CENTS LYING ON THE ROAD.

AS LIFE WAS GENTLY LIFTED

THE THOUGHT WAS SENT OUT

FOR ALL THAT YOU ARE SCARRED AND BATTERED YOU STILL ARE FIVE CENTS

IN FACT TRUE TO LIFE YOU STILL HAVE YOUR SELF WORTH.

AFTER HAVING A SERIOUS ACCIDENT THAT STOPPED MY CAREER AS A MEDICAL REPRESENTATIVE IT WAS NECESSARY TO ATTEND PHYSIO AND DOCTORS 3-4 TIMES A WEEK FOR MONTHS.

EACH MORNING FOR A WEEK I PICKED UP A 5 CENT COIN OUTSIDE THE PHYSIO DOOR, THEN FINDING ONE NEAR THE BEACH AS THE SUN WAS RISING AND NOTING THE COIN WAS BATTERED THIS POEM WAS WRITTEN. EXPRESSING THAT ALTHOUGH INJURED, NOT WORKING, MY SELF-WORTH WAS STILL THERE.

TO THIS DAY A 5 CENT COIN REMAINS AN AFFIRMATION TO HOW STRONG OUR INNER POWER IS.

HEALING 15 YEARS LATER IS NEARLY COMPLETE. I DO NOT GIVE UP AND MY FAITH IS TRUSTING THAT EXPERIENCE IS NEEDED TO WATCH WHAT WE ASK FOR.

CONFIDENCE/FEAR

When we realise what the goal is for our life-where we want to go, we then become aware that opportunities occur to clear each obstacle we learn as we grow. One of the things that we get the opportunity to deal with is fear. Fear is one of the greatest obstacles man has to learn about. Modern man daily introduces thoughts of fear into his, her day. Fear manifests itself in many ways. Fear means we are uncertain. It is really more of the unknown, where confidence is the assumption of success or having done it before. To stay in our comfort zone is not to go beyond that which gives us opportunity for growth; so if movement is required in any direction for change it is better to try than not try at all. This is why friends often say; " Why did you change? It is natural for the soul to want to learn and to seek opportunity to do this. This is the reason we have come to earth. So if you feel fear, uncertainty or lack of confidence that is normal because you are looking at the unknown. So let us try to put aside that feeling and instead look at our objective.

We are starting something new. We have an objective that requires new skills. Accept that you have the necessary skills for success. What do we need to do to succeed? First of all we must be aware of exactly what it is we are required to do. Is this something that requires a minute, a day, a week or a year to achieve? In other words do we divide the objective up so that our energy can focus on each part in its turn leading to completion? If we do not look at it in this way the sheer size of the task might well daunt us and leave us in a state of indecision. When thought is on a positive level one can set goals and plan how it is going to be achieved. We can consider how we are going to implement the plan and in what time scale? In this way reaction becomes action.

This is not to say we suddenly become very confident but while we are in action mode there is movement instead of being still or in a state of

agitation. This is a lesson that we are here to learn. Too do or not to do, be aware of an in between state that does not need to exist.

Look at what is possible to happen in any given situation and look at the probabilities of the outcomes that may well give courage to achieve. While it remains merely a probability or a possibility there is nothing you can do.

You can only take the steps that you have planned to achieve the final goal and if any of these possibilities happen then you will deal with them as they arise. The action of that will take away the thought of fear if your mind is engaged in active doing.

Where there is love for ones self there is no fear. There is courage, confidence and achievement through action. Basically there is trust, faith in the inner love to succeed.

FOCUS ON THE BEAUTY

FOCUS ON THE BEAUTY IN EVERYTHING YOU DO
EVEN OTHER PEOPLE WITH A DIFFERENT POINT OF VIEW
LISTENING TO OTHERS AS THEIR STORY IS TOLD
SILENCE WITHIN AS THEIR VERBAL PICTURE UNFOLDS

YOU ONLY CREATE WAVES OF RESISTANCE
WHEN YOUR MIND IS DIVIDED IN TWO
HALF LISTENING WHILE THE REPLY
IS ALREADY COMING THROUGH

BE THE BEAUTIFUL PERSON YOU ARE
REACH YOUR FULL POTENTIAL
BY FOCUSING ON THE BEAUTY
YOU WILL HOLD THE JOYS THAT ARE ESSENTIAL

ATTITUDE HAS THE POWER TO CREATE
YOUR TRUE WEALTH
LOVE ON YOUR JOURNEY ALLOWS
THE STRENGTH TO BE YOURSELF

FOR REACTION TAKES US OFF THE PATH
AMONGST THE ROCKS AND WEEDS
SO WHAT DO YOU WANT TO PLANT IN LIFE?
YOU HAVE THE CHOICE OF THE SEEDS

FOR WHEN THE DAY IS ENDED
IT IS THE BIG PICTURE THAT REALLY MATTERS
FEELING LOVE INSIDE AND AROUND YOU
WILL HALT THE CONSTANT CHATTER

START TO SOW WHAT YOU WANT

DESTINY IS IN THE SEEDS
THAT YOU CHOOSE TO SOW
FREE WILL IS THE DECISION
TO REALISE WHAT YOU KNOW
FOR ACTIONS RETURN TO COME
BACK WHERE THEY START
WOULD YOU WANT THIS THOUGHT
TO COME BACK TO YOUR HEART

SO SEND OUT THE SMILES
ADOPT A POSITIVE POINT OF VIEW
CARING FOR OTHERS
AS IF THEY WERE YOU
SHARING YOUR GIFTS
FOR THEM TO MULTIPLY
THAT YOU FEEL LIGHT IN THE HEART
AS IF YOU ARE IN THE SKY

FOR DESTINY HOLDS THE FUTURE
FOR THE JOYS AND SORROWS THAT WE SOW
SHOULDN'T WE BE FULL OF FAITH
REALLY HAVE A GO!
SUPPORTED BY OUR THOUGHTS AND ACTIONS
TO SHOW WE REALLY CARE
BRINGING IN ALL OUR COLOURS
TO CROWN OUR GLORY WHILE WE ARE HERE

REALISING THAT OTHERS OFFER SEEDS OF WISDOM
FOR US TO EMPLOY
AN ENERGY OF THEIR LOVE
A GIFT INSIDE OF US TO ENJOY

WE ALL SOW IDEAS
THAT OTHERS MAY TAKE ON
HOW WONDERFUL THIS GIFT OF LOVE
WHEN GIVEN ITS HIGHEST SONG

FEELING UNLOVED

One appears to have unsurmountable obstacles.

Why do we feel unloved? There are so many questions. One must seek and keep asking. Please look for other questions. Is there a trigger point; at a gathering or when we are by ourself, you live alone, with family or another relationship? What is the background; brothers, sisters, parents, adopted or no family ties. What do you perceive this relationship to be like, write it out or meditate on the information you have? You are looking for a key to help yourself to clear this unloved feeling. I.e. Divorce is the trigger: the reaction being rejection. Can cause you to lose confidence in yourself. Possibly lost father through divorce, so there is a trigger point of male loss. Therefore, a deep longing within to have a loving male relationship or even being critical of the male relationships in your life as judgement on your fathers behaviour as you perceived it. If you identify the key you can re-establish your own action to take you back to strength. You may be measuring the present relationships against hopes of the past; this gives you no possibility of living in the present with the relationship.

If one desires to live in "the now" without measurement one must first of all learn to forgive and forget. This will enable one to stop making comparisons between the past and the present. In this way one is enabled to recognise and appreciate that "the now" is the beautiful new state to which one can look forward with joy to the future. "The now" from existing in that beautiful new state from where you can grow further. We are here to clear that which impedes us. First we must acknowledge it exists in our subconscious. When we feel unloved we should also ask ourselves where we are giving love. Giving carries us over the gap until we feel loved. We are not talking about physical relationships here. These are as noises we create to distract us from facing reality. Just as with constant hurried activities that prevent us being at one with the silence that allows us to go within.

Love is very beautiful. We have come here to become whole. To become total love; so it is right to say that we do not feel alive without love whether we are giving or receiving love. Without either a person is not dedicated to a kindly way of life. If their mental energy is in a negative pattern and is being used in that way they may be completely materialistic with their base on money issues and use people. They may be unaware of their path as being different from others.

Even what they call love will have a measurement and a receivership back to themselves of having earned what they are getting, or that it is due to them. "Love or ignorance, the two actions." This quote is said to be used in the early eighteen hundreds by a well-known author. When first I heard it, I thought how beautiful that someone realises that when it is not love the individual is certainly unaware that other than love between each other is done through the ignorance; not realising they sow that action to come back onto them self. Having read the autobiography of the author the realisation came to me that the statement was in reference to performance of the sexual act performed for the benefit of only one of the parties involved. Those that have a soul that has identified the path toward white light, the wholeness of love, become more sensitive. They need the balance of giving or receiving love. The receiving of love is not ours to demand. We live in a world where the balance is a little bit one sided, for some people are in a habit of taking; of thinking they are looking after self first in a selfish way. Many times the strong person that gives so much in love is neglected for the assumption by others is that they are all right. That they give so much that they cannot feel like others. Fortunately their faith in growing towards total love sustains them. One day more will discover the joy of giving and the energy force will rapidly increase as the vibration is increasingly given around the world.

Feeling loved opens a world to all things are possible. The beginning is identifying loving others as we love ourself. Do you love others? Do you love yourself by identifying with your inner child to care and protect

your own soul? So many neglect themselves and look for the love outside when it must radiate from within. Love the inner child by identifying the strengths and discarding negative thought. Focus on balance through positive thoughts to attract supporting energies of self-worth and feeling loved. Love is abundantly present. Love supports to conquer challenges. No love = No confidence + A challenge is a mountain.

My Secret Garden

What will I plant in my garden
Beginning with a seed.
Perhaps I should prepare the soil
By removing all the weeds.

Others may not see them
The vines that hold tight
Of fears and pains that bind me
Away from others sight.

My heart feels soft and tender
It begins to open wide
The love is there to flower,
I see a seed inside.
The faith of god is mine in love
When I let the voices pass.
That constant negative chattering,
A pattern to end at last.

Looking at your thoughts
That cast seeds of pain to grow.
Pity, anger, greed:
Things we all know.
Identify the weeds
You have sown in your garden.
Decide not to feed them
For all is forgiven, there is a pardon.

For love the perfect energy
Of god and grace above.
Sits ever at your table
To fill it full of love.
Open up your heart
Acknowledge the seed of love within.
For the love of god holds us
As we face this world we are in.

THE FIRST STEP

A JOURNEY BEGINS WITH THE FIRST STEP
NO MATTER HOW MANY MILES
WE TRAVEL THE DISTANCES BEST
WHEN WE PAUSE, REFLECT A WHILE
FOR ENJOYMENT IS THE KEY
INNER BALANCE FROM WITHIN
THAT YOU FOLLOW OUT YOUR PATH
KNOWING NOW THAT YOU WILL WIN

FOR LIFE GIVES US OUR JOURNEY
TO IDENTIFY AND MEET OUR NEEDS
THEY REQUIRE CONFIDENCE AND COURAGE
SO THEY GROW LIKE LITTLE SEEDS
SO IF YOU FEEL CONFUSED
HALT FOR A WHILE
TAKE NOTE OF ALL LIFE'S WONDERFUL JOYS
TO BRING BACK YOUR SMILE

THE NEWNESS OF THE DAY
IS OPEN FOR NEW BEGINNINGS
LIVE FOR THIS MOMENT
WITHOUT FEAR OR MISGIVINGS
ACTION IS THE KEY
FOR LETTING GO OF DOUBT
RELEASING THE THOUGHTS OF WORRY
YES! THAT IS WHAT LIFE IS ABOUT

ENERGIES AFFECTING OTHERS AND ONE'S SELF

There is a force of belief and not believing. The force made up of positive and negative attitudes. These create energies that we can re-act on, often without being aware of them. When we realise we can either ignore or add in a different thought to create a new result.

Sadly conditioning from childhood, and even lessons from the past are often the very things that prevent us acknowledging that we are much loved. The very person correcting us might in fact, be the person in search of approval. We need to ask the question and to be aware that at least eighty percent of our observation is derived from learned experiences. These experiences are not necessarily positive.

Living in the moment without measurement releases bondage for approval, not feeling loved. The joys to experiencing being in the bush, the songs of the birds or the whistle of the wind! Watching the sun appear to rise or set. Being still to enjoy the sunset with the moon and stars in the sky. This is true love that represents God in that moment.

It has been said that certain people always behave in a violent way and have done so for centuries. This is not so much through choice that may appear contradictory as we are responsible for our own actions, so much as observing that first we must see that we want change. Others may not. We have this energy active within us and we may feel like repeating our last action. Until with a new understanding we will become a new energy. This then becomes our dominant force.

Life is constant change. Without realising it we change other peoples lives. A friend has told me he is worried about his daughter who is expecting twins. The daughter has lost three babies before and nearly died each

time, the father fears the worst. To change the outcome a new energy is required. If close people fear-repetition, they hold that energy around her. The daughter must believe in positive out-comes as must those close to her. The new energy can then operate leading to give a different outcome. One can project something onto someone else. Ones thoughts must be positive to attract the best outcome.

When we are sufficiently strong our thoughts control our destiny. When we are not strong, the thoughts of others control our destiny. Our thoughts are passed to others who often take them as their own and carry them through. There are those who intentionally do this, controlling others. The law of karma of 'do unto others as you would be done by' attracts the balance for such an action. We do manifest other people's energies. Since we are responsible for our own actions it is important to be in touch and focused on outcomes for our soul. To be focused on the action required manifesting our visions to reality. To do this we have to achieve the ultimate destination of oneness of our soul back to the source of white light, higher intelligence, the source of love. We are all a part of this source. The journey of our soul to total love removing negative energies is the prime purpose for our life in the physical form. We do not say it ends the cycle on earth for the difference between energies of the developed soul and the young soul is so great that for further tempering of the steel a different environment is required for maximum opportunity to grow. There is help along the way, but each soul must achieve its own destination so graduation to the next class or stage is necessary. With all qualifications natural progression takes you on to new opportunities. So yes, who says where we further all our learning and in what form?

Earth's basic learning is on the physical, emotional and intellectual planes that are best manifested in the male and female forms we know.

This wonderful world is made up of different energies that we are aware of to the degree of our development. Some people seek the energy they have identified as necessary or release that they choose to let go. It may be as simple as deciding it is time to smile instead of going around looking unhappy. Both are forms of energy. We often allow the surrounding energies from other people to become ours. Once this is recognised we can choose to control our destiny by deciding if this is really how we wish to be. If not you can become the new energy by several methods.

Thought power.

Experience.

Taking it on from another.

We are seldom aware of others sensitive trigger points. They develop not only from this life, but can often remain there to clear from a past life. Remember we are accumulation of everything we have ever known and are able to apply the learned experience of the past lives. Energies are recognised through our senses. We feel from touch, from interpreting how we sense things, also sight and hearing. All these receive and send energies. If we observe self we can hopefully become positive with that energy surrounding us and attracting like people. We are what we think.

CLAIMING TODAY

Walk the day as new
From deep inside of you.
Comparing yesterdays memories
Will obscure, change the view.

The newness of the moment
Is there for you to have.
Life has this balance
To be happy, to be glad.

Trust in your faith,
Let go of the fear.
There are many new experiences
Just do it, be aware.

Knowledge from yesterday
Is yours, what you have.
It will colour, change your day
Remove the newness if you compare.

So many opportunities
Are there in our life.
Do we let them happen,
Postpone them once or twice.

For life is a circle.
Our opportunities come around again.
So reach out, enjoy them.
Your life will never be the same.

SEEING OUR SELF

LESSONS COME IN MANY WAYS
TO TEMPER UP THE STEEL.
GIVE THANKS THAT WE SEE THEM
TO HELP OUR SELF BE WELL.
FOR UNKINDNESS THAT WE THINK
IS SAD FOR US TO SEE.
CAN THAT INDIVIDUAL
REALLY BE ME?

SO TAKE THE LESSON
TO BE A NICER SOUL.
YOUR JOURNEY HAS THIS PURPOSE.
IT IS MANS INNER ROLE.
KEEP ON TRYING FOR EACH
DAY CAN BE NEW.
SO WATCH YOUR THOUGHTS, SHAPE THEM
WITH LOVE YOUR EXPRESSED VIEW.

SEEKING DIRECTION

Knowing one needs a new direction is the beginning of ones quest. Identifying the difference between your Hearts choice and your Ego's is the importance in identifying two different roads. The road of the heart will contain purpose that reflects joy, inner values, self worth, fun and laughter. This, however, does not mean the road of the heart will be easy because it demands courage to be true to self. However, trying to fit into a system, society, or wanting to appear normal is the conditioning of the child. (Refer, chapter on conditioning) This is when the Ego or head rules. The Ego works from the subconscious with positive or negative reinforcement. Hence, when your Heart indicates the true path over Ego there has to be consultation supporting this path. That way, through positive attitude, one's heart's dream will be realised. Too often low self-esteem and self worth destroy the dream.

Awareness of self is the greatest gift we have to bring order into one's life. Free will is the gift to develop self. When one is asked the most important thing in life we may answer food, water or shelter. But, if these are without love, trust and faith, life is without direction of the heart. The energy of love is one's spiritually, and it alone leads to new life. Materialistic achievements count for nothing.

The present, the now opens up to a new day with the future as one's friend - for what is past is past remains in the past. Yesterday must not be allowed to prevent us from having today. How can this be achieved? The constant chatter of your subconscious mind holds decisions from the past that the conscious can take as fact to form action. This works well when we build on confidence, courage, and self worth. But when the subconscious holds fear, doubt worry, we have a foundation of a heavy load on our back. How much better to walk free without the load, for love, confidence and self worth are not a weight to carry. They lift us for an easy stride through each day.

When yesterday is the load there is no today so make sure you are not stopping yourself this day. We are given the strength to deal with this day. The future is our friend. The opportunity is there for hope, faith and love. Each day opens to a new stage. When you go to a play you do not expect them to keep repeating a scene. When the curtain opens you look for the next act, the moving on. Life they say is a stage. One must make each day new by living it to the full. One must look for the beauty of the day while one is continuing to dream from the heart so the new day allows one to bring those dreams to reality. One has to live one's life – not others. We all share the same energy. Are we being pulled off course, how do we know? In a world so fast and loud one needs time of quietness to meditate, to be still, ask the question what is my dream if my life was ending now, what would one wish to have done? Today provides the opportunity to manifest ones dream. One must not let go. Maybe one can find another who has found it. One does not need to start again. Things that are new to one are not new to the universe. One must open one's spirit to the beauty of the flower within: that is one's uniqueness. Ones basic being is always one's foundation. One has to make sure it is sound on which to build. Preparation is of utmost importance.

So whence are ones decisions coming from? Am I happy? Is there lightness, laughter and joy in one' step or is each step heavy- lack of confidence and self-esteem?

To come rediscover one's centre one needs first to acknowledge that it's discovery is necessary - that one wants to do it. How does one become centred and focused? What makes one flow? Enjoying music, walking, friends, or solitude. When the day is busy with noise, rushing, no stillness the beautiful child within is not having its needs met. The longer you continue to wander off one's special path away from one's destiny the more uncomfortable one will become until the day arrives when one might even come to a standstill. The heart will always seek recognition for only

journeying on the path of the heart when it is effortless. One still has to do things but each step moves into where you want to be. Life should be like this - a joy. When one is flowing in harmony with one's heart one will accomplish so much more as one enjoys the journey. Its choice is yours – be happy, make the most of today.

QUIET TIMES

Those rocks give me comfort as I
Sit and gaze over the sea.
This view with its beauty gives me
The stillness to be free.
Thoughts dance through my mind;
They are not there to stay.
Watching as with shadow until
They softly pass away.

The stillness of the moment with
This mirror here to see.
All my thoughts reflected as they
Dance in front of me.
Learning to let go of doubt and
Learning to be calm.
My morning meditation sets the
Path to protect from harm.

This time is mine each day.
The gift to inner peace.
When all the world is rushing around.
When will it all cease.
It isn't surprising that they have no
Time for them self.
That special time of silence which is our own real
wealth.

Allow the stillness to expand.
You will do far more.
For each day will be full of things
You wish to explore.
The fear and uncertainties will slowly
Leave your life.
As you travel on your journey on a Path with out the
inner strife.

COMMUNICATIONS GIFT

The gifts of life are many,
They come in different ways.
Those special little dew drops.
They brighten up our day.
They can be big or small.
In fact the gift may not
Be held at all.
For when the gift is one of love.
We can give it as it is above.

It can be under standing,
A special moment held.
The look, that says I love you
Has a very special spell.
Keep on sharing with the love
Coming from deep within.
When all of us see this way
There is strength to not give in.
Patience is the key to love;
That and communication.
Happiness the joy to share,
Gives strength to all the nation.

MEDITATION

Meditation means order.

We search subconsciously for agreement and acceptance against what we already know. We may consciously re-act when others appear to have a different opinion. What does it take for the individual to accept that difference? Being true to self is the way to good health. The more one attempts to fit in with others the more uncomfortable one will become. As others make statements should we not listen to what they say? After all we all seek recognition. So why not let others seek theirs? This is the meaning of the Indian peace pipe. Each one would hold it for a specified time during which they expressed their opinion. The others would then respond, "This is what you are saying" and if the interpretation was accurate the next in the circle of completeness took the pipe and spoke. So the pipe was passed from one to the other until complete understanding was reached. Acceptance of differing opinions is much to be preferred over seeking power over others is the observation each one needs to be aware of for their own healing. This is why realisation of self by meditation forms the basis of bringing order into one's life. So does it matter to offer an opinion? Will it bring conflict or love to the other person? There is a balance.

Finally is the energy beautiful that we create? We need to consider and meditate that what one sows one reaps – often from the most unexpected quarters. Ones best friend is the little child within. One has to put one's house in order. The individual struggles with self- purpose. It is easy to do what one already knows. Identifying what makes your heart sing gives joy to life. The question is; who am I? Who do I want to be? As one takes a step each day along the journey of the heart life's burden will lighten. Hills and oceans will be an opportunity to experience life instead of a load. So go for it. When the day comes for you to realise life is moving on it will all be worthwhile knowing that you walked the journey of your dream or

dreams. So give your inner child the love, and the recognition that you both walk as one: you need never be lonely again. Support your inner child within. This is the nine tenths of your brain the experts say we do not use. The moment when one realises that one can accomplish anything it is then that it is completely heart centred. Your journey starts with the first step on the path of the heart. So how do you know you are walking your hearts path? Can you remember watching the joy and excitement of a child as they are offered something unexpected to enjoy. Its heart sings doesn't it! Then suddenly the situation may change and the gift may not be available. Its heart drops in loss. So your heart should be joyful to lift. When you recognise the lifting of your heart you know it is your personal journey. Go after this dream until you complete it or you do not feel the joy. The time has come to open your new direction. It is safe to be you.

FREEDOM WAITS

EACH MOMENT IS AVAILABLE
TO BE FREE, TO BE TRUE.
TO ENJOY LIFE'S EXPERIENCE
TO OUR SELF WE MUST BE TRUE.

FOR THE UNIVERSAL ENERGY
PULLS US FROM ALL SIDES.
WE OFTEN GO IN ALL DIRECTIONS
LIKE THE CHANGING OF THE TIDES.

OBSERVING OF THE ENERGY
WITHOUT TAKING IT ON.
LEAVES US FREE TO BE OUR SELF
ON THE JOURNEY WE BELONG.

SO LET OTHERS GO THEIR WAY
IT IS NOT RIGHT OR WRONG.
JUST BEING AWARE. TRUE TO SELF.
WILL FILL YOU FULL OF SONG.

NOW THE SKY IS CLEAR
WITH BLUE SO QUIET AND CALM.
THE CLOUDS HAVE GONE AWAY.
NO CAUSE FOR ALARM.

BE STILL, LET GO FOR JOY.
JUST LET IT ALL RELEASE.
SO IT IS INSIDE,
THE BEAUTY, AT LAST THE QUIET PEACE.

ONENESS

GATHER THE PICTURE AROUND THE WORLD
AND SEEK FOR YOU WILL FIND.

IT IS NOT THE COLOUR, THE RACE OR CREED
WHICH MAKES A DIFFERENCE TO EACH MIND.

EACH BELIEF OR RELIGION
HAS THE BASE OF BEING LOVE.

WHEN EACH ONE COMES TO RECOGNISE AND
CHOOSES TO LIVE BY LOVE.

THEN AND ONLY THEN WILL ONE ENERGY
BE GIVING ONENESS TO THIS EARTH.

THEN AND ONLY THEN WILL WE KNOW
OUR OWN SELF WORTH.

FOR THAT WE SHARE WITH OTHERS
AND FOCUS ON OUR SELF.

IS WORTH NOTHING IF WE DO IT
FROM THE STRENGTH OF WEALTH.

FOR LOVE COSTS US NOTHING
UNLESS WE OFFER LESS.

EACH DAY GIVES US OPPORTUNITY
TO LEARN AS WE PROGRESS.

SHADOWS OF THE PAST SHOULD
NOT BE THE DRIVING FORCE.

BE STILL AND BE THE MOMENT
WITHOUT REACTION OR REMORSE.

People's memories are the joy of
Where we once have been.

The focus should be now
For the beauty yet not seen.

Each chapter of courage opens
New doors to share our love.

Helping to close others as we
Learn with patience from above.

Thank you for this day
Which has really touched my heart.

Forward in the moment
To play my own true part.

CATEGORIZE

When we see or hear something we compare it with the known in the subconscious mind. If it was previously pleasant we want it. When not pleasant we wish to reject it. There is so much we have not experienced. So much that we do not know. Is it possible that in the comparing for sameness we miss the now? Possibly, energies surrounding us with their intensities control our responses? We may be experiencing feelings of loss, rejection, isolation or other concerns that trigger concerns from our childhood. If we can identify our parents' response to each other from early childhood, then we have vital additional information. Were you conceived in love, lust, wanted, not wanted. These comprise the first energies that entered your subconscious. Without realising it these energies may have been your measurement in all relationships to date.

They say that frequently there are family patterns not only of behaviour but also of family illness. Is this due to common factors at conception, past family behaviours and thought patterns? Could it be the conditioning of observation and instructed behaviour? That is you are right, you are wrong, good, bad, clever, even stupid. All this conditioning can form who we think we are. Where there is a negative attitude we can break the tie by changing that thought pattern in our subconscious. The use of an affirmation that is positive, reinforced by use to become the new present thought pattern " I do make good decisions" replaces the negative thought pattern " I do not make good decisions" when the new subconscious memory changes for positive changes success, and self esteem will build in your life as you support yourself from within. Naturally you will continue with your internal housework. It is important to not be unhappy or angry as you identify negativity. Enjoy the opportunity and recognise your ability to become the person you really are. The loving individual then manifests the opportunities to achieve their path with a heart. This unique person is now meeting its inner needs. Once this opportunity is taken joy comes

into our day. In fact time can cease to exist as the individual follows its heart-path without the constant chatter of the unfocused mind. The action of the mind supporting the heart's path ends time. Ever noticed that when you feel truly happy there is inner joy, no blockage, things happen in less time than when your heart is not following you heart path? When the road is heavy take your faith, confidence, courage in yourself and be still to ask the question. What do I need to do to meet my needs for learning for growth?

OUR TREE

LIFE AND LOVE HAS THE TREE.
SO MUCH KNOWLEDGE PASSED
DOWN FOR HUMANITY.
THE ROOTS TO THE EARTH AND WATER.
ITS LEAVES TO THE AIR
AND THE FIRE OF THE SUN.
THE BALANCE OF NATURE
IS THERE IN THE TREE.
IT IS THERE TO HEAL
FOR YOU AND FOR ME.

THE BRANCHES REACH OUT
LIKE SO MANY PATHS.
WHILE THE ROOTS FIRMLY
HOLD THE TRUNK SO STRONG.
ITS LESSONS ARE MANY
AS THE SEASONS GO BY.
LEAVING THEIR MARK,
BUT THE TREE STILL GOES ON.
UNTIL FINALLY DROPPING
A SEED ON THE GROUND.
IT PRODUCES AGAIN
FOR THE CIRCLE TO GO AROUND.

CARETAKER TO MAN
IN SO MANY WAYS.
IT CLEARS UP THE AIR
ALL OF ITS DAYS.
GIVES OF THE ENERGY
IT DRAWS FROM THE EARTH.
ALL YOU DO IS PUT YOUR ARMS
AROUND ITS GIRTH.

BUT MAN IN HIS WISDOM
KNOWS WHAT IS BEST.

So he cuts down the tree
As he has done with the rest.

One day he will realise
Too late to his cost.
That the tree is his friend
For humanity lost.
So get it together
For all of mankind.
For the tree has been here
From the beginning of time.
Our tree will keep going
If we allow it to be.

Plant them, enjoy them and nurture
Them well, from now to the end of eternity.

REACH FOR THE STARS

A YEAR OF TRUST AND BEAUTY
AS YOU LEARN UPON THIS EARTH
THAT THE SIMPLE JOYS EACH DAY
DEVELOP YOUR SELF WORTH

THE COURAGE TO EXPERIENCE
AND TO TRY WHAT IS NEW
WITH CONFIDENCE TO EXPRESS
YOUR UNIQUE POINT OF VIEW

SHARING SPECIAL MOMENTS
WITH DEAR ONES NEAR YOUR HEART
FOR LOVE IS THE PATHWAY
THAT MEANS WE WILL NEVER BE APART

YOUR INSTINCTS WILL SUPPORT YOU
WITH SENSITIVITY AND CARE
FOR COMMUNICATION TO OPEN DOORS
WITH DEAR ONES WHO ARE NEAR

SO SET FORTH WITH TRUE FAITH
AND THE STRENGTH OF INNER LOVE
THAT HAPPINESS IS YOURS TO RADIATE
AS YOU REACH FOR THE STARS ABOVE

ENVIRONMENT

The world is a complex of energies. Each person is capable of a different thought pattern that joins with like vibrations that impact on the world. An example is the trees that use carbon dioxide and produce oxygen. Trees benefit the world by cleaning our air. They provide shade, hold the soil; some grow beautiful flowers and berries for the birds. There is so much more. Clearing the carbon dioxide from the air produces our essential oxygen. It is hard to think of another living thing that contributes so many essentials towards the well being of our planet and human life.

Ever stood against a tree? Trees feel! What do we humans contribute? It is said the world is perfection but the nature of man seems always to assume control. Is mankind looking for the beauty or constantly attempting change? With so much aggression amongst so many on the planet one must eventually have a cause and effect.

Gentleness is the quiet achiever. Aggression eventually returns to the sender. When all people become aware of their personal vibrations that they send out, laughter anger, materialism, love the cause and effect of the individual response of their vibration not only on themselves but also on our earth then and only then will the world claim the real power of the universe. Only love cannot be fragmented. All other vibrations the sender eventually allows to control their path, greed etc. their inner path of the heart is not identified. They are not yet aware this is available to them.

Do we have an energy pattern that is inherited? Whether it comprises interests, likes or dislikes? Is this limiting, confining us to a fraction of the potential that is ours? Maybe it is the pattern that we have come to learn from. Many of our responses are reaction. Not knowing right from wrong. Being still allows energy to halt. In this state, one of just being there - no movement, neither forward nor stepping back. All energy comes from the one universal force. We shape it by our attitude.

All matter is energy. The frequencies of vibrations vary at different locations both internally and externally. Our circulation is important for carrying internal blood. Our life force constantly on the move. Energy can be activated to form attitude. It is acknowledged that the human embryo takes on energy from twenty-one weeks after conception. We are already whole in our being. The taking on of non-loving energies has consequences for changing that child's life to experience less than love. The gift is to go into yourself, your heart. You have the truth. The path to wholeness is yours to put your own house in order. You are on your path to happiness now. When one becomes aware of the things that caste a shadow on one's path one has the means, through thought, of becoming that which one chooses to be. By using a new affirmation, the negative thought form of the present is one's current affirmation. Positive new thoughts create new actions from self and that can bring new responses from others into your life for even greater joy. What messages are you sending out? Attract the love into your life by continuing to send love into your life as you send love out. Vitality will grow in the world. You can live in this world without conflict. When enough individuals are becoming the action of love the world will lift in vibration for higher awareness.

They say that opposites attract. We learn and grow in so many ways. It can be when we acknowledge something lovely that we recognise in ourself or in another. Life should be simple. In the beginning there was light: referring to light as the white light of love that is pure in all its forms. Light being the thought form, the beginning to produce or sow the experience we will have. When all thought is love the energy produces all the bounty required for a life of bliss. The journey towards wholeness in love is non judgemental. Our observations and awareness are the beginning. Newness to the attitude takes us to where we are now. Wonderful isn't it! How is today going? Looked at a tree, a bird, smiled at a stranger, talked with a friend? Recognised yourself in some way? Loneliness is locking the beauty

of the day out. Others will not always make the first call. Show initiative. Make the approach. Someone you know or someone new. Your uniqueness is a special flower that blossoms and grows all of your life even if you are not aware of it. So look at your inner self and smile, laugh and enjoy the little child within that is you. Love starts with self. Once we learn to love self, love attracts love and people around us benefit as love reaches out towards them. The heart opens.

Time doesn't exist. Time is created through expectation, fear, jealousy, doubt, any attitude that is not love. Within each of us is a dream. When that dream becomes our focus and we move into the path towards it, each step will take us towards manifesting our reality. So take the first step.

Remember if you have negative attitudes like a huge rock, all with names "I cannot" "Too late" etc take them down and put in new attitudes of "now is the time" "I commence with this action" "People support me" "Friends support me"- you have the rest of your life: the importance is to start. Do not put the clock on with impatience, disappointment with past actions. The universe has a natural action to allow movement of love into your life through your trust, confidence and faith. Good self-worth, high self-esteem will reflect the person you are the most comfortable with for inner happiness. How do you see yourself? Your heart needs to be able to travel the path that gives you the greatest meeting of your needs for your inner joy. Change to a new path to travel the path of the heart. Remember emptiness, sadness, heaviness can be indications that your attitude is not supportive or this is not your hearts path.

Good communication is rare. How do you communicate with others or with self? Do you listen to what the other person is saying or what you think you need? When others are talking to you do you listen, or do you immediately focus on yourself to tell your story? Everybody needs and deserves the respect to be listened to. Self-worth, self-esteem are mirrored in our behaviour. Give yourself time each day. Use your intuition and listen to your inner knowing. The other nine tenths of the brain rarely used. There

has to be time each day for self, as you tidy, feed your garden so you should attend to self with love, honesty, patience and joy. Laughter always helps so keep your sense of humour. There are no winners or losers in life. Just this moment, the now, to fulfil life's purpose to total love - in the world but not of the world. Confidence builds confidence. Change allows movement instead of stagnation. Take opportunities for growth through living new experiences with existing people and new people. Allow recognition that endings are simple - the beginning of a new chapter. Let the newness be refreshing. Let uncertainty pass. Newness is not the known. Enjoy taking this opportunity for new beginnings. Without the heavy load of assumed problems: freedom is the easy step you take. Unconditional love is allowing another to be true to self without judgement or expectation. New attitudes based on love amongst people allow loving relationships when based on honesty and integrity. Continue to be aware. Your reality is formed by your thoughts. The world's energy is all part of this wholeness, so add your love to it today. Live in the type of world you want to be in, you are the world. You are part of the light of the world. Talking negativities in the world adds to supporting the manifestation of that attitude. Thinking with love can stop, delay or change the outcome. Do you want to be a player for world peace? Each thought is the opportunity to sow love. The author Newbolt impressed me when he wrote, "it isn't if you win or lose, but how you play the game."

So how is your day going? Have you noticed it is the wonderful small things that give inner happiness to most people? Each day has enough joy in it when you allow opportunity to recognise it.

Recognising the uniqueness of self allows love of self. Feeling different, not good enough, puts distance between love and your real self. Acknowledge life is a gift. The gift of love to be love, give love and receive love. So give thanks to each day for the day. During my counselling there have been

individuals of wealth, others with very little. The causes of unhappiness are the same.

The lack of love for self and a true faith in their future, no identification with the purpose of life; the days of both these groups of people generally see lack: whether their concerns are finances, security, friendships or self-esteem. No identification with a purpose of life. Happiness within attracts happiness into our life - new day for seeking the opportunities that support the inner child. You should finish the day knowing you didn't let your inner child feel unsupported. Be your own best friend by recognising the love that is your inner child. There is always enough trust, faith, honour or your beliefs to be true to your inner self. Love is your right. Claim your love by trusting in the universe and yourself. Think big - you are big. Bring out your tool kit. Your potentials are your uniqueness. Live your miracle today: today is every day. The strength of your inner light can inspire others when it is brilliantly lit.

Within each of us is the inner knowing of our true identity. Observe, when necessary negate the observation so you are not living from reaction. So many people go from one reaction to the next having to take action on their reaction instead of being still and choosing their own informed decisions. Everything, everyone has something to teach us. Acknowledge the learning and love the experience. Focus on what you are doing right. Observing joy brings joy. Why ask for anything else? Remember decisions allow our choice of action, while reactions generally take us off the path. You are the biggest teacher of your self. Watch and learn, by observing self, making changes you live the life you choose. Questions often give us opportunity for positive changes to our attitude.

How do you respond when you share?

How do you respond when you do not?

How do you respond when you compliment?

How do you feel when you criticise?

How do you feel when you are criticised?

Be careful what you ask for. What is your pattern?

You are your own thoughts and deeds. Practice what you preach. If not you are cultivating the opposite. Do you allow your mind to go quiet by becoming still or does it constantly chatter? For most people stillness means putting them selves into a meditative state by music, imagining a scene to go to, sitting in a certain position. All of these can be beneficial, but true meditation is order -of-the- mind. The mind that cannot be still is a mind that creates unrest. Consider picturing a rose or something of beauty and keep on picturing it until your mind ceases to chatter and race: all other thoughts are gone. Each day is new as we have opportunity to live the day with total love. Today is always the first day with God. To genuinely repent we need to end the negative pattern through self-awareness and the new thought-form for positive change. It isn't saying sorry only to repeat the action. The same is true of others – letting go of their errors towards us. It doesn't make it right, but accepting that they are also on the journey and do not know any different allow compassion and tolerance. The world can then continue to grow in love.

LIFE ISN'T A RISK LIFE IS AN OPPORTUNITY

WHEN WE TRY OUR HEART CENTRE OPENS
WE SEEK FOR ANOTHER DOOR
WHAT INNER DEPTHS OF KNOWLEDGE
BECKON WHEN WE START TO EXPLORE

FOR NATURE IS THE BEAUTY
THAT SOFTLY OFFERS MORE
THE BIRDS, THE FLOWERS AND THE TREES
THAT WE DO ADORE

THOSE LITTLE INSPIRATIONS
THAT KEEP OUR LIGHT AGLOW
AS WE REAP IN THE BOUNTY
FOR OUR INNER WORTH TO GROW

WHERE LOVE OF LIFE IS THE KEY
SOFTENS US WITHIN
LISTEN FOR THE MESSAGE
THAT HELPS US TO BEGIN

FOR FAITH ON THE JOURNEY
IS OUR REAL STRENGTH
CONFIDENCE IN OUR PROGRESS
TO HANDLE EACH EVENT

EVER-STRONGER FORWARD
FOR THE OPPORTUNITY IS THERE
THANKYOU FOR THIS DAY TO LEARN
ACKNOWLEDGE THE LEARNING THAT IS HERE

IT ISN'T A RISK TO TRY
THE PURPOSE OR OUR SOUL
COME ON WE CAN DO IT
THE WISH TO ARRIVE, BE WHOLE

THE EGO

What is the ego that
Has this opinion.
Who is the ego
To try to change my vision?
My heart speaks out with joy
With new chapters to write.
Then the little ego tries
To block them out of sight.

Sending thoughts of doubt
Buried in the past.
Take courage, let them go
The shadows need not last.
There is but one voice of joy.
It comes from the heart.
Like a child without measurement
It allows you to start.

Many experiences on the path
As we travel along.
Those without calculation
Fill our day with song.
As destiny directs and we
Fulfil our path.
Enjoying life to the full
As we stop doing things by half.

Higher Intelligence

Internal dialogue - Channelling

Insight, intuition, a hunch; write them down when you get them.

Often we ignore the message. In hindsight we often realise that had we acknowledged and heeded the insight the action or response we would have made would have created a better result. Once you get used to identifying and noting the benefit when your response is to use the action to support life insight, confidence adds this natural gift into your life. The isolation goes. You are not unique to channel. Everyone has this gift available. Each individual takes the journey to wholeness in different ways. Knowledge is available in many different forms. It could be one sentence you take note of, a book, a response or an action of another. Once you are aware to collect all the pieces of your jig saw puzzle that are joyful and supportive of self, the final placement of the pieces can only be the joy of living. Lifestyle can raise or lower your vibrations. When your vibrations are too low you will not be able to connect with your intuition. Too much heavy food, alcohol, loud music, aggressive life- styles, negative chatter all lower your vibrations isolating you from the support that you can receive when your vibrations are high. Light food, soft music, gentle-life style support your vibrations to lift. Then communication is available from your higher self for support. Then you can walk on the path with universal wisdom and knowledge to support you. The Akashic record is where an everlasting record is kept of everything that has ever happened in the world - everything that is happening and therefore the probabilities of what may happen. It is like a never- ending cinemascope where the film never ends. Imagine being able to go to the Akashic records to see how a country and the people looked thousands of years ago or even yesterday that live there. The records hold all of this information. For me being given a person's birthday date opens their subconscious to reveal information to assist their healing. It isn't always so much to tell

them what is going to happen tomorrow. Why repeat the pattern that is not following your heart. Often their blockages in attitudes are shown to me and then when revealed to the person they can understand and choose to travel the path of their heart without the heaviness. Learning to protect your self from non-loving thoughts from not only this dimension, but particularly from other dimensions is essential. Love surrounding an individual protects. Your free will to implement action or reaction is yours. It is vital that you understand before leaving yourself open to channelling any thought forms.

Let love light your way. 'Let there be light and there was light'. Thoughts of love create a loving result. Thoughts of negativity, anger, jealousy and more create a negative result. So where does it all start? In a world of love there would be real freedom. Real freedom comes from total wholeness of thought that the content is love, thereby creating or increasing the love on the earth. Each moment we have free will to take on the energy around us. Recognising through observation, sensitivity, feeling and intuition, that the energy is love that is uplifting or negative that lowers our vibrations. Have you ever walked into a meeting and felt unwelcome? This doesn't necessarily mean you are not wanted. It could be the majority of people in the room feel unwanted so the energy is dominant. Once we develop our awareness we can put ourself outside this energy. Can you imagine why we ever put our self outside of love! It is a conscious choice that sadly we walk a path without love. The good news is that there may appear to be a lot of repetition throughout these chapters as they reinforce the action open to change your conscious and subconscious to walk in the world where our every thought sows love. There are several ways to do this. One of these is just to let the energy pass. Another is to picture a mirror so it reflects off you. You could also picture love in the area. All these strategies stop, reduce or repel the unwanted energy. Now are you really having a bad day or just taking on other people's vibrations. Attitude

is everything. Attitude is already past for it is a preformed opinion. When you experience the 'now' there is no comparison, simply what 'is'. Stillness is the gift of no thought, no chattering. A television needs an aerial to receive the picture. A computer needs electricity to work. So it is with us. When we are in a world of noise without the capacity to be still within we are on the outside of the circle. This reduces our vibrations. That is to say that when we are still our inner hearing has the capacity to engage universal energy. Imagine being able to listen to any lecture in the world. Read any known records on becoming whole. When we are connected we can do this. Our free will allows us to accept or reject the information. Most importantly we are not alone. We can assimilate the universal information for our wellbeing. It is natural for us to move towards wholeness. The information can build self-esteem - self-worth when accepted and used to add love to self. This automatically increases the love available to our planet. Only love holds its form. All other energies are divisible. In their fragmentation other attitudes are created. Love holds or multiplies love. Once again it is stated that thought creates the action of what you think. What you sow you reap. Wouldn't it make sense to be aware what you are bringing into your life? Watch, listen, be still when you need to. Let yourself have love. Are you a victim or being given the opportunity to know yourself through experiencing grief, anguish, pain, judgement or low self-esteem, only to rise from the depths to an understanding with insights to have high self-esteem. Letting go of doubt to acceptance, respect and the highest love of self will be the result. Until the individual has respect for them self there will not appear to be acceptance from others as they look for it subconsciously. We do look for acceptance from others whether we are aware of it or not. Do we join in, get asked to join in, are we agreed with or disagreed? Do we wear what we feel comfortable in or attempt to please others? Once the individual learns to self observe this awareness identifies attitudes of strength that are supportive of the beauty of self. Awareness also identifies weakness

that loses the true identity of self. This gives an opportunity to make change. Through this change the individual continues to grow in love towards self. Let go the victim identity and do not take on the thought form, thereby being outside that force. After all it was the individual's perception, the conditioned expectation that gave the thought form. The people around give us the opportunity to acknowledge our inner beauty, to remove our sores and warts and rough edges. Sandpaper is rough but the end result of its use is a smooth surface. Life is like that: enjoy lifting your awareness so that you have a softer, smoother knowing of self. The layers of attitudes you have put up over time will be shed with each new lesson learned. Free will enters - why add more layers through negative attitude? When one lives in the moment one just is! The known may feel safe but the beauty just to be in the moment is true freedom. In the stillness we just are. It is often said that nothing is real. The answers are all there. Let your best friend be your self. So who is your opponent? Whence comes the negative force? Could it be from your self? How are you dealing with the issues? One must be still to know. The mind quietens and in the observation of your thoughts, even in another's presence where there is verbal communication or action one has the moment to observe what you the individual are expecting. Whether from the relationship, the action, judgement in that expectation is the sowing of the seed that can come into form in your life. The other person is the one that is making your doubts, lack of self-worth become a fact. When you sow seeds of positive worth about yourself the action will change. New people will come into your life that you can respond with to the new positive person you recognise as yourself. Sometimes it appears easier to find fault, this action only takes your power away and possibly theirs. Relationships commence by looking for something to love in another. Frequently, generally within two years the relationship can change to one of looking for what could be wrong. The distance between the parties can grow. Possibly to separation or hopefully through self-observation what

they have been reacting to and start taking actions that are responsible and based on love towards themselves and to others. Sadly some of us keep the score sheet subconsciously. Look to write on the love side instead of the negative side. Life will lift to see and enjoy the new day. There are still concerns for how else would you recognise the beauty within as you trust and take action for resolution instead of stirring up the pot. You can never be too positive. This doesn't mean letting the inner child be put down and accepting this behaviour from others. Learn to negate their negativity, it can return to sender or others that claim it.

Sweet song

The seeds have been sown
With care and love
That they will multiply
Throughout the years with love

Peace comes through giving
Without thought of return
Increasing with experience
As we live and learn

The world is for learning
That we may be free
The purpose for being here
Throughout eternity

There is no end
As the energy goes on
When we serve from the heart
With love our own sweet song

PLAY THE GAME

IT IS NOT IF WE WIN OR LOSE.
BUT HOW WE PLAY THE GAME.
KNOWING THAT WHICH WE GIVE,
WE WOULD LIKE THE SAME.
EVERY ACTION FOR US TO DECIDE
SOWS OUR FUTURE ON THIS EARTH.
EVERY ACTION ON OUR PART GIVES
US THE CHANCE TO SHOW OUR WORTH.

WE ARE ONE WITH THE UNIVERSE

Thought the component, the creator. In our immediate environment the thoughts we had yesterday or years ago come into form. The years of youth add our own and others presumed opinions of us into our subconscious. These become our memory bank of self-esteem and self-worth. When it is positive we look for respect in all forms, when negative it appears we expect to be treated in the manner of our subconscious. Sadly instead of living in the moment we listen to another's words to see if they are behaving in the manner of our subconscious. This is our expectation, our conditioning. Once we recognise that it is ourself that is shooting ourself to bring negative conditions into our life we can set an objective to not give control to negative thought form. Now the journey towards freedom can begin. Self-observation and awareness is the key to opening the doors to joy and inner love. Awareness of non-loving measurement gives us the opportunity to either ignore it or put a positive affirmation into its place. "I am not any good" becomes "I love and respect myself daily and so do the people I meet." The subconscious changes the message when you constantly apply the positive affirmation. This is when an individual journey takes on the happiness and high self-esteem that is available for all of us in our lifetime. So we create the day.

LOVE COMES

LOVE COMES DAILY WHEN YOU
OPEN UP YOUR ARMS.
LOVE IS THE FAITH
WHICH KEEPS YOU FEELING STRONG.
FOR COURAGE IS THE JOURNEY
WHICH PROTECTS YOU FROM ALL HARM.
COURAGE IS THE KNOWLEDGE
TO FOLLOW RIGHT FROM WRONG.

MARRIAGE IS THE OPPORTUNITY TO SHARE.
RECOGNISE YOUR OWN SELF WORTH.
TO BE THERE WITH SUPPORT
THROUGH THE SMILES AND THE TEARS.
CHILDREN BRING THEIR MOMENTS
TO SHARE THIS GLORIOUS EARTH.
YEARS GIVE US THE LEARNING
TO LET GO OF ALL OUR FEARS.

GOING FOR YOUR DREAMS TO ALLOW
THEM TO BE REAL.
RESTING WHEN YOU NEED TO,
TO FOCUS ON YOUR STAR.
KNOWING LOVE WILL SUPPORT YOU
IF YOU HAVE IT AND YOU FEEL.
MOVEMENT COMES FROM STILLNESS
WHEN YOU GO FROM WITHIN YOUR HEART.

A LIFETIME IS THIS MOMENT,
NO BEGINNING AND NO END.
GIVING LIFE THE PURPOSE
WE CHOOSE TO HAVE AND SHARE.
FOR LOVE IS LOVE AND ONLY LOVE
FOR US TO COMPREHEND.
WITH FAITH, HOPE AND COURAGE
TO SUPPORT OUR LIFE TIME HERE.

On loves terms

We all look for opportunity
To demonstrate our power
Natural as breathing
Every minute throughout each hour

Mutual respect for each other
With co-operation together
Forms relationships that travel
Through rough waters, any weather

There are logical consequences
To each action that we take
Consideration should be made
To the decisions that we make

Good behaviour to belong
To contribute and co-operate
Give freedom to each one to travel
With space the open gate

Equality for the individual
For each one to live free
Gives unity of purpose
That excludes just thoughts of me

We have opportunity to guide and direct
But not to impose our will
Let love be the example to unite
The terms to be fulfilled

With encouragement there is interest
In all things new
We want to learn about them
With new opportunities to create and do
When a team moves together
With inner harmony
The sharing with each other
Will give happiness the sweetest melody

MARRIAGE

To love, honour and obey.

Today is the wedding pledge. What will make this pledge different to the other pledges that fragment? The dictionary explains pledge as "something given as a security." "One who becomes surety for another." The dictionary then has a surety as a certainty, one who is bound for another. This is a serious day, do we understand that love cannot be fragmented. Where love exists love is real in the action of the moment whether in thought or the deed as a response to thought. Observe the relationships around you now, including the relationship with you - yourself. Where there is no love your thoughts sow the seed for tomorrow. One needs awareness to negate negativity. Have you got the courage just to be, to let go of your constant analysing? The individual has his or her own choice of making decisions on the journey to freedom. Years of authority, division of religions, and wars have intensified antagonism between people and nations. We respond out of fear or loss or to animalistic behaviour. There are many generations of subconscious conditioning. It is for each individual to shed the layers to reveal the inner love that has always been there. Our journey towards wholeness reduces the separation between people and the energy of love. When in the now of love aloneness goes restoring us to eternal peace. Life the journey to wholeness to cultivate what is good and to eradicate what is evil. Being aware of self one has the capacity to love and allow the beauty that is within to blossom. When thought stills or halts there is a quietness that removes the separation from love. Love unites - thought controls and compares. Are you living from your subconscious? Thought is always in the past - the response of memory. Provided what you do is ethical you are sowing reality within self. Do not look for approval: love yourself for this moment of love for you are perfect now. Love is neutral - it isn't positive or negative - love doesn't seek an outcome. It has no expectation or manipulation. Love doesn't judge. Love allows one to be. Love doesn't

seek to claim the energy of another. As long as there appears to be us, or them, the thought process will create separation. This sometimes becomes very pronounced in the name of religions. The beginning is identifying the base of self, your own principals of a loving person. The path towards love is always in process. Love and death travel together. Lessons come in all experiences. We laugh, feel joy, we hold and touch. In the expectation of wanting to hold onto the experience we sow the seeds of doubt, loss and grief. When we are in love we feel safe in being held - not alone. Our learning in life indicates that part of our life experience is to live with our faith instead of leaning on others. Eventually the journey identify's the need for love to be sent out for it to come in. Understanding, that each person is made in God's image, they are their own creator. The author will write their own page or play for all life's experiences in their lifetime. Given as the first cause. From each cause there is an effect. Namely us. Man has written the good book as represented by the different religions. Written as the "Word of God." Sadly different cultures, families fight in the name of God and ask for support to win. Love is not asked for.

It is written that the human being transgressed away from love to take the negative form that has become established practice for behaviour. Away from the love that is God. Time was created, so we do not follow the Good Book. People call this movement from love the Devil. "Be still and know that I am God. Life is made up of each moment within each day. The message is "a day at a time." In the beginning, there was thought. God, the creator formed the world. Ever watched your thoughts? These thoughts are beginning of creating what comes into your life - sometimes formed in that moment, sometimes after years. When you sow love and wisdom you reap that. You do have the power to change your life. Each individual has free will - the freedom to create the world he/she wants to live in. The beginning is to put our own house into order. That of love where there is no end, there just is. There is so much more. We will briefly look at spirit. The opportunity is there for each individual to learn their own truth

from their own experiences. Personal truth is not taught from school or lecturing, it becomes unquestionably the persons understanding - their own truth. Today I heard a minister proclaim the evils of clairvoyance. How clairvoyance is the devil, so evil. The description of a clairvoyant is one that sees without eyes. For many years it has referred to the wise men, the prophets, the witches and so the list goes on as even Kings and Queens have sent for their wise person to tell them of the future. We sadly are off the track and this is why individuals live in a world of pain and suffering of their own creation, yet blame God.

THE CHALLENGE

THAT WHICH WE DO WITH CONFIDENCE
IS WHAT WE ALREADY KNOW.
THE GREATEST CHOICE OF LEARNING
HELPS US TO REALLY GROW.
LETTING GO OF WHAT WE HAVE,
TO HOLD ONTO THE BEST.
TO GIVE FULL FOCUS WITH SOMETHING
NEW, IS CERTAINLY THE TEST.

WHEN THE CHOICE COMES FROM THE HEART
FOR WHERE WE NEED TO BE.
THEN THE GAIN WILL SHINE THROUGH
LOVE FOR EVERYONE TO SEE.
IT ISN'T WHAT YOU LOSE,
FOR YOU HAVE BEEN AND DONE.
YES MY FRIEND YOU CONQUERED,
CERTAINLY YOU WON.

LET EACH ONE BE A PART
OF WHAT THEY NEED TO DO.
THE STRENGTH WITH LOVE SUPPORTS YOU
TO HELP YOU SEE IT THROUGH.
ENJOY YOUR NEW CHALLENGE
WITH THE STRENGTH WITHIN YOUR HEART.
THE LOVE YOU HAVE WILL BRING YOU THROUGH,
AS EACH ONE PLAYS THEIR PART.

POETRY IN MOTION

THE ENERGY OF GOD
IS BEAUTIFUL TO FEEL
MANIFESTED THROUGH THE INDIVIDUAL
ALLOWS IT TO BE REAL

FEELING THE LOVE
AS IT RADIATES THE AIR
GIVING OF THIS POSITIVE FORCE
FOR ALL OF US TO SHARE

FOR WE COME FROM GOD
RETURN TO GOD
OUR ETERNAL FLAME GROWS
EXPANDING AS A SPROUT BURSTING FROM A POD

RELEASING OF THE PAST
THAT ISN'T TRULY REAL
FOR NOW OUR EYES ARE OPEN
AT LAST WE LIVE, WE FEEL

FOR THIS LITTLE CHILD
HAS EYES THAT HAVE OPENED
THE PAIN RELEASED AT LAST
FOR THE INNER VOICE HAS SPOKEN

FREE WILL FOR EACH ALONG THE ROAD
WITH MANY PATHS TO CHOOSE
EACH EXPERIENCE FOR OUR GROWTH
ENSURES WE NEVER LOOSE

SO CLEANSE YOURSELF
LET THE PAINFUL MEMORIES GO
THE ENERGY OF LOVE
THIS CALMNESS SUPPORTS YOUR INNER GLOW

NUMEROLOGY

Numerology is recorded as being the first mathematics developed five hundred years before Christ by Pythagoras. There are numerous books available on numerology, the study of numbers without writing on the meaning given to the numbers in this book.

Everyone has the ability through faith, trust and the courage to manifest all that is needed in life through positive loving thought. Then we are part of the universe in its totality. Positive living is being God-like, negative living is allowing the Ego to cast doubt and fear into our life. Feeling comes in many forms. Awareness is the factor through observation that if you are thinking something that is destructive towards yourself or others you can stop it by putting something loving into it's place. Where there is a pattern, end the pattern. If in childhood you were made to feel you were always being attacked, that others were better than you or you were unloved that is the message you are carrying in your subconscious. Whatever people say you may compare to this factor and decide that it is not true and they do not really care about me. There is quite a bit of housework to do. Those attitudes need to be released and replaced with new positive loving ones. People do care, I can succeed, I have no fear, I am my faith, and I trust myself, acknowledging my thoughts make my day. I am creating my life. When you give a child a new bike you have to trust that they will look after themselves. So why then do problems occur? That is because you have been given free will. As a child grows they must be allowed to be true to themselves and live their life. Each has the opportunity to live with love. Then life will flow for us. When it doesn't we can only blame ourselves, not God.

So now that you have learnt to love the inner child, your observation will allow you to drop the anguish and put in the loving support that this little child has waited for from within. They never need to be alone again. So love that child by putting in confidence, courage and faith. Move into the

world and claim your power. Claim the real you. You are not here to please others. You can share the love, the caring and respect, but not at a cost. The little child within you is the little child that you can put in a house of love to reach your self worth. Claim that child now! What other people think really doesn't matter if you are not saying or doing anything to hurt them. Just get on with your life. You are here to live your life.

GOD BLESS THE CHILD WITHIN

ALL THESE YEARS OF SEARCHING
NOT KNOWING WHAT TO FIND
AT LAST THE FLOWER BLOSSOMS
IT IS NOT INSIDE MY MIND
FOR DEEP WITHIN MY HEART
GOD'S LOVE HAS HELD ME STRONG
THIS BOUNTY HAS ALWAYS BEEN THERE
AND TAKEN ME ALONG

NOW THE VIEW HAS CLEARED
TO LET ME SEE INSIDE
LIFE WILL BE FOR THE MOMENT
WITH A JOYFUL RIDE
RELEASING OF THE BURDENS
THAT SIT INSIDE MY MIND
TO WALK STRONGLY FORWARD
WITH ACTION AT THE TIME

FOR NOW WITHIN THIS CHILD
I SEE THAT I AM LOVED
A CHILD TO FULFIL THE GIFT
THE MAGIC FROM ABOVE
THE LOVE FROM OTHERS AND THE
LOVE OF OBSERVING SELF
HAS GIVEN ME MY FREEDOM
THIS LOVE IS MY REAL WEALTH

OPENING THE HEART

WHAT JOY! WHAT PEACE! WHAT TREASURES
TO SEE THEM FORMULATE
THERE ARE MY INNER DREAMS COMING
THANKYOU IT IS NOT TOO LATE
FOR DESTINY HAS A JOURNEY
FOR EACH AND EVERYONE
DESTINY GIVES THE OPPORTUNITY
FOR RELEASING FEARS TO OVERCOME
WHEN WE STOP AGITATING
OVER SILLY INCONSEQUENTIAL THINGS
THEN THE GATES OPEN
FOR OUR DREAMS TO REALLY SING

ACCEPTING WE CAN HAVE OUR
DREAMS AND SEE THEM BECOME REAL
GIVES MAGIC TO THE MOMENT
WE ARE ALIVE, AT LAST WE FEEL
THIS IS WHAT IT IS ALL ABOUT
HOW WE SHOULD BE
LIFE IS FOR THE LIVING
FOR NOW TO ETERNITY
THANKYOU FOR THE BLESSING
THAT HAS COME MY WAY
AT LAST MY HEART IS HAPPY
I AM LISTENING; NOW MY HEART HAS THE SAY

MIRACLES OF LOVE

It was in 1990 that I started to write. Very often what we write to share with others is what we need to bring our own house into order - claiming our given birthright, the beauty that can be in our life.

There have been several times in my life where I have been saved. We do have a guardian angel watching over us. There was an incident when I was approaching a set of traffic lights. The green light indicated my right away when another car came through on their red light heading straight at the middle of the side of my car. My car was lifted and the next thing I knew I stopped across the other side of the intersection. The other car stopped across their forward direction of the intersection. I was shaken but realised it wasn't my time to be taken or to experience the accident. The universe had saved me.

Another time I was driving at about one hundred kilometres an hour at four thirty am when I came across a huge dead steer on the road. It covered the whole of my side of the road. My small Suzuki car couldn't miss it. I got the message "get your feet off the pedals Teresa" and steered to the right going over the already dead animal. The car veered off to the right going down into a drain and hit the fence post that made the car rebound back across the two lanes to my side of the road. The car motor stopped, and the car came to what appeared to be an immediate stop as well. If my foot had stayed on the accelerator pedal I may not be writing this. Over four hundred and fifty kilometres still to travel to my fathers place. I turned the key and the motor started. There is more to the story, I reached my fathers home safely. It was father's day and I said to my father, " I have brought you a present Dad." My father replied, "I do not believe in those things." "You may want this gift Dad." I said this as I showed him the car and he saw the smashed up side and back of the car. "The gift for you is me home safely Dad. I could have been killed."

I have been saved other times. Often it is the instinctive gut feeling or message not to go, or to go. I am sure there are memorable times in your life. Miracles are truly what these were, done by supernatural powers.

Once I was repeatedly delayed by slow traffic as I drove my twin brother to see the Queen Elizabeth leaving the harbour at Sydney heads. We thought we would miss it. When we finally got there the ship was just coming towards the heads so I stayed on the side of the road in a driveway and remained in the car while my brother crossed the road to see the ship. Kindness showed when the owners of the house saw and called out "Park in our drive if you wish." There I was looked after again and able to give thanks as I joined my brother to bring my dream through. The joy is there if we ask for it.

There are so many books out there now on how to put one's life into order. Achieving wealth. Manipulating others. There is nothing new, it has all been written before. However 'Freedom from within' is based on recognising the love of God is within your Heart and healing and altering your thoughts to those of love in your life. Then the life of joy we came to live and the bounties can be ours. This is the life God gave us in God's image. There is one factor that is very important. That is the understanding of why one needs to put one's life in order, and that you can do that if you want to. Never in the world before have there been so many people that are so unhappy with low self-esteem, loss of identity giving up hope. Just wondering why they are ever here. They do not really believe that they can have a better world. Yes there are books that others have written, "I have changed my life." Somebody asked me the question "what does it really take to make people change?" let us go back to the beginning because when a child was conceived without love, the child can feel unwanted. Probably there was no intention of having a child. The child may claim this sexual energy too. There is no energy or thought power that is lost in the universe. So if you feel that no one bothered about you have a look at

your parentage. Often you haven't met all your grandparents, family do not talk about them or really share things. Possibly they felt abused, unloved or not wanted. What a difference when a child knows they are wanted, told they are beautiful. Has the confidence to know whatever they try they can achieve it. Unfortunately these children are very rare. We all become very good at trying to please other people. Right from a little child there are things we do to get attention. We are told we are clever. They may be smacked or sexually abused. These are the messages that are held in the subconscious of having no worth. This is the message the child then compares things to. Most go to school at five years of age. If they are abused at home they may not feel they belong or that by fooling around they get attention. Where the child lacks confidence in their ability in the classroom they may become the joker of the class to gain attention even though this can attract an attempt to change the behaviour by the teacher. At least getting punishment is recognition, especially when the other children give their attention. At home this child doesn't get attention unless there is violence or negativity. Possibly one of several children and they do not really feel bonded to the family without recognition of their talents. They may not feel clean when they compare themselves mentally to the other children to assume the other children have so much more than they do. The child may even sit in the school grounds feeling unwanted. That is where they feel safe to be. There are those who naturally need quiet time on their own. They may be naturally revitalising themselves by the sight of the trees, the song of the birds, the beauty of the sky with the clouds floating by. Unfortunately so many are not aware where their stillness can come from for inner peace and harmony. They do not take the time to enjoy the greatest gifts we have in the environment. Without the trees there would be no oxygen for our life. Let us go back to the beginning to change our life, claim our joy, happiness through our courage to work with the universe. Why is it we cannot go straight into being free from within? Christ did, Budda did. They didn't hold onto condemnation from other people. The

whole of their heart supported their trust and belief in the purpose of life. They felt worthy to do the job they felt they were given towards the healing example for the world. They didn't take on any negativity as they travelled. Every thought was positive - understanding that the thought you send out returns to you. Through their faith they always thought in the thought pattern of love. God is sad when we have pain, not responsible for our negative thoughts. Recognising that God is love and in that love we are forgiven. It really is time for individuals to stop blaming God.

If you observe yourself you will see that there is frequently a double conversation going on when someone is talking to you. Imagine you are being asked if you would like to do something but your head sends the message you do not fit in. I will be tied there. No I am not really wanted. No I am not going to go. That thought from the Ego is the separation from joy. It stops you from being true to yourself. The more often the separation occurs from the Ego, the more your true personality is lost. Now you have become a people pleaser or a person that avoids others. If the Ego didn't chatter away you would be free to just enjoy the day and the response would be honest and true to your inner self. If you wanted to go you would respond, "Yes, I would love to." If you didn't you would simply state "Not today thankyou, thankyou for asking." There would be none of the juggling around of the Ego. Recognising what is in your heart, having the courage to follow it. The more frequently you follow your heart the less frequently the Ego will be given control. Eventually positive affirmations will become the pattern allowing you to move forward from past negative patterns. The more positive you become, the higher your energy and vibrations to connect with more joy in your life. Often people say "I was on a high yesterday, had a great day." When the Ego controls the response may be, I was feeling really low yesterday, had a bad day." The statements are true in that what we think raises or lowers our vibrations. The more we follow our hearts path of joy, confidence, courage and above all our faith we walk from our heart. The path of life will offer the opportunity for the

individual to become free. Each moment will be free. No comparison or expectations, time will cease to exist.

Now when you look at this book it will contain a lot of statements other books have but it will remind you from time to time to use the chalk duster to rub out the Ego's message and for you to put a positive affirmation in its place. "I am lovely, capable and my faith and love takes me forward to joy and happiness. Sharing with others, my wealth is the love and respect for myself. I am supported in everything I do." When you first start you may think it is just an exercise, but you will observe that things start to improve in your life and you can continue to write the joy by positive loving thought.

THE FRONT OF THE QUEUE

TOSS THE KEY AWAY
LET YOUR HEART FLY FREE
ADVENTURE IS THE KEY WORD
FOR IT IS A TIME FOR ME

GIVING ALL TO OTHERS
WITH FEELINGS FROM THE HEART
AT LAST I SEE THE PICTURE
FOR JOYS TO REALLY START

FOR AT THE END OF THE LINE
IS A LITTLE CHILD THAT IS ME
THANKYOU FOR THE STRENGTH
TO HEAL THAT LITTLE GIRL THAT IS ME

FOR DEEP WITHIN HER HEART
ARE THE SONGS THAT ARE YET TO RING
LITTLE JOYS AND TREASURES
TO MAKE HER HEART SING

EACH DAY WILL BE A PLEASURE
AS I MAKE HER DREAMS COME TRUE
YES, THANKYOU FOR THE MESSAGE
BRING HER TO THE FRONT OF THE QUE

TIME WILL OPEN WIDE
THE DOOR OF HER HEART
RELEASING FEARS TO FOCUS
ON COURAGE IS THE PART

SO GENTLY ENCOURAGE THIS CHILD
WITH LOVE, CONFIDENCE AND FAITH
AT LAST THE JOURNEY HAS SHOWN MY CENTRE
YES! MY PLACE

ENJOY THE EXPERIENCE

DECIDE TO ENJOY THE EXPERIENCE
THAT WILL LET THE ENERGY GO
THE POWER PERCEIVED WILL RELEASE
TO PUT YOUR LIFE IN FLOW

MOVING WITH THE TIDE
INSTEAD OF FIGHTING AGAINST THE WAVES
WILL OPEN UP YOUR LIFE
FOR HAPPIER CARING DAYS

FOR DEEP WITHIN YOUR ASSUMPTION
THAT LIFE IS VERY CRUEL
IT IS YOUR ACCEPTANCE
THAT YOUR JOYS ARE VERY SMALL

SO FOCUS ON THE MOMENT
THAT NOTHING EVER LASTS
ALREADY THIS MOMENT IS OVER
YES, IT IS THE PAST

RECLAIMING OF THAT TIME
PREVENTS THE JOYS OF NOW
SO SET THE SCENE, IT IS POSSIBLE
COME FORWARD TO TAKE A BOW

FOR YOU ARE OUT THERE ON THE STAGE
ONE OF MANY SCENES
WOULDN'T YOU DO IT A DIFFERENT WAY
TO BRING IN YOUR OWN DREAMS?

SO LOOK TO YOUR DREAMS
AS SOMETHING FRESH AND NEW
NOW YOU CAN SEE IT
FROM A DIFFERENT POINT OF VIEW

Gone is the indecision
Connected with the past
Releasing of the time of doubts
When you wondered if it would last

Start your dream and live the moment
Feel that you are free
At last this wonderful peace
My actions are really me

A child of freedom
Without conditioning of the past
Free in the moment
Not wondering if it will last

For timeless is the moment
That's filled me full of grace
Freedom just in being
Without a feel of pace

Feeling one with the world
With no boundaries around
Feeling connected with my vision
Stillness: yes no sound

TIME

We have created time, or should one say time exists when there is thought of desire and expectation. One can just keep on going all day with a task until suddenly there is the feeling, time to go. When one allows things to happen all things are possible to achieve. Not just on your own, but with others that just arrive or contact us to assist. After all there really is no hurry, for it is said that when we come to the end of this earth experience there will always be a list of thing we wanted to do. Stress is something we create ourselves, an attitude of not accepting from others or our own behaviour. If you do not like it, change it or negate it. Life is about ending patterns. Experiencing new life is to live in the beauty of the world. We have created disorder through negative deliberation in our thought process. To err is part of the human condition. The dictionary has the word think as the process to solve by a process of thought, to consider all the consequences relating to a course of action before taking it. Freedom is living in the moment, experiencing the unknown. Thought has not resulted in a soul that lives in harmony and peace. It is time for the human race to let go and be still to experience this peace. To forgive means to let go. Difficult relationships give us the opportunity to heal, the opportunity to put our house into order. Total love is order. The natural order of the universe brings retribution. It is not for us to judge. Evil for evil creates evil. Forgiveness builds love and allows us to move on without the heavy burden of resentment and anger. To negate something is to make something ineffective, imply it is non-existent. Let any reaction go. Be still. You are the world and consciousness is part of the whole. Thoughts are our illusions. When we walk with desire, pain, joy, feeling happiness these are our illusions through thought. When one ceases to be in the common consciousness one has real intelligence: the intelligence that is recognised and referred to as higher intelligence that we can access by using the other nine tenths of the brain. The freedom that is available outside

common consciousness. Follow your heart, with self-esteem, self-worth in your world that is constant change. Your heart is the key, not your head. Intuition is natural to us all. The capacity to be still allows us to achieve the state within where the heart opens to wholeness. Love is an energy that can be felt as the love within you expands others can feel it by being in your presence. The world will benefit by this greater sea of love. Like the ocean the waves of love keep coming in.

Give thanks for the new awareness for the opportunity to follow a new path with courage and self-worth and the power that you are claiming. From the time that we are born there is a higher power looking over us. Whether we recognise a guardian angel, an ancestor, we are not alone. Conditioning can close down the intuitive support. Awareness to desperate times gives us the moment to observe that our intuition offers solutions. Right action moves us through and the clouds open for new beauty. Be still and seek what is there, always has been and if you recognise it love will always be there. Once upon a time intuition was not openly discussed. Certainly clairvoyance was frowned on. Now there is curiosity, a sense of reaching out for help as more people seek spiritual help. All being well they meet genuine intuitive people that are able to give them insights they are currently unable to connect to and receive them selves.

Creative intelligence, you put the slides in so what are you projecting now? What do you really want to do? Make the commitment that you always do what is in your heart. People do not need to learn to think positively. They need to learn to always project positive form. It is time to let the negative thoughts go. These are not the purpose of affirmations. Becoming the action of the words is the movement towards freedom. Let today count, this moment to be focused on the beauty and to be there. Faith is the power to trust. Let go of fear and claim your power. Love is to provide security, pleasure, honesty, trust, vulnerability, intimacy and caring. The result will be a reduced state of loss. Respecting freewill gives the power to accept

or reject joy in your life. Remember you are asking for the experiences amongst the birds, bush, sky, rain and the sun - the relationships available to us from all life forms. Our total universe is connected in every way to all the created vibrations that have been formed. Remember that we the people have the creative intelligence for everything in the universe. May each one of us enjoy ourself and live by trusting in our faith that we will contribute to the healing of this planet with love. Let your body enjoy good health, believe in it by eating well and above all give yourself loving attitude.

All energy forms something. The quantum mechanics is that energy reforms into other combinations that give something new. It doesn't actually ever end so awareness to energy you are attracting or sending out is important. Everything needs positive reinforcement. To identify something wanting, the supplement for the individual is essential health mentally, physically and spiritually.

You may be asking, what does energy mean? Are you feeling tired, energetic, positive or negative? Glad to be here with a dream to achieve, high self-esteem and self-worth. These are the attitudes that make your inner strength. They either open the day with enthusiasm or the day without direction, drive or creativity. This is your energy. When your energy is one hundred percent positive you will be motivated, positive in attitude and in the state of mind to enjoy the day.

ATONEMENT

Time exists for man
As a purpose to an end.
To undo thoughts not of love
That the universe can mend.
The purpose for creation
Went right off the path.
When the miracle of love
Was broken; did not last.

Ever watched your thoughts
As they dance in your mind.
We have the means to change,
To alter, to be kind.
Thoughts of love
Are the miracle of creation.
The healing thoughts of love available
To heal the nation.

LIFE IS A WONDERFUL

LIFE IS A WONDER.
IT IS ALL AHEAD OF ME.
SO MUCH TO CHOOSE FROM.
MY THOUGHTS CAN LEAVE ME FREE.

BY SELECTING WHAT I WANT TO DO
WITH FEELINGS FROM THE HEART.
I WILL KNOW WHAT I WANT AND
BEGIN TO MAKE A START.

THE ROAD HAS MANY DAYS,
SO TAKE THEM EACH IN TURN.
YOUR DIRECTION CAN BE CHANGED
TO GIVE YOU YOUR RETURN.

FOR FEELINGS JOY INSIDE
WITH A SMILE ON YOUR FACE.
GIVES ONE THE HAPPINESS
TO LIVE IN CONSTANT GRACE.

GOD, I AM.

Life in the physical sense is the opportunity we have chosen even before the sperm successfully achieved fertilisation in the egg. To reproduce on earth there is male and female. In writing or speaking about God the majority refer to God as he. God is not made up of physical form. Not identifiable as male or female. God as described in most religions is love in action. Described by God's thought of "Let there be light and there was light". Indications being, that thought creates the form of the thought. Thought that is one hundred percent total love creates immediately. The given response to Moses on Mount Horeb when he asked, "Who shall I say you are?" was "I AM that I AM." (Exodus 3:14) Each individual is made in God's image. Our thoughts create our day. That individuals blame God or do not believe in God always indicates they have no faith. God doesn't impose hardships, challenges, injury, losing a life on individuals. Acknowledging that we are made in God's image with free will is the beginning to working towards freedom – with an understanding that each individual is his/her own creator with respect to conscious and subconscious form. Experiences, health, relationships, all reflect our attitude to life. Life becomes real as our purpose opens to the fact that through our own thought we are the "I AM" responsible for creating love. When we pass on in death, we hopefully go in love with joy and our faith. Many, however, choose to go with fear, anger and thoughts that this is the end. Why would you take these? Think about it? Questioning can bring truth. Truth that becomes real to you. If the truth in you is love you will look for the beauty in your day. This doesn't mean that there will be no concerns. But it does give the understanding not to blame, not to react. To be still and in that stillness loving action will be available. Let your thoughts be your best friend. May your ' I AM 'create the love for life.

EACH POEM IS A MEDITATION FOR YOU TO GROW IN LOVE ON THE JOURNEY TO FREEDOM.
ENJOY THE PROCESS. YOU CHOSE THIS OPPORTUNITY.

MAY YOU CONTINUE TO WALK THE PATH, REALISING THAT NOW YOU UNDERSTAND YOU
WILL NOT GIVE UP AND ENJOY EACH OPPORTUNITY FOR FURTHER GROWTH.

FAREWELL THE AUTHOR TERESA ALEXANDER

FAREWELL AS IN "FARE THEE WELL" AN EXPRESSION FROM SCOTLAND.

A GIFT OF LOVE

Inspirational verses to uplift the soul

ACKNOWLEDGEMENTS

My special thanks to Bill McKean. A true friend throughout the twenty four years I shared with him before he passed away. My first friend when I came to Australia, Bill was always there for me.

Aunt Agnes Anderson of Scotland who left me the money to purchase the dictionary that has given me confidence and support of love each time I use it.

Peter Hawking for the book on computers that "worked". Many little things make big things happen.

Charles Gerussi for the setting up my computer. Just phone and Charles was there. Thankyou Charles.

There is a dear friend that doesn't want recognition. This is because her understanding of life is very real and honest. Our walks together as I discussed my writings were very encouraging. My friend thankyou for just being you and sharing with me as my thoughts opened to these writings.

MESSAGE FROM THE AUTHOR

'My continuing enquiry into life led me to accept and believe that we are never alone'

My life is dedicated to the joy of life on the journey to wholeness. Meditation is for order within. These poems have been written to assist with healing within the planet.

Dedicated to my dear friend Mary Irwin. The Scottish friend that mothered me, loved me like a daughter and I her as a mother.
Her words "you can do it" inspired me to believe and to trust myself and go ahead with my publishing. God bless you Mary.

In each persons life there is some one who changes our life forever. Mary's joys and her pains have empowered me to blossom. Death is not the end. Until we meet, Thankyou Mary, my love always.

Special dedication to all who seek purpose for this life,
May you travel with courage from the centre of your heart!

ABOUT THE AUTHOR

Born in New Zealand, teresa alexander is a twin and one of seven children.

After experiencing the early knocks of life, Teresa left New Zealand for the United Kingdom, where she lived for 10 years before arriving in Australia and making it her home.

It was in Australia during moments of solitude amid nature that her writing began to evolve. It has graced greeting cards and been used for meditations.

Teresa's balance comes from the oneness with nature; believing the purpose of life is self-growth and total love. Faith in acceptance that God is love and that we have been given free will to create our experiences by our thoughts. acceptance that the moment is our reality. Walking the journey in love or fear is a choice we have. Teresa's intuitive strength has given her the connection to believe and sustain her.

Teresa writes her works for all who seek and question life for their inner growth towards becoming one with God. That the world has an opportunity to survive by the growth of inner love that can heal all life forms on this earth.

THE LEAF OF LIFE

I AM ON MY LEAF OF LIFE
FLOATING ON LIFE'S RIVER.
NO MATTER WHERE LIFE TAKES ME;
I WILL NOT FEEL BLUE OR SHIVER.
FOR DEEP WITHIN MYSELF
I ALWAYS DO MY BEST.
KNOWING FINALLY WHEN I GO TO BED
THAT I HAVE EARNED MY REST.

MY WORLD IS OPEN, THE CHOICE IS MINE
FOR ME TO CHOOSE DIRECTION.
MANY ROADS SEEM THE SAME,
SO I CHOOSE FOR SATISFACTION.
TIME IS MINE TO LEARN,
TO BUILD THE PEACE WITHIN.
LETTING GO OF CONFLICT
FOR THE SUN TO SHINE RIGHT IN.

HOME WITH MY FAMILY,
IN A HOME THAT IS FULL OF LOVE.
EACH DAY I GIVE THANKS
FOR THIS BLESSING FROM ABOVE.
WE LAUGH AND CRY TOGETHER
AS WE SHARE EACH THING NEW.
YES MY LIFE IS HAPPY,
FOR I CLEARLY SEE THE VIEW.

Do it your way

Go through life your way.
Try not to conform.
Walk your own road
For the reason you were born.
Being kind to others,
Staying true to self.
Allows you a full life
To know your own true wealth.
No time for regrets,
Of things you wish to do.
Each day as you fulfil your heart
Allows you to be true.

Time passes swiftly for each
And every one.
Know with a song these are
The things you wanted done.
Many opportunities come
Along the way.
Get up, enjoy them,
Make today your own day.
Smile from your heart
As you move from place to place.
Know you have done your best
When you look at your own face.

For others are not your judge,
They do not walk your way.
Each their own destiny
As we share some things each day.
Continue on with love
For each and everyone.
Leave them to their own road
With blessings from above.
When you know that you have lived
The best that you could do.
Peace will come within
With each day so new to you

LIFE IS FOR LIVING

So you have a challenge,
A further chance for growth.
Just how to go about it
To ensure you gain the most.
Stay at the top of where you are
With your spiritual insight.
Follow your faith to focus there
To turn darkness into light.

For doubt or judgement brings you down
When you focus on your plight.
Energies are passing; so be your faith,
Stay up in the positive white light.
Know that learning comes from
Courage in believing who you are.
Continually working upward.
A happy sparkling star.

Pick your gifts to help you.
Faith, courage, love.
Know you are a winner when you
Engage the higher energies from above.
For happy is the moment
When we take our self in hand.
Happy is the moment when
At last we understand.

That freedom is our choice
With loving attitude.
The choice is always ours
To be the positive point of view.
Other people notice.
It is nice to feel you near.
Laughter, joy and caring
Light the world right here.

WHEN THE WORLD CAN SEE THAT HOW
THEY FEEL IS IN THEIR HANDS.
THEN THE KNOWLEDGE GAINED
WILL MAKE THEM UNDERSTAND.
THAT INDEED WE ARE FREE.
OUR WILL IS OUR OWN.
SELECTING POSITIVE ENERGIES
TO SAFELY HEAD FOR HOME.

MAGNIFY THE POSITIVE ENERGIES
AS OTHERS TAKE THEM ON.
INCREASE THE JOY OF THE WORLD
AS EACH ONE FILLS WITH SONG.
WHEN EACH ONE ACCEPTS RESPONSIBILITY
FOR HOW THEY WANT TO FEEL.
THE JOY, THE FAITH, THE COURAGE
WILL CREATE THE INNER WORKING SPELL.

THE BIRDS WILL BE HEARD TO SING,
THOUGH THERE HAS ALWAYS BEEN THEIR SONG.
THE MUSIC OF THE WATER AS IT
TRICKLES OR RUSHES STRONG.
THE TREES IN ALL THEIR GLORY WILL BE
VIEWED WITH ALL THEIR SHADES OF GREEN.
WITH THE COLOURS IN THE HEAVENS,
THE BRIGHTEST WE HAVE EVER SEEN.

THANKYOU FOR THE BLESSINGS
AVAILABLE EACH DAY.
LOVING, SHARING, GIVING AS THEY
GENTLY COME EACH DAY.
A BREATH OF AIR IS SLIGHT,
BUT KEEPS US ON THIS EARTH.
THANKYOU FOR THE EXPERIENCES
WE ARE GIVEN FROM OUR BIRTH.

Our healing park

There is peace today within the park.
With natures beauty to heal the heart.
The trees full of glory
Have burst out with spring.
While the birds in their joy
Start to sing.
Water reflections across the pond,
Give joy to this day which
Forms quite a bond.
For stillness and beauty
Can all be yours.
When nature and man
Have the same rapport.
As you become one with
This beautiful scene.
Relax, be still, it is yours;
Not a dream.

MY GUIDE

Thank you for your hand;
Yes, it has always been there.
But now as I see to understand
You have always been right here.

Knowing that you watch my step.
You never give up, or show regret.
If you have the love
To always watch over me.
Then I have the courage on this journey
With growth to set me free.

The cleansing of the rain
and life force in the sun.
Now I am not afraid
Of anything or anyone.

No expectations

The slate is clean,
All promises fulfilled.
My way is clear.
I have done my best.
Nothing lost,
Each day to gain.
Joyful life
Through the sun and the rain.
Chains of the past release
To set me free.
Love in its beauty in the
Moment, now care free.

Magic is the moment,
Beauty everywhere.
Patience from within
Allows others to be whole.
Giving them their place
Without judgement to compare.
Allows each one to go their
Way to fulfil their own role.
Gratitude in the day
For everything that has been.
Look for the beauty to
Note just what you have seen.

PLAY THE GAME

IT IS NOT IF WE WIN OR LOSE.
BUT HOW WE PLAY THE GAME.
KNOWING THAT WHICH WE GIVE,
WE WOULD LIKE THE SAME.
EVERY ACTION FOR US TO DECIDE
SOWS OUR FUTURE ON THIS EARTH.
EVERY ACTION ON OUR PART GIVES
US THE CHANCE TO SHOW OUR WORTH.

OBSERVATION

WHEN ONE TRULY LOVES, THEY LOVE
WHEN IT IS THE ENERGY FROM ABOVE.
FOR LOVE HOLDS NO JUDGEMENT
OF OTHERS OR OF YOURSELF.
KNOWING LOVE IS WHOLE
IS OUR TRUE WEALTH.

TRUE WILL GIVES CHALLENGE ALONG THE
WAY FOR EACH AND EVERYONE.
KNOWING YOU CAN MAKE CHANGES
SHOWS THE VICTORY CAN BE WON.
DO NOT LOOK AT OTHERS TO JUDGE
THEM OR BE UNKIND.
FOR TIME CAN GIVE THE STILLNESS
TO GIVE YOU PEACE OF MIND

THE CHALLENGE

THAT WHICH WE DO WITH CONFIDENCE
IS WHAT WE ALREADY KNOW.
THE GREATEST CHOICE OF LEARNING
HELPS US TO REALLY GROW.
LETTING GO OF WHAT WE HAVE,
TO HOLD ONTO THE BEST.
TO GIVE FULL FOCUS WITH SOMETHING
NEW, IS CERTAINLY THE TEST.

WHEN THE CHOICE COMES FROM THE HEART
FOR WHERE WE NEED TO BE.
THEN THE GAIN WILL SHINE THROUGH
LOVE FOR EVERYONE TO SEE.
IT ISN'T WHAT YOU LOSE,
FOR YOU HAVE BEEN AND DONE.
YES MY FRIEND YOU CONQUERED,
CERTAINLY YOU WON.

LET EACH ONE BE A PART
OF WHAT THEY NEED TO DO.
THE STRENGTH WITH LOVE SUPPORTS YOU
TO HELP YOU SEE IT THROUGH.
ENJOY YOUR NEW CHALLENGE
WITH THE STRENGTH WITHIN YOUR HEART.
THE LOVE YOU HAVE WILL BRING YOU THROUGH,
AS EACH ONE PLAYS THEIR PART.

TRADITION

A FAMILY OF ETHICS
THAT LIVE BY THE CODE.
A SENSE OF VALUES TO FOLLOW
AS THEY TRAVEL DOWN LIFE'S ROAD.
FOR GENETIC IS THE LESSON
FOR OPPORTUNITY TO BE WHOLE.
LIFE THE EXPERIENCE TO LEARN,
TO BE FREE, TO KNOW.

LESSONS AND EXAMPLES
WHEN WE ARE KNEE HIGH.
PUT OUR FEET UPON THE PATH
WITH ASPIRATIONS FROM ON HIGH.
WHEN THE DAY COMES THAT
WE START TO QUESTION WHY.
THE FOUNDATION OF THE FAMILY
WILL LIFT US UP ON HIGH.

FOR GRANDMOTHER HELD THE
COMMANDMENTS UP IN HER HAND.
GRANDFATHER TOOK NO NONSENSE
FOR HE DIDN'T BUILD ON SAND.
THE ROCKS OF FAMILY VALUES
WERE THE BASE ON WHICH WE WALKED.
THEY WERE ALWAYS ALL AROUND US
TO SEE IF WE DID NOT TALK.

SO IT IS WITH THANKS THAT MY
HEART GOES OUT TO THEM
THAT WALKED THE PATH AHEAD OF ME.
MY THOUGHTS DO NOT CONDEMN.
THE LOVE IS REAL, THE CONFLICT,
THE PAIN AS THEY WALKED.
I WISH THAT I HAD KNOWN THEM
SO THAT WE COULD SHARE, HAVE TALKED.

NEW CHAPTERS

LIFE HAS MANY CHAPTERS
FROM THE FIRST ONE TO THE END.
MANY PEOPLE WRITE ON THEM
THROUGHOUT OUR LIFE TIME HERE.
THE MOST IMPORTANT CHAPTERS
ARE THOSE WE WRITE OUR SELF.
THOSE SPECIAL DECISIONS WE MAKE
THAT SHOW OUR OWN TRUE SELF.
IT OFTEN TAKES MANY YEARS
TO LET GO OF THE PAST.
TO WALK FREE AND STRONG, WITHOUT THE
SHADOWS WHICH DO NOT NEED TO LAST.
EACH DAY CAN BE NEW AND FREE
FOR US TO FULLY EXPLORE.
WITH ALL THE MAGIC COLOURS OF LIFE
THERE IS SO, SO MUCH MORE.
MONEY CANNOT BUY IT.
THE FREEDOM OF THE HEART.
THAT SPECIAL LITTLE SOMETHING WHICH
MEANS TRUE LOVE IS NEVER APART.

Smile on the day

Flowers every colour
Smile on the day.

They brighten up our life
In so many special ways.

Their colours come to meet us.
Some with perfume have a plus.

They blend into our wealth;
For these beautiful colours
Are a reflection of our self.

BE STILL

LET THE SILENCE ENTER THAT LITTLE
CHAMBER FILLED WITH LOVE AND LIGHT

THAT IN THE SPACE ONE MAY SEE
AND BE GIVEN MORE INSIGHT.

A HEART OF JOY IS FILLED WITH GOLD,
COURAGE AND STRENGTH FOR A FIRM FOOTHOLD.

SO REMEMBER THE PEACE FROM WITHIN
WHEN YOU WERE STILL.

FRIENDSHIPS LIKE A RIVER

FRIENDSHIP IS LIKE A RIVER
WHICH FLOWS AROUND ROCKS AND BENDS.
THE WATER STILL AND QUIET,
OR RUSHING TO END UP AS A FALL.
WHERE IT DASHES PAST THE ROCKS
TO FLOW OFF FAR BELOW.

YES, FRIENDSHIP IS A RIVER
WITH MUCH FOR BOTH TO SHARE.
THE SADNESS AS WITH DROUGHTS AND FLOODS,
WHERE NATURE BATTLES ON.
SO IT IS WITH FRIENDSHIP
AS THE RELATIONSHIP TRAVELS ON.
EACH ONE BEING THERE.
THE SPARKLE TO HOLD A SONG.
SO MUCH TO SEE TOGETHER;
THE VALUE JUST TO SHARE.
LOVE IS THE WATER,
WHICH GIVES US LIFE AND JOY.

YES, FRIENDSHIPS LIKE A RIVER,
FOREVER FAR YET NEAR.
THE FORCES OF THE WATER
CHANGE LIFE, SHAPE AND FORM.
JUST AS OUR CENTRES CHANGE WITHIN
FROM THE MOMENT WE ARE BORN.
SIT WITH A FRIEND, FEEL A SPECIAL
PEACE, THAT STILLNESS, BUT STILL SPACE.
WITH EACH ONE IN THEIR OWN WORLD,
YET THE ENERGY OF ONE.

YES , FRIENDSHIP IS A RIVER
WITH MUCH FOR BOTH TO SHARE.
WHEN THE WATER BECOMES MURKY
THERE IS MUCH THAT SHOULD BE DONE.

FOR LIFE TO REALLY SPARKLE
THE CLEANSING MUST BE WON.
DO NOT FIGHT OR STRUGGLE,
OR SWIM AGAINST THE TIDE.
WELCOME THE STILLNESS,
WITH YOUR ARMS HELD OPEN WIDE.
FROM STILLNESS COMES JOY
OF SEEING WHERE YOU REALLY ARE.
THE CHOICE IS YOURS OF WHAT TO TAKE
AND WHAT TO LEAVE BEHIND.

YES , FRIENDSHIPS LIKE A RIVER,
FOREVER FAR YET NEAR.
SOME TRIBUTARIES REFORM TO MEET THE MAIN
FLOW AS IT CONTINUES ON ITS WAY.
WHILE OTHERS TRAVEL ON THEIR WAY
NEVER TURNING BACK.
SO IT IS WITH FRIENDSHIP
OF THE SPECIAL KIND.
THE WATERS FLOW DEEP AND HOLD THEIR PLACE
WITH LOVE SECURE TO PASS THROUGH TIME.

COURAGE

COURAGE ISN'T ALWAYS WHAT
OTHER PEOPLE THINK.
MANY PEOPLE HAVE IT,
THAT EXTRA SPECIAL LINK.

IT SAYS KEEP ON TRYING
WITH WHAT WE HAVE TO DO.
THE INNER STRENGTH IS THERE
TO FIGHT AND TO BRING YOU THROUGH.

EACH ONE MUST IDENTIFY
JUST WHAT THEY HAVE TO DO.
SO EACH DAY CAN BE A PLEASURE
WITH EVERYTHING AS NEW.

LIFE IS ABOUT WINNING,
EACH IN THEIR OWN WAY.
GIVE THANKS AT NIGHT WITHIN,
LOOK FORWARD TO TOMORROW THE NEW DAY.

FRIENDS AROUND LOVE YOU
AS THEY SEE YOU OVERCOME.
WE OBSERVE YOUR WINNING WAYS
AS YOU JOIN LAUGHTER AND FUN.

KEEP SMILING AND REACHING
FOR ALL THE GROWTH ABOVE,
MY FRIEND YOU HAVE SUPPORT
FROM ALL OF US WHO LOVE.

FOR TODAY

ANOTHER DAY, ANOTHER YEAR.
A TIME TO CELEBRATE THE SOUL IS HERE.
EACH DAY WE LIVE, EACH DAY WE LEARN.
TO WALK THROUGH LIFE WITHOUT CONCERN.

THE MIRROR PLACED ON THE WALL.
ALLOWS US TO REFLECT AND TO SEE IT ALL.
IF WE WISH, WE CAN MAKE CHANGES.
THE PURPOSE OF LIFE THROUGH OUT THE AGES.

IT ISN'T WHAT OTHERS SAY.
IT ISN'T WHAT OTHERS DO.
EACH HIS JOURNEY FOR HIS SOULS SAKE.
EACH RESPONSIBLE FOR THE WORDS AND
THE ACTIONS THEY TAKE.

CHRISTMAS

For all that we share
Each day of the year.
Our laughter, our joy,
Our fears and our woes.
We just keep on smiling
With the joys in our heart.
The love which we share
Sets no day apart.
Now that it is Christmas
We pause to say.
Thank you for the love
Which came our way.

We acknowledge , give thanks
With a wish from the heart.
That the new year will bring joy
Right from the start.
If Christmas makes us pause
To see what we have.
Then life will be brighter,
Not nearly so bad.
If we can give to others,
Instead of seeing self.
The gift of love will be treasured
As value more than wealth.

BIRTHDAY BEGINNINGS

A BIRTHDAY IS THE BEGINNING
OF YOUR OWN PERSONAL YEAR.
AN EXTRA SPECIAL TIME FOR FRIENDS
TO SHOW HOW MUCH THEY CARE.
MY FRIEND I WISH YOU HEALTH AND JOY
ON THIS YOUR SPECIAL DAY.
MAY EVERY DAY THERE AFTER
BE FILLED WITH LOVE AND LAUGHTER.

AN OPPORTUNITY TO BENEFIT FROM THE
GROWTH OF THE PASSING YEAR.
IF WE TAKE THE TIME TO LOOK
IT GIVES STRENGTH AND PURPOSE
FOR THE COMING YEAR.
WISDOM MAKES US YOUNGER
AS WE TEMPER UP THE STEEL.
THOUGH MANY OF US FEEL
IT IS A SPECIAL KIND OF HELL.

IN FACT IF WE ACCEPT THE CHALLENGE
AND FACE IT TO THE END.
WE USUALLY FIND BEFORE TOO LONG
WE FEEL SAFE, AT PEACE AGAIN.
WITH CHANGES COMING AROUND US
AS WE JOURNEY ON OUR PATH.
TAKE TIME TO REFLECT ON ALL THE BEAUTY
OF THIS SPLENDID EARTH.

THANK YOU FOR TODAY

WHAT NOURISHES AND FEEDS US
UPON THIS EARTH TODAY?
BRINGS US TO A STANDSTILL
AND REALLY MAKES OUR DAY.
THE RIVER FLOWING BY
AS IT GENTLY CURVES AND BENDS.
FLOWING ALWAYS ONWARDS.
ON ITS JOURNEY TO THE END.

BIRDS ON WING SEEK DAILY
FOR THE TREES WHERE THEY CAN LAND.
GENTLY TAKING NECTAR
FROM THE FLOWERS AS THEY STAND.
OUR GARDEN IS THE GLORY
FULL OF SENSES THAT DELIGHT.
FULL OF JOYS AND COLOUR
FOREVER IN OUR SIGHT.

OUR TREE

LIFE AND LOVE HAS THE TREE.
SO MUCH KNOWLEDGE PASSED
DOWN FOR HUMANITY.
THE ROOTS TO THE EARTH AND WATER.
ITS LEAVES TO THE AIR
AND THE FIRE OF THE SUN.
THE BALANCE OF NATURE
IS THERE IN THE TREE.
IT IS THERE TO HEAL
FOR YOU AND FOR ME.

THE BRANCHES REACH OUT
LIKE SO MANY PATHS.
WHILE THE ROOTS FIRMLY
HOLD THE TRUNK SO STRONG.
ITS LESSONS ARE MANY
AS THE SEASONS GO BY.
LEAVING THEIR MARK,
BUT THE TREE STILL GOES ON.
UNTIL FINALLY DROPPING
A SEED ON THE GROUND.
IT PRODUCES AGAIN
FOR THE CIRCLE TO GO AROUND.

CARETAKER TO MAN
IN SO MANY WAYS.
IT CLEARS UP THE AIR
ALL OF ITS DAYS.
GIVES OF THE ENERGY
IT DRAWS FROM THE EARTH.
ALL YOU DO IS PUT YOUR ARMS
AROUND ITS GIRTH.

BUT MAN IN HIS WISDOM
KNOWS WHAT IS BEST.

So he cuts down the tree
As he has done with the rest.

One day he will realise
Too late to his cost.
That the tree is his friend
For humanity lost.
So get it together
For all of mankind.
For the tree has been here
From the beginning of time.
Our tree will keep going
If we allow it to be.

Plant them, enjoy them and nurture
Them well, from now to the end of eternity.

LOSS, THE JOY OF HAVING

YES MY FRIEND YOU HAVE HAD A LOSS.
THE ONE YOU LOVED, YOU WILL FEEL LOST.
THE THINGS YOU SEE, YOU FEEL AND TOUCH.
REMIND YOU DEARLY OF SO MUCH.

TAKE TIME TO BE STILL AND COUNT THE WAYS.
THESE THINGS WERE BLESSINGS OVER THE DAYS.
YOU SHARED WHAT MANY HAVE NEVER KNOWN.
YOUR YEARS SO FULL HAVE REALLY FLOWN.

SMILE ON THE MEMORIES EACH DAY.
REMEMBER A SOUL, A THOUGHT,
IS NEVER FAR AWAY.
LOOK AT WHAT YOU HAVE TO KEEP.
THE LOVE IN YOUR HEART WILL GIVE YOU PEACE.

LOVE SHINES FORTH FROM UP ABOVE.
YOU ARE COVERED BY THIS HEAVENLY LOVE.
REACH OUT YOUR HAND IF YOU FEEL LOST.
MY FRIEND OUR LOVE WILL NEVER COST.

MOTHERS GIFT

MOTHER'S DAY MEANS MORE TO ME
THAN WORDS CAN EVER SAY.
WHEN FIRST I HELD YOU IN MY ARMS
I KNEW YOU WOULDN'T STAY.
A TINY SOUL, A ROSEBUD,
ON LOAN FROM UP ABOVE.
SO FRAGILE AND TRUSTING.
A GIFT OF JOY AND LOVE.
TO NURTURE THROUGH THE EARLY YEARS
WITH LOVE AND UNDERSTANDING.
 TO SET YOUR FEET UPON THE PATH,
TO MAXIMISE YOUR LEARNING.

OUR DAYS SO FULL OF LAUGHTER,
OF SHARING EACH THING NEW.
AS YOUR EYES GREW BIG AS SAUCES
IN THIS WORLD SO NEW TO YOU.
YOU WOULD HOLD MY HAND IN WONDER,
A SIGN OF YOUR TRUST.

YES, MOTHERS DAY IS EVERY DAY.
THERE IS SO MUCH TO REMEMBER.
NOW THAT YOU HAVE GROWN AND
YOU SEEK OUT YOUR OWN PATH;
I PRAY THAT GOD WILL HELP YOU
ACHIEVE EVERYTHING YOU ASK.

REACH UP YOUR HEART TO GOD WITH TRUST
AS ONCE YOU DID WITH ME.
THAT LOVE WILL ILLUMINATE
EVERYTHING YOU DO.
THANK YOU FOR THE JOY OF OUR
EARLY DAYS TOGETHER.
YES, MOTHERS DAY IS EVERY DAY,
THERE IS SO MUCH TO REMEMBER.

FATHERS GIFT

A FATHERS THOUGHTS ARE MANY
FOR HIS LITTLE CHILD.
THE EXTRA DAYS OF WONDER
MAKE IT ALL WORTHWHILE.
A CHANCE TO SHARE THE BEAUTY
GATHERED ON THIS EARTH.
A CHANCE TO SHARE THE VALUES
WHICH GIVE US OUR SELF-WORTH.
THOSE LITTLE EYES THAT SPARKLE
AND FILL FULL OF JOY.
IT DOESN'T REALLY MATTER
IF IT IS A GIRL OR BOY.
CHERISHED ARE THE MEMORIES
OF THINGS SHARED ALONG THE WAY.
THEY BUILD A BOND TO SHOW HE CARES
AND CHERISHES EACH DAY.

EACH STAGE A DIFFERENT LEARNING
WITH NEW THINGS TO SEE AND DO.
A FATHER AND A FRIEND WHO
DOES EVERY-THING WITH YOU.
MAKING THINGS, RIDING A BIKE,
EVEN HOW TO FISH.
WHO BUILDS THE FIRE TO COOK IT.
IT IS STILL MY FAVOURITE DISH.
YES FATHERS CAN BE SPECIAL
WHEN THE YEARS DO NOT COUNT.
WHEN BOTH OF YOU ARE CHILDREN.
YES, THAT IS WHAT IT IS ABOUT.
NOW WHEN I AM ON MY OWN,
MY THOUGHTS GO DEEP WITHIN.
FOR MEMORIES SAFELY IN MY HEART
ARE ALWAYS THERE OF HIM.

WHEN EACH ONE HAS THE LOVE
THAT EACH ONE IS A PART.
THEN WITH CONFIDENCE AND LOVE
THEY WILL ALWAYS KNOW WHERE TO START.
SO IT IS WITH THANKS,
TO BE GIVEN TIMES TO SHARE.
THAT I WAS ABLE TO TELL HIM
WHILE ON OUR JOURNEY HERE.

SELF OBSERVE

Self observe as with a mirror
To observe your thoughts within.
With love of self and patience
Those hard times will pay dividends.
They lead to learning on all things
To clearly show us here.
That love is love and only love
Which keeps it uniquely dear.

OPENING YOUR HEART

LIVING FOR THE MOMENT WITH
TRUE FEELINGS FROM THE HEART.
WITH JOY OF KNOWING THAT
GIVES US THAT SPECIAL PART.
THE MANY YEARS OF GROWING,
OF SEARCHING FOR THE BEST.
TO FINALLY ARRIVE AS WE
TAKE ON THE REAL TEST.
OUR PATH THAT GIVES US WHOLENESS
WITH JOY AT OUR HEART.
HELPS US IDENTIFY
EXACTLY WHERE TO START.
THE ART OF OBSERVATION
OF OTHERS AND OUR SELF.
THAT WE MAY MAKE THE CHANGES
WHICH GIVE US OUR TRUE SELF.

THIS MOMENT

This world is mine to take
In the time that I am here.
To experience and learn
Everything I can.

Each moment is a chance
To work on the big plan.
The joy of being here
To evolve as you can.
Pain is not lasting,
Anymore than joy.
As with a child in the moment
As it plays with its toy.

Observe the moment and know
It does not last.
Everything that has been
Is already in the past.

THE ROAD TO SUCCESS

THE DISAPPOINTMENT PASSES.
LET THOSE EMOTIONS GO.
PUT IN DETERMINATION
AND GET ON WITH THE SHOW.
NOW THAT THERE IS A CHALLENGE
TO BRING COURAGE RIGHT TO HAND.
FROM THIS COURAGE CAN GROW GREATNESS.
REMEMBER WHERE IT ALL BEGAN!

ALL THINGS PASS

ALL THINGS WILL COME TO PASS.
MOVEMENT IS AROUND.
FOCUS IS ON THE DREAM
WHICH MAKES IT VERY SOUND.
EACH STEP BRINGS IT CLOSER
AS OPPORTUNITIES UNFOLD ALONG THE WAY.
THE COURAGE TO KEEP ON TRYING
MAKES IT POSSIBLE EACH DAY.

CREATION IS THE KEY
WITH DELIGHT WITHIN THE HEART.
KNOWING TRULY WHAT ONE WANTS,
SO THE FOCUS SHOWS US WHERE TO START,
LETTING GO OF ANGER, FEAR AND THINGS NOT SEEN.
ALLOWING FOR THE FLOW OF TIDES
TO ENHANCE YOU'RE EVERY DREAM.

EACH DAY IS FOR CREATION
FROM DEEP WITHIN YOUR HEART.
FEELING THOSE GENTLE MESSAGES
WILL SHOW YOU WHERE TO START.
FORGET THE HILL OR THE SWAMP,
JUST SEE YOUR PATHWAY GREEN.
YES, YOU WILL CONQUER. IT WILL
BE MORE BEAUTIFUL THAN YOU HAVE EVER SEEN.

IT DOESN'T HAVE TO COME FROM HERE
OR END UP OVER THERE.
AS LONG AS IT IS JOYFUL
FOR THE TIME THAT YOU ARE RIGHT THERE.
LIVING FROM THE HEART
WITH INSPIRATION FOR ALL TIME.
ENSURES A COMMON FACTOR
AS WITH LOVE OUR PATHS ENTWINE.

Life is good

Feel good! life is good!
Each happening for a purpose.
So take courage and enjoy
Each experience upon this earth.
You have your faith to keep
You strong;
With true belief
This cannot be wrong.

We are tested for our faith
Along the way.
Enjoy the experience
Of each day.
For endurance brings success
Others cannot see.
It allows us to handle our experience
With joy and love to victory.

COUNT YOUR BLESSINGS

PERCEPTION IS MINE
TO VIEW THE WORLD AROUND.
THE JOY COMES BACK
IF WE OBSERVE WITHOUT A SOUND.
FOR OTHERS CHOOSE TO LIVE THEIR LIFE
IN MANY DIFFERENT WAYS.
THE PEACE FOR US IS TO GENTLY LIVE
IN A KINDLY WAY.
NATURE'S BOUNTY THERE TO SEE
SHOWS US SO MUCH EVERY DAY.
IF WE CHOOSE TO ENJOY IT MORE
THE INNER PEACE WILL COME OUR WAY.
FOR SIMPLE SOLUTIONS
ARE USUALLY THERE TO FIND.
IT IS A MATTER OF NOT RUSHING,
LET EACH DAY HAVE ITS TIME.
FEAR TAKES THE PRESENCE
MAKING US DO WITHOUT.
HOW MUCH HAPPIER WE COULD BE
IF NOT FILLED WITH THE PAIN OF DOUBT.
SO LOOK AT ALL THE THINGS YOU HAVE,
THOSE BLESSINGS SHARED WITH YOU.
COME ON AND LAUGH, TAKE HEART,
KEEP A POSITIVE POINT OF VIEW.

BIRTHDAY CELEBRATIONS

CELEBRATIONS DEAR ONE
FROM ALL YOUR FRIENDS TODAY.
IT IS THE DATE YOU WERE BORN ON
A FEW YEARS AGO.
EACH FRIEND WILL OFFER GROWTH TO YOU,
YOU MEET ALONG THE WAY.
IT IS THE PATH WE CHOSE TO WALK
THOSE LIFE TIMES LONG AGO.
YOUR SOUL CHOSE THE LEARNING
IT NEEDED ON THE WAY.
A WORD OF LOVE, A FLASH OF ANGER,
THEY ALL HELP US TO GROW.

BE STILL AND SEE WHERE YOU ARE AT
SO YOU CAN SET YOUR HEART.
TO CONTINUE ONCE MORE DOWN THE PATH
WHERE YOU FEEL A SPECIAL PART.
YOUR YOUTH OF COLOURS IN THE BUSH
GAVE YOU THE EYES TO SEE.
NATURE AT ITS GLORY TO SUSTAIN YOU
WITH ITS FRESHNESS AND BEAUTY.
REACH INSIDE FOR THE TREASURES
YOU HAVE WITHIN YOUR HEART.
SEE THEM AS WE DO AND YOU
WILL NEVER FEEL APART.

YOUR STRENGTH WILL COME WITH CONFIDENCE
AS YOU LAY CLAIM TO YOUR TRUE SELF.
LOVE THE ONE WE ALL KNOW,
YES MY DEAR, YOUR SELF.
WHEN OTHERS ACTIONS HURT AND THEIR
WORDS SEEM HARSH AND WRONG.
TRY TO BE DETACHED; RELEASE THE PAST
TO BRING BACK YOUR SWEET SONG.
THEIR WORDS RELEASE OUR DEEPEST FEARS

FOR OTHERS AND OUR SELF.
SO WE SHOULD SEEK THE WAY TO CLEAR
AND BE CONFIDENT WITHIN OUR SELF.

RELEASE THE VOICES OF THE PAST
SO YOUR HEART IS FREE WITHIN YOUR SOUL.
SO THE SUBCONSCIOUS DOESN'T COLOUR
IMAGES AND CHANGE YOUR OWN TRUE ROLE.
THE WORDS WE HEAR COME FRESH AND NEW,
WE HAVE A NEW POINT OF VIEW.
HAPPINESS, GOOD HEALTH AND WEALTH
IS THE PRAYER FOR YOU.
MAY EVERYTHING YOU REACH FOR
AND IN YOUR DREAMS COME TRUE.
TO SERVE AND HELP THOSE WE LOVE
WITH BALANCE FROM ABOVE.
HOW WONDERFUL TO SHARE THE LEARNING
WITH THOSE WE REALLY LOVE.

THE JOY OF THE YEARS

Thank you for the blessings
Of the learning of the years.
Thank you for the joys and love
Which help when there are tears.

I love the flowers and the trees;
The beauty of the seasons.
The growth of the universe
With experience for a reason.

My love of people,
The moment to share.
Allowing the blessings
And giving the care.

Life is so full,
Each day seems so short.
Those precious moments of time
Which cannot be bought.

Past years have been kind
When I see what is mine.
The vast inner knowledge
Which grows giving value to time.

To loved ones who share
My journey while here.
Thank you, my heart fills with
Love for all of you there.

LITTLE BOY

Give me the space to let me be good
And I will respond in kind.
Surround me with energies of love
To keep them in my mind.
When I feel all alone,
That nobody really cares.
Then I do those awful things
To bring others very near.
Unfortunately the damage
Kicks up a mighty row.
With others being angry
Which gives their face a scowl.
There never seems to be a day
When my slate is ever clean.
What will it take to show I care,
I'm nice, can be good and clean!

THERE IS A ROOM IN THE HEART

GOODNESS IS QUIET. IT DOESN'T
NEED TO PROCLAIM.
WHILE EVIL MAKES MUCH NOISE
WITH A NEED TO EXPLAIN.
FOR CONSCIENCE IF ONES LUCKY
TAKES THE TIME TO REFLECT.
HELPS US SHED THE HARSH LINES
WHICH BIND US IN A NET.
FOR GOODNESS IS THE MOMENT
OF TRUTH, WARMTH AND LOVE.
THE CHOICE WE HAVE OF FREEDOM
TO LIVE LIFE WITH A SOFT KID GLOVE.
TO LET THE PAIN PASS BY
AND LIVE WITHOUT REACTION.
PAUSES BEFORE OPINION OR
TAKING ANY ACTION.
THE ROOM AROUND OUR HEART SOFTENS
AND FILLS WITH LOVING CARE.
ATTRACTING LOVING PEOPLE TO US
WHO ENJOY BEING NEAR.

ONENESS

GATHER THE PICTURE AROUND THE WORLD
AND SEEK FOR YOU WILL FIND.

IT IS NOT THE COLOUR, THE RACE OR CREED
WHICH MAKES A DIFFERENCE TO EACH MIND.

EACH BELIEF OR RELIGION
HAS THE BASE OF BEING LOVE.

WHEN EACH ONE COMES TO RECOGNISE AND
CHOOSES TO LIVE BY LOVE.

THEN AND ONLY THEN WILL ONE ENERGY
BE GIVING ONENESS TO THIS EARTH.

THEN AND ONLY THEN WILL WE KNOW
OUR OWN SELF WORTH.

FOR THAT WE SHARE WITH OTHERS
AND FOCUS ON OUR SELF.

IS WORTH NOTHING IF WE DO IT
FROM THE STRENGTH OF WEALTH.

FOR LOVE COSTS US NOTHING
UNLESS WE OFFER LESS.

EACH DAY GIVES US OPPORTUNITY
TO LEARN AS WE PROGRESS.

SHADOWS OF THE PAST SHOULD
NOT BE THE DRIVING FORCE.

BE STILL AND BE THE MOMENT
WITHOUT REACTION OR REMORSE.

PEOPLE'S MEMORIES ARE THE JOY OF
WHERE WE ONCE HAVE BEEN.

THE FOCUS SHOULD BE NOW
FOR THE BEAUTY YET NOT SEEN.

EACH CHAPTER OF COURAGE OPENS
NEW DOORS TO SHARE OUR LOVE.

HELPING TO CLOSE OTHERS AS WE
LEARN WITH PATIENCE FROM ABOVE.

THANK YOU FOR THIS DAY
WHICH HAS REALLY TOUCHED MY HEART.

FORWARD IN THE MOMENT
TO PLAY MY OWN TRUE PART.

LIFE'S DESTINY

SING FROM THE HEART.
SING INTO THE WORLD.
LET ALL YOUR DREAMS AND ASPIRATIONS
SURFACE AND UNFURL.
SUNSHINE IN THE MOMENT.
LAUGHTER FROM WITHIN.
ENJOYING NATURES BOUNTY
OR LIFE DEVOID OF SIN.
FOCUS ON THE POSSIBLE TO
MAKE IT ALL COME TRUE.
COURAGE IN THE MOMENT WHEN
FACING THINGS THAT ARE NEW.

LIVE THE FULLNESS OF YOUR DESTINY;
BE FREE OF THE MOULD.
LET ALL OF YOUR TALENTS SURFACE
TO CREATION AS THEY UNFOLD.
KNOW THAT THROUGH THE YEARS
NOTHING HAS PASSED YOU BY.
THAT YOUR CHALLENGES HAVE BEEN MET;
THERE WAS NO NEED TO DENY.
NOW THE YEARS ARE MANY
I LOOK AND FEEL WITH JOY.
THE PASSING YEARS HAVE GIVEN
ME MUCH LEARNING TO DEPLOY.

NATURES BOUNTY

MORNING BREAKS AS THE SUN
RISES IN THE EAST.
THE COLOURS DANCE IN THE SKY,
A JOY, A WONDERFUL FEAST.
THIS NEW DAY OF CREATION
AS THE BIRDS BEGIN TO SING.
ENCHANTED WITH THE JOY OF LIFE,
IT HAS A WONDERFUL RING.

LOVE FOR THEIR MATE
IS SOUNDED OUT ON HIGH.
THE DORMANT SEASON ENDS IN SPRING
WHEN YOUNG BIRDS HATCH AND FLY.
WHEN ALL OF NATURES BOUNTY
STARTS TO GROW AROUND.
THE FEELING OF THE UNIVERSE,
THE PERFUME, THE COLOUR, THE SOUND.

JOYFUL IS THE MESSAGE
OF NEW LIFE IN EVERY FORM.
WITH EACH ITS JOURNEY ONWARD,
EVEN THROUGH A DROUGHT OR STORM.
WONDERFUL ARE THE COLOURS
ON LAND SEA OR SKY.
CREATION THERE IN EARNEST
WITH THE GLORY FROM ON HIGH.

FOR NATURE HAS A BALANCE
WHICH SEEMS TO BALANCE THROUGH.
REMINDS US TO KEEP ON TRYING
WITH EVERYTHING SO NEW.
LOVING, CARING, SHARING,
FOR EACH AND EVERY AGE.
WITH EVER CHANGING BEAUTY
FOR EACH AND EVERY STAGE.

BEAUTY TO ENJOY

JUST THE JOY OF BEING HERE
WITH BEAUTY TO ENJOY.
GIVES THAT SPECIAL MOMENT
OF LIVING IN THE NOW.
TREES, BIRDS, PEOPLE,
ALL HAVE THEIR OWN FLOWER.
KNOWING THAT THEIR ENERGY
IS LOVE THE REAL POWER.

THE WORLD IS FULL OF OPPORTUNITY
FOR EACH TO REALLY GROW.
SHARING JOY WITH OTHERS
THAT WE MEET AND GET TO KNOW.
EACH THEIR DIFFERENCE FOR A PURPOSE
TO MAXIMISE THEIR LEARNING.
LET GO, FEEL THE PEACE AND FREEDOM
AS YOU RELEASE ALL YOUR YEARNING.

A SPECIAL FRIEND

It takes a very special friend
To open up your heart.
A friend who knows how you are
Though you may be apart.
They show their emotions and
You take all the flak.
You can bless them though,
For the friendship stays intact.

Yes, a friend is a friend
Through the rough and the smooth.
They help us to grow
And get us out of the groove.
They help us to learn our lessons.
While they go through the pain.
Thank you my dear friend,
You have given me the gain.

If we can share our lessons
And both put in our gain.
Each will save the others need
To experience it again.
So my friend I thank you,
For friend indeed you are.
May love shine and bless you
To protect this little star.

ONCE IN A WHILE

Once in a while we meet someone
For whom we really care.
Time gives us comfort to adjust
To a life for both to share.
True love starts when both can talk
Of things which give them pain.
So when a word is said it does not
Trigger hurt; it simply reminds one
That life is lived again.

Each day must be new
For both to experience joy.
There must be agreement for each
To clear their image of things
That do annoy.
When both can work at love
In everything they think.
Life will be the elixir for
Each moment that you drink.
Patterns of the past must
Be prepared to change.
This wonderful word called love
Can heal and make you whole again.

BEAUTY IS AROUND

BEAUTY IS AROUND US
IN EVERY SHAPE AND FORM.
FOCUS ON THE HAPPINESS
TO AVOID THE PERPETUAL STORM.
LOOK FOR IT AND ADD YOUR SMILE,
LIFE IS SO VERY WORTHWHILE.
POSITIVE APPROACH AND COURAGE
ENSURES LIFE IS NOT A TRIAL.

WHEN THE DAY COMES TO AN END
AND YOU KNOW YOU HAVE DONE YOUR BEST.
THE INNER GLOW OF KNOWLEDGE
WILL MINIMISE THE STRESS.
EACH DAY SHOULD BE A PLEASURE
WITH EVERYTHING AS NEW.
OBSERVING AND ACKNOWLEDGING
EACH OTHERS POINT OF VIEW.

MANY PATTERNS ON THE PATH.
EACH THEIR ROAD TO GO.
GIVES A DIFFERENT PICTURE
TO EVERYONE WE KNOW.
ALLOW FOR THE DIFFERENCE,
EACH ONE HAS THEIR OWN CHOICE.
YOUR STRENGTH AND PURPOSE
ARE YOUR OWN AND INNER VOICE.

OPEN PATHWAYS

LIFE HAS MANY CHAPTERS
FROM THE FIRST ONE TO THE END.
THE DIFFERENT ONES WHO SHARE THEM
EVERY NOW AND THEN.
THE ROAD IS OURS TO TRAVEL,
TO LIVE AND UNDERSTAND.
THAT EACH DAY IS THE ONLY DAY
WE HOLD WITHIN OUR HAND.

WITH FREEDOM FOR TODAY
THE WORLD IS AT OUR FEET.
PATHWAYS ARE OPEN,
EXCITING AS A TREAT.
TAKE THIS MOMENT TO FULFIL
THE EXPERIENCE OF THE HEART.
KNOW THAT DEEP WITHIN YOU
HAVE LIVED YOUR FULLEST PART.

ENCHANTMENT IN THE MOMENT

SMILE FOR TODAY.
LET THE STRAIN GO AWAY.
LIVING FOR THIS MOMENT
IS THE ONLY WAY.

SUNSHINE IN YOUR HEART
WHERE EVERYTHING CAN BE,
BRINGS THE WORLD OF ENCHANTMENT
INTO REALITY.

ARRIVING WHERE WE ARE
IS WHERE WE ARE TO BE.
KNOWING THAT OUR WORLD IS HERE,
THE THOUGHTS TO SET US FREE.

KNOWING IS ENOUGH
TO LIGHTEN UP THE LOAD.
THE HEART JOYFUL BECKONS
TO INDICATE THE ROAD.

PUT OUT YOUR HAND

OPEN YOUR ARMS OUT.
LET LOVE COME INTO YOUR LIFE.
RECOGNISE HOW IT HAS ALWAYS BEEN
WHEN YOU FELT FULL OF STRIFE.
FOR BEAUTY IS OURS
TO TOUCH AND TO FEEL.
PUT OUT YOUR HAND,
RECOGNISE THAT ALL IS WELL.

GENTLE TIME

FOR MY FRIENDS I SEND THEM JOY
TO KNOW THEIR OWN TRUE WORTH.
TO ENJOY THEIR JOYS AND CHALLENGES
AS THEY LEARN UPON THIS EARTH.
TO SHARE THEIR JOYS AND SORROWS
WITH OTHERS NEAR AND DEAR.
FOR NONE OF US ARE ALONE
DURING OUR VISIT HERE.

LOVE ONES UNITE TO SEARCH
AND SEEK THEIR COMMON GOAL.
THE JOY OF BEING HERE TO LEARN,
THE EXPERIENCES TO MAKE US WHOLE.
OUR FACE IS THE MIRROR THAT
REFLECTS WHAT IS INSIDE.
EACH HEART CONTAINS THE LOVE TO EXPAND
AND TOUCH THOSE WHO TRAVEL BY.

IF EACH ONE SHOWS THEY CARE FOR OTHERS
AS THEY WOULD WISH DONE TO THEMSELVES.
OUR WORLD WILL BECOME THE CHOSEN LAND
THAT REFLECTS OUR OWN TRUE WEALTH.
UNSELFISH GIVING FROM THE HEART
DOES NOT LOOK FOR RETURN.
IT DOESN'T MEASURE ANYTHING
BUT TAKES EACH DAY TO LEARN.

I LOVE YOU AS YOU ARE

I love you as you are
For my heart can see the child.
With all the possibilities that
With your courage you will reveal.
Mine is not to judge
The journeys of the past.
Time is but fleeting
For we know it doesn't last.

Each day is ours to choose
Just what we want to do.
Giving each one the opportunity
To their own point of view.
Where you go is yours to choose;
It is your own concern.
May the choice be from the heart
And not to reactions that burn.

For joyful is the journey
When others choose to care.
Joyful is the journey when others
Let you know that they are there.
Should you choose to walk away
And take a path alone.
May stars shine brightly overhead
To show you your way home.

HONEST LIVING

REJECTION ISN'T WHAT OTHER PEOPLE THINK.
THE PAINS OF THE PAST ARE OUR REAL LINK.
WE FEEL WE ARE NOT WORTHY
THAT WE CANNOT PASS THE TEST.
IF THE TRUTH WERE KNOWN
WE ARE UP THERE WITH THE BEST.

LACKING CONFIDENCE IN OUR OWN SELF-WORTH WE
WITHDRAW.
LOOSING OPPORTUNITY, NEVER KNOWING
WHAT IS BEHIND THE NEW DOOR.
GIVING WHAT WE HAVE TO OTHERS
WITH NO VALUE FOR OUR SELF.
WE OFTEN PAY THE CONSEQUENCE
WITH CONCERNS AROUND OUR HEALTH.

WHEN THE SUNSHINE BRIGHTENS AND
OPENS UP THE DAY.
WE SEE WHAT WE ARE DOING
AND DECIDE TO MAKE A CHANGE.
OUR DAY HAS COME TO SHARE
EVERYTHING WE HAVE BEEN GIVEN.
THE KEY IS IN OUR HAND,
THE ONE FOR HONEST LIVING.

FEELING NEW

The first step is the beginning
Of a journey.
A chance for new direction
To open up the door.
Letting go of doubt
To let the sun shine in.
Believing you will receive strength
To achieve much more.

Picture what you want to
Come true for you.
One dream is worth a thousand
Negativity's on your mind.
Step by step it happens
For your dreams to come true.
So show how much you love yourself.
Go on be truly kind.

Show the love to your self
That you would wish from others.
Open up the door to love
For it to magnify.
As you love your self
As you would love another.
Your inner peace will come to you
As life takes on a high.

Knowing what you think
Is what you will get.
Sets an attitude to be
Positive and true.
With insight into life
Without pain or regret.
For wonderful things come to us;
For us to feel as new.

HOME IS WHERE THE HEART IS

A HOUSE GIVES US SHELTER
FROM THE WIND AND THE RAIN.
SOFTLY PROTECTS US AS NIGHTFALL
COMES AGAIN.
FILLED WITH OUR MEMORIES
OF FRIENDS WE HOLD DEAR.
SHARING OF THE LOVE WHEN THEY
HAVE BEEN THERE.

NOW THE TIME HAS COME TO MOVE
OUR HEART HAS CHOSEN WELL.
FILLED FULL OF EXCITEMENT;
IT IS ALMOST LIKE A SPELL.
WITH ALL OUR THINGS AND THOSE
WE LOVE BY OUR SIDE.
THE WORLD IS OURS TO HAVE AS WITH
THE TURNING OF THE TIDE.

United

For all that I have had
And all that will be;
Thank you now for this path
To eternity.
Love in full bloom
Expands to fill.
This wonderful day
Of inner joy and thrills.

The place in my heart
With love for you there.
Excited and happy to
Finally be here.
May your wishes be filled
Today and forever.
Let the path of your hearts
Be your sweet surrender.

LOVE COMES

LOVE COMES DAILY WHEN YOU
OPEN UP YOUR ARMS.
LOVE IS THE FAITH
WHICH KEEPS YOU FEELING STRONG.
FOR COURAGE IS THE JOURNEY
WHICH PROTECTS YOU FROM ALL HARM.
COURAGE IS THE KNOWLEDGE
TO FOLLOW RIGHT FROM WRONG.

MARRIAGE IS THE OPPORTUNITY TO SHARE.
RECOGNISE YOUR OWN SELF WORTH.
TO BE THERE WITH SUPPORT
THROUGH THE SMILES AND THE TEARS.
CHILDREN BRING THEIR MOMENTS
TO SHARE THIS GLORIOUS EARTH.
YEARS GIVE US THE LEARNING
TO LET GO OF ALL OUR FEARS.

GOING FOR YOUR DREAMS TO ALLOW
THEM TO BE REAL.
RESTING WHEN YOU NEED TO,
TO FOCUS ON YOUR STAR.
KNOWING LOVE WILL SUPPORT YOU
IF YOU HAVE IT AND YOU FEEL.
MOVEMENT COMES FROM STILLNESS
WHEN YOU GO FROM WITHIN YOUR HEART.

A LIFETIME IS THIS MOMENT,
NO BEGINNING AND NO END.
GIVING LIFE THE PURPOSE
WE CHOOSE TO HAVE AND SHARE.
FOR LOVE IS LOVE AND ONLY LOVE
FOR US TO COMPREHEND.
WITH FAITH, HOPE AND COURAGE
TO SUPPORT OUR LIFE TIME HERE.

A Mother's World

A mother's dreams are everything
For her baby child.
There are basic things which mum can
Share to show her love and care.
The precious gift of life is where
It all begins.
Each one on their journey
With time ahead of them.
For some this time is short,
While others have many years.
The experiences in between
Give opportunities to learn.

Some will share with others
The lessons they have learned.
Each can only give the realisations
They have earned.
Judgement must be soft
As we realise from outside
That others cannot give what they do
Not have inside.
When you know they have shared
What is in their heart.
You will understand they have
Never been apart.

A SPECIAL PERSON

A FRIEND IS A SPECIAL PERSON
WHO TRUSTS YOU WITH THEIR HEART.
THEY LET YOU TAKE A LOOK INSIDE.
THEIR FEELINGS, THEY DO NOT HIDE.

YOU HAVE THE CHANCE TO HELP THEM
OR PAIN THEM AT THEIR HEART.
THE WAY MUST BE FREE OF RESTRICTIONS
FOR EACH ONE TO GROW STRONG.

TO LEARN THROUGH OBSERVATION
THE SELF SEES NEED TO CHANGE.
THE FRIEND CAN GIVE THE GUIDANCE
IF BOTH CAN SEE THE BALANCE.

BUT BOTH MUST WORK WITH LOVE
FROM WHERE THE OTHER STANDS.
TO GIVE THEM WHAT THE OTHER NEEDS
AND NOT YOUR OWN PLAN.

WE ALL ARE VERY DIFFERENT.
ALLOWANCE MUST BE MADE.
UNTIL THE SOUL IS READY
FOR CHANGES TO BE MADE

Forever there

With thanks in my heart
I think of those friends held so very dear.
Some are many miles away,
But somehow they are near.
For deep within my heart
With love they re-appear.
The thought that brings you together
Like yesterday is very clear.
When you held each other in your arms,
Just as if it was today.
So my special friend;
Know that I am truly here.
Whenever you think of me
Our love will re-appear.

WHAT IS A FRIEND

A FRIEND KNOWS OUR SECRETS
AND KEEPS THEM AT THEIR HEART.
THEY HEAR OUR PROBLEMS WITHOUT QUESTION
AND ADVISE US HOW TO START.
THEY SHARE OUR JOYS AND SORROWS
AND HELP US WITH OUR FEARS.

TIME BRINGS A TRUST, A CLOSENESS,
WHICH MONEY CANNOT BUY.
IN FACT A FRIEND IS EVERYTHING
TO KEEP THE WORLD ON HIGH.
SO MY FRIEND I THANK YOU
AND HOPE WE NEVER PART.
FOR MY FRIEND I TREASURE YOU.
YOUR LOVE IS IN MY HEART.

THE ROSE

THE ROSE IS A GIFT
WHICH GROWS AND BLOOMS.
WITH FLOWERS SO SOFT
AND FULL OF PERFUME.
WE NOURISH AND PRUNE IT
SO IT FLOWERS EACH YEAR.
A ROSE IN THE ROOM
BRINGS BEAUTY AND CHEER.

SO SOFT ARE THE PETALS
TO LOVE AND TOUCH.
WHEN THEY FINALLY FALL,
THEY HAVE GIVEN SO MUCH.
THEY LIE SO SOFT
AGAINST THE RAIN.
AS WITH A RAINBOW
THE ROSE FLOWERS AGAIN.

THE CYCLE GOES ON
AND THEY GIVE MORE AND MORE.
THOSE ROSES WE LOVE,
ALL OUR FRIENDS DO ADORE.
FROM NOW TO ETERNITY
MAY PEACE BE A ROSE.
LET ITS BEAUTY SPREAD
THROUGH THE WORLD
WHEREVER IT GOES.

THANK YOU ROSE
FOR ALL MANKIND.
MAY YOU BLOOM AND GROW
FOR ALL TIME.
YOUR COLOURS SO MANY ,
SO BRIGHT AND TRUE.
THANK YOU DEAR ROSE;
WE DO LOVE YOU.

MY TROUBLED FRIEND

WORDS MAY NOT SEEM IMPORTANT
UNTIL THEY ARE NOT HEARD.
THE SMILE IS TAKEN FOR GRANTED.
ONCE GIVEN IT IS GONE.
LIFE IS ABOUT FEELING
SO MANY PRECIOUS THINGS.
WE CANNOT UNDERSTAND SO MUCH,
SO MANY LITTLE THINGS.

IN TIME WE COME TO REALISE
THE JOY LIFE HAS TO BRING.
THE LITTLE THINGS THAT MATTER
AND MAKE OUR HEART SING.
WHEN WE SHARE WITH OTHERS,
A DOUBLE BLESSING IS OURS.
FOR GIVING IS THE JOY OF LIFE
SINCE THE WORLD BEGAN.

WHEN SADNESS COMES, THOUGH TEARS MAY FALL,
WE KNOW THAT TIME WILL HEAL.
WHEN LOVED ONES WORDS AND SMILE,
WILL CHASE AWAY THE TEARS.
WHEN LOVE IS TRULY IN OUR HEART.
THERE IS NO DOUBT OR FEAR.
A SONG IS EVER IN OUR HEART
WITH THOUGHTS TO BRING GOOD CHEER.

TRUE LOVE

As we venture along life's path we change
And give or take from our friends.
We grow then rest a while
As life leads towards the end.

Love comes as a shadow
And opens many doors.
Which one we take is hard to know
And so we must explore.

We try so many doors by hand.
So many of them blocked.
The biggest joy of all,
Is the one that is unlocked.

At this door we learn love,
In so many different ways.
That it always will stay open
Throughout our many days.

It is the joy of loving one another.
Being true to our self.
In fact, we learn the precious joy
That true love knows no self.

GREETINGS MY FRIEND

When life becomes hard
And the road seems all up hill.
Your heart feels full of dread.
People are unkind
For reasons of their own.
You wonder if they stay that way
When in their own home.

From observing other people,
We find much to learn.
Even if it is to realise
Their own lessons they must learn.
Life has a purpose
For each and every soul.
For each to seek and follow
To achieve their own goal.

Some will seek out riches
With adornments around their neck.
While others seek out pleasure
And only look for sex.
Blind to the beauty the world
Puts in their way.
No joy in life for them they say,
Unless they drink night and day.

Put aside all these things,
For god has promised more.
The joy, the laughter and the learning
Must be behind another door.
Money cannot buy it,
Not any amount of wealth.
The joy we seek is in our heart,
Deep within our self.

Keep faith as you travel,
Be still and rest a while.
As you glimpse the path once more,
Your face will light up with a smile,
What you do is up to you,
Every moment counts.
Your thoughts, your speech,
What you see, sends energies without.

Our soul takes in the learning
To guide us another day.
No experience is wasted as we learn.
More to help us on our way.
For life is a circle
Until our life is whole.
One filled with love and joy
Which has now another note.

To help others as they stumble by,
Shining forth a light.
If they take the time to listen,
They may avoid a nasty plight.
Travel on for self-growth my friend,
For you glow for others to see.
Who knows one day where you will
Help to soften misery.

The best is wished for you;
That you get the chance to be
Free in love and beautiful
For all the world to see.
May your heart be free of ties
As it takes on its true song.
That you may serve others now,
With your faith you will be strong.

GREETINGS BROTHER

GREETINGS BROTHER , ALWAYS NICE TO KEEP
IN TOUCH; JUST TO SAY HELLO
AND FEEL HOW MUCH I LOVE YOU,
WHICH GIVES AN INNER GLOW.
YOU ARE OFTEN IN MY THOUGHTS
TO BRING YOU VERY NEAR.
THE MEMORIES THAT ARE HELD
KEEP YOU VERY DEAR.

YEARS GO PAST IN WONDER
AS WE EACH EXPERIENCE LIFE.
MAY YOUR JOURNEY GIVE YOU PEACE
AND NOT SEEM FULL OF STRIFE.
TAKE TIME TO LOOK AT WHERE
YOU HAVE BEEN.
NOTE ALL YOU HAVE ACHIEVED.
IT WILL LIGHTEN UP YOUR LOAD.
GIVE CONFIDENCE ON YOUR ROAD.

YOU HAVE GIVEN THINGS TO OTHERS
WITHOUT THOUGHT OF RETURN.
MAY YOU GET YOUR REWARD WHICH
GIVES YOU PEACE IN YOUR TURN.
MONEY CANNOT BUY IT,
THAT SPECIAL PEACE WITHIN.
IT IS BECOMING LOVE
AND LETTING GO OF SIN.

MY BROTHER

IF I COULD CHOOSE MY WORLD
OF PEOPLE AROUND ME.
IT WOULD BE ONES LIKE YOU
WHO ALLOW ME TO BE FREE.
AS MY BROTHER AND MY FRIEND,
MANY EXPERIENCES HAVE WE SHARED.
BUT NONE SO DEAR AS NOW
AS WE BOTH HAVE BECOME MUCH MORE AWARE.

THE GIVING AND THE SHARING
TO ALLOW EACH ONE TO BE WHOLE.
GIVES A SPECIAL MEANING
AS WE BOTH FULFIL OUR ROLE.
YOUR BEAUTY FROM WITHIN
IS APPARENT TO ME HERE.
AS YOU STRIVE TO LEARN, ENJOY,
EVERY MOMENT AS YOU GROW.

THE LEARNING IS NOT PAINLESS,
BUT COURAGE ON THE ROAD.
NOW ALLOWS YOU TO SEE YOU
HAVE GAINED A GOOD FOOTHOLD.
MAY YOUR JOURNEY BE HEARTFELT
WITH LOVE AROUND YOU HERE.
THAT ALWAYS YOU FEEL LOVED
AND THAT PEOPLE ARE REALLY NEAR.

LOVES DECLARATION

THANK YOU FOR OUR YEARS.
FOR THE JOYFUL TIMES WE HAVE SHARED.
ALL OUR LOVING MEMORIES
FILL ME FULL OF LOVE.

EACH DAY WE ADD IN MORE
IN THIS BEAUTIFUL WORLD OF OURS.
OUR LOVELY CHILDREN
TRULY MAKE US PROUD.

THE PICTURE IS OF UNITY.
HELD WITH LOVE AND SOUL.
AS EACH ONE PROGRESSES TO FULFILMENT
IN THEIR OWN ROLE.

SUNSHINE WILL BE OURS
AS TOGETHER WE GO FORTH.
TO JOURNEY THROUGH OUR YEARS
IN THE MOMENT NOT THE PAST.

THERE IS NO TIME FOR FEAR,
DISAPPOINTMENT OR TEARS.
LIFE IS FOR LIVING
TO MAXIMIZE OUR YEARS.

SO KNOW THIS LOVE IS IN MY HEART
TO ALWAYS BE RIGHT HERE.
IT IS ENOUGH FOR ME TO KNOW
THAT YOU ARE ALWAYS THERE.

REACHING OUT

THANK YOU FOR CARING.
IT SHOWS THROUGH YOUR TOUCH.
THANK YOU FOR THE SHARING.
JUST BEING THERE MEANS SO MUCH.
WHEN THE ROAD SEEMS LONG
WITH NO END IN SIGHT.
A FRIEND IS A JOY
WHO WILL SHARE THEIR INSIGHT.
I REMEMBER YOUR KINDNESS
AND ENCOURAGEMENT ON THE WAY..
WHICH SHOWS THAT TOUGH TIMES NEVER LAST,
BUT TOUGH PEOPLE ALWAYS DO
AT THE END OF THE DAY.

IN MY HEART

CAN I LOOK INTO MY HEART
AND LET IT DECIDE?
THE HEAD SEEMS TO STOP ME
FROM DECISIONS AND OVERRIDE.
THE DISTANCES AND TIMES AWAY
HAVE KEPT US PHYSICALLY APART.
DEEP INSIDE IN TRUTH I FEEL, YOU
HAVE ALWAYS BEEN IN MY HEART.

EACH CELEBRATES FOR THE OTHERS JOY
AND SUCCESS ALONG THE ROAD.
YET DEEP INSIDE THE WISH TO SHARE
MORE FROM THE SAME ABODE.
TIME TO BE TOGETHER,
NO NEED TO WALK ALONE.
FOR BOTH HAVE LEARNT TO LOVE THE SELF.
THERE IS NO NEED TO ROAM

FAMILY LOVE

A family brings its joy
When the home is full of love.
When each one can identify
With true love from up above.
The love that holds us firm
When things do not go our way.
The patience that we use as
We go from day to day.

Tolerance the lesson when we feel
For another's mistakes.
Perhaps it is a question of the
Different road they take.
They all lead to learning
for the time that we are here.
With true love we stand by to
Allow others the time to become aware.

When we feel disappointed
We should stop to ask our self why.
For the lesson is with us.
Do not let this opportunity pass by.
People come into our lives
To teach us what our lessons are.
The ones we feel make us suffer
Can take us very far.

IN THE GARDEN

There is a garden for two
Which is in the heart.
The seeds have been planted where
They may flourish to beautiful colours
Where that love plays the part.
The path is open that both may choose
To live in the moment upon this earth.
The strength that each is free, united
In love to hold their self worth.
Come feed it to flourish
With confidence true.
That you know in your heart
That my love is for you.

THE JOY OF SHARING

THANK YOU FOR TODAY.
THERE IS GLADNESS IN MY HEART.
THE SHARING AND DISCUSSION
HAVE ALL PLAYED A PART.
TWO HEARTS WHICH BEAT AS ONE,
YET STAY AS INDIVIDUALS.
TWO HEARTS WHO LOVE AND SHARE
TO ALLOW THE OTHERS FULL POTENTIAL.

THE JOY OF FULFILMENT OF
THE OTHERS TALENTS.
SHOWING SUCCESS FROM EFFORT
SO VALIANT.
OPENING DOORS FOR THE FUTURE JOYS
WITH A TRUE EXPONENT FOR OTHERS TO LEARN FROM.
A CHANCE FOR TWO SOULS TO RADIATE LOVE.
A LOVE THAT WHITE LIGHT SHINES DOWN UPON.

Come my friend

New times, new friends,
Occurring every day.
Living for the moment
With experiences along the way.
Learning to be still when life
Is in full flight.
Letting go of anguish
To bring in faith and light.

Being there for those we love,
Yet freedom of our own.
To carry out our destiny
Where we choose to roam.
Freedom with our choice
To open up each day.
Courage to be true in side
With each experience along the way.

Asking for the closeness we feel
Within our heart.
For those we love dearly,
But have spent the time apart.
So open up the lines
Of communication and of care.
We can be together
With both of us standing here.

Thank you for being there
To let me see my heart.
Giving me the insight and faith
To make a start.
Each day is the moment
Where it begins and ends.
The magic and the newness;
To journey around another bend.

In this life together

Joined for a reason
In this life together.
Brother, sister, friends,
As long as we remember.

For destiny has set us
With distance in between.
Yet caring flows between us
That is real, not a dream.

Coming together reinforces
Genetic traits which are the same.
Gives us reflections
Which give a smile as we play the game.

For unique the individual
With joy ahead of them.
When they realize that courage
Stops fear to support the child within.

YOUR INNER CHILD

THE NEEDS OF YOUR INNER CHILD
ARE BURIED DEEP WITHIN.

SO BE STILL AND RECOGNIZE THEM
SO YOUR REAL LIFE CAN BEGIN.

FOR YEARS OF PLEASING OTHERS
AT THE EXPENSE OF YOUR SELF;

STOPS YOU BEING REAL
TO LIVE WITH YOUR TRUE WEALTH.

SO ENJOY YOUR SOLITUDE,
DO NOT FEEL ALONE.

FOR THE DREAMS WILL SURFACE;
AT LAST YOU FEEL AT HOME.

BE KIND TO THIS INNER CHILD,
DO NOT DENY THE SELF.

GOD BLESS AND KEEP YOU
AS YOU DISCOVER YOUR TRUE WEALTH.

Birthday remembrance

What has been will never pass away.
What will be, we will share another day.
The laughter, the tears,
The joy and the pain.
Make it so special until we meet again.
The love never dies,
This door has stayed open.
When you care for another
The friendship is not broken.
May joy surround you where ever you are.
With your soul in touch
With its heavenly star.
Today is your birthday
So special for you.
May its joy be with you
The whole year through.

WRITE YOUR DREAMS

THE DREAMS WE SEE CAN BE REAL
WITH BOTH OF US INDEPENDENTLY STRONG.
OUR LOVE UNITED WILL GREET EACH DAY
TO FILL IT FULL OF SONG.

I WANT TO SHARE THE WORLD WITH YOU.
TO SPEND OUR LIFE TOGETHER.
TO SHARE OUR LOVE THAT EACH CAN FEEL
COMPLETE THROUGH THE STRENGTH OF THE OTHER.

UNDERSTANDING COMES AS WE SEEK
TO BOTH FULFIL OUR DREAMS.
THE TIME IS NOW TO MAKE IT REAL,
THE HAPPIEST TIMES WE HAVE EVER SEEN.

WRITE THE DREAMS AS THEY COME,
FLOWING FROM THE HEART.
NOW IS THE MOMENT TO CREATE
FOR YOU AND I CAN START.

THE PROPOSAL

WHEN FIRST I SAW YOUR FACE,
MY HEART LIT A LITTLE SPARK.
THERE HAS BEEN DISTANCE, TIME BETWEEN,
STILL YOU STAY. IT IS NOT A DREAM.
COME BE WITH ME AND LIVE OUR LOVE
FOR ALL IS STILL IN YOU.
YES MY LOVE WE BELONG TOGETHER.
ONLY YOU CAN MAKE IT TRUE.

COME TO ME, BE WITH ME.
SHARE OUR LIVES TOGETHER.
BE THE LOVE IN OUR HEARTS
SO OUR LIFE WILL BE FOREVER.
EACH THEIR DREAMS TO FULFIL
INSPIRED BY THE OTHER.
LOVE ABOUNDS TO GUIDE THE WINDS
INTO OUR SAFE HARBOUR.

FOR OCEANS CALL FOR US TO SHARE
EXPERIENCES FROM OUR LEARNING.
THE WAVES, THEIR COLOURS,
EACH A CREST OF LEARNING.
COME TAKE MY HAND AND BE WITH ME,
OUR LOVE IS YET TO BLOOM.
MY HEART IS SOFT AND GENTLE
WITH THOUGHTS OF YOU, NEAR AND IN THE ROOM.

LIFE OFFERS MANY CHANCES
TO TAKE US DOWN THE PATH.
THIS ONE MY DARLING
ALLOWS FOR IT TO EXPAND AND REALLY LAST.
FOR EACH DAY IS A MOMENT.
THE BEGINNING AND THE END.
EACH DAY FOR ETERNITY.
THE DESTINY WHICH HAS NO END.

SHARING FOR THE MOMENT

IT IS NOT THERE TO TAKE,
FOR THAT WOULD BE THE END.
SHARING FOR THE MOMENT
GIVES AN EXPERIENCE WHICH DOES NOT END.

LETTING GO OF EXPECTATION
WITH NO THOUGHT OF RETURN.
ALLOWS A TOTAL LOVING
FOR EACH TO HAVE THEIR TURN.

THE FOCUS IS ON BUILDING,
WITH SMILES, JOY AND LAUGHTER.
A ROCK TO BUILD WITH LOVE
TO EXPERIENCE EVER AFTER.

TAKE MY HAND AND SHARE OUR LIFE
AS WE COME TOGETHER.
MY LOVE THIS MOMENT OFFERS
AS WE GENTLY BOTH SURRENDER.

Graces Christmas

I looked with joy and wonder at the gifts under the tree.
They held the gift of Christ for all humanity.
The first gift was patience representing endurance, calmness and quietness.
There is time for everything on the path to wholeness.

The second gift was kindness for humanity with sympathy and good feeling.
Goodness from the heart to the world for inner balance, to stop it reeling.
Our third gift is peace, bringing calm. Freedom from war, yes good order.
That the universe can mend, bringing down all forms of borders.

Wrapped in pink were charity, goodwill and generosity in all forms of giving.
For the gifts of loving attitude form the base of joyful living.
One parcel offered vulnerability, the courage to be true to self.
Secure in your wholeness and trusting the identity of your real worth.

Wrapped in gold was faith giving belief that prompts loving action.
Observing of the self with purpose, not reaction.
For the gift of Christ is clear in thought, action, yes your deeds.
With thoughts that are loving thoughts sow only beauty as the seeds.

Music, nature's sweet harmony, the birds and the wind in the trees.

The friendship in another's voice in gladness as they talk to you.

Yes! There is much to Christmas when we reflect on the day.

An opportunity to show we care in so many ways.

So each day of the year that is ahead of me.

There will be opportunity to use these gifts so special beneath the tree.

Spiritual love multiplies to spread throughout the world for all.

Use your Christmas day. Recognise your gifts and let your banner unfurl.

FAMILY CHRISTMAS

CHRISTMAS TREE, OH CHRISTMAS TREE,
THE SEASONS AT AN END.
FAMILY REJOICED, EACH IN THEIR OWN WAY
AS THEY STOOD BEFORE YOU ON CHRISTMAS DAY.

SO MUCH IS GIVEN,
IT IS NOT ALL GIFTS OF PRESENTS.
A NOD, A SMILE, A SONG, A GRIN,
IT REALLY DOESN'T MATTER.
THAT EACH COULD BE THERE TODAY
SOWS A SEED FOR NEW BEGINNINGS.

IF ONE COULD LEAVE THE IMAGES
WE CARRY FROM THE PAST.
TO SHARE IN THIS MOMENT,
HOPE IT ALL WOULD LAST.
IT TAKES A SPECIAL EFFORT OF
WANTING TO SUCCEED.
IF EACH COULD CARRY THIS DAY ON
THEY WOULD NEVER BE IN NEED.
MAY THIS TREE OF HOPE WITH ALL ITS TINSEL,
SPARKLING LIGHTS AND DECORATIONS
ALWAYS REMIND US WHY WE ARE HERE,
THE REASON FOR CREATION

COURAGE MY FRIEND

When you feel you must give up;
The road has been too long.
Stop, be still and rest,
Renew your heart with song.

For courage has carried you to
Victory this far on your journey.
Recognize your inner worth
To continue with your learning.

Destiny is the story
You planned and wrote for your self.
That you could learn and experience
To give you your true wealth.

Maximize this time ,
That you have chosen to be here.
Smile with the glory of the right
To the challenges as they appear.

A TIME OF PARTING

Share the joy of being there
Through the years together.
The love you shared was well expressed
And felt within her heart.
It was not for you to share
That journey at the end.
May the love sustain you,
Give strength to you my friend.

MY BIG SISTER

WHAT IS IT LIKE TO HAVE A SISTER
WHO SHOWS LOVE AND REALLY CARES?
WHAT IS IT LIKE TO HAVE A SISTER
WHO BRUSHES AWAY YOUR TEARS?
THE EXTRA YEARS HAVE HELPED HER
TO LEARN SO MANY THINGS-
TO RIDE A BIKE, RUN REALLY FAST.
GO SO HIGH ON THE SWINGS.

NOW THAT WE HAVE GROWN,
MY SISTERS GONE TO WORK.
I PATIENTLY WAIT FOR CAST OFFS.
OH! WHAT A BEAUTIFUL SKIRT.
THE BOYFRIENDS COME TO VISIT,
I AM TOLD TO GO AWAY.
THEY SAY THAT I WILL UNDERSTAND
IN TIME IN MY OWN WAY.

THE BIG DAY OF HER WEDDING
WITH ME AS BRIDESMAID HERE.
MUM AND DAD SO PROUD OF HER,
SO BEAUTIFUL STANDING THERE.
MAY THEY BOTH BE HAPPY
AS THEY START THEIR LIFE TOGETHER.
MY BIG SISTERS LEFT THE NEST,
THIS DAY A DREAM TO REMEMBER.

LIFE TIMES SHARED

IT HAS NEVER BEEN WRITTEN
HOW I FELT WHEN FIRST I SAW YOU.
LOVE IN THE MOMENT BECAUSE
I FELT I ALREADY KNEW YOU.

WE TRAVELLED AND WE TALKED
OF ALL THINGS IN THE WORLD.
EVERYTHING ACCEPTED.
OUR MINDS IN QUITE A WHIRL.

EXCITED IN THE MOMENT
WITH SO MUCH TO SAY AND SHARE.
IT HAS ALWAYS BEEN THAT WAY
WHETHER CLOSE OR JUST RIGHT HERE.

SHOWING VULNERABILITY
WITH CARING FOR EACH OTHER.
LETTING GO OF FEAR
TO BE THERE FOR ONE ANOTHER.

ACCEPTING THE EXPERIENCES
WITHOUT JUDGEMENT OR SCORN.
REALIZING THEY WERE PLANNED
FOR GROWTH BEFORE WE BOTH WERE BORN.

TO BE THERE ON THIS EARTH
WHEN THE OTHER IS IN PAIN GIVES A JOY TO BE THERE
UNTIL WE SMILE AGAIN.

IT HAS BEEN A HARD JOURNEY
TO TEMPER UP THE STEEL.
WHEN TIME SAYS BE QUIET;
WE EACH REST FOR A SPELL.

DELIGHTING IN THE VICTORY'S
FOR EACH ALONG THE WAY.
SHARING OF THE KNOWLEDGE
MAKES IT EASIER EACH DAY.

LIFE TIMES SHARED CONT

MY PRAYER FOR YOU IS SELF WORTH
TO HELP YOU CARRY ON.
SEEING YOU SHARE WITH OTHERS
TO HELP THEM TO BE STRONG.

MAY YOUR TALENTS BE THE FOCUS
TO FILL YOUR HEART WITH JOY.
THAT GRADUALLY PAIN FROM OTHERS,
NO LONGER CAN ANNOY.

FOR LIFE HAS MANY CHAPTERS
FROM THE FIRST ONE TO THE END.
A NEW ONE IS BEGINNING
WHICH WILL CHEER YOU UP NO END.

HARD TO BELIEVE, BUT GIVE IT
ALL YOU HAVE GOT.
MY FRIEND MY HEART SINGS FOR YOU.
I BELIEVE YOU CAN HAVE THE LOT.

SO WE WILL KEEP ON LAUGHING,
SHARING ALL THINGS NEW.
THANK YOU FOR PUTTING ME
IN THIS WORLD ALONG WITH YOU.

THE KEY

SOME ONE ONCE SAID THAT THE WORLD
COULD BE MINE.
THAT EVERYTHING I WISHED FOR
WAS POSSIBLE IN TIME.
LONG AGO I DID NOT KNOW
OR EVEN UNDERSTAND.
THAT WHEN THE KEY OF LIFE IS HELD
OUR HEART PUTS OUR DREAMS INTO OUT HAND.

COURAGE IN THE MOMENT
TO FOLLOW FROM THE HEART.
TRUSTING IN THE FUTURE
TO ALLOW ME TO PLAY MY PART.
FOR JOYFUL IS THE MOMENT
KNOWING IT IS REAL.
FREEDOM FROM WITHIN HAS A JOYFUL,
HAPPY FEEL.

CONTINUE ON YOUR WAY,
KNOWING YOU ARE SAFE.
ATTRACTING SUPPORTING ENERGIES THAT WORK WELL WITH
YOU IN YOUR PLACE.
A JOY TO SHARE WITH OTHERS.
THE QUEST OF LIFE IS LOVE.
SUPPORTED WITH HIGHER ENERGIES
AVAILABLE FROM ABOVE.

DESTINY

DESTINY IS OURS
ON A PATH FULL OF LOVE.
AS WE CHOSE TO BE TOGETHER
WITH THE GUIDANCE FROM ABOVE.
WHEN ONE LIVES FROM THE HEART,
BEAUTY IS REFLECTED FROM INSIDE.
LIVING FOR EACH DAY AS WITH THE
MOVEMENT OF THE TIDE.

WITH THE RISING OF THE SUN
A NEW DAY APPEARS.
HOW WONDERFUL TO EXPERIENCE LIFE
WITH ALL THE BEAUTY HERE.
FOR FOCUSING ON WHAT IS REAL,
INSTEAD OF LITTLE DOUBTS.
GIVES MEANING TO THIS LIFE
AND WHAT IT IS ALL ABOUT.

LIFE HAS MANY GIFTS
FOR EACH ALONG THE WAY.
TAKE TIME TO BE STILL,
TO RECOGNIZE THEM EACH DAY.
WHEN THE DAY COMES TO AN END
AND YOU SETTLE DOWN TO REST.
KNOW THAT YOU HAVE GIVEN ALL
AND DONE YOUR VERY BEST.

QUIET TIMES

Those rocks give me comfort
As I sit and gaze over the sea.
This view with its beauty
Gives me the stillness to be free.
Thoughts dance through my mind;
They are not there to stay.
Watching as with shadows
Until they softly pass away.

The stillness of the moment
With this mirror here to see.
All my thoughts reflected
As they dance in front of me.
Learning to let go of doubt and
Learning to be calm.
My morning meditation sets the
Path to protect from harm.

This time is mine each day.
The gift to inner peace.
When all the world is rushing around.
When will it all cease.
It isn't surprising that they have
No time for self.
That special time of silence which
Is our own real wealth.

Allow the stillness to expand.
You will do far more.
For each day will be full of things
You wish to explore.
The fear and uncertainties will slowly
Leave your life.
As you travel on your journey on a
Path without the inner strife.

SMILE AS YOU LEARN

THIS JOY IS MINE ALONE,
A LOVE OF SELF AND TRUE WORTH.
THE REALIZATION OF THE JOURNEY.
THE REASON FOR OUR BIRTH.
EACH DAY IS A JOYFUL MOMENT
WITH BLESSINGS FROM THE HEART.
TO BRING HAPPINESS TO MY WORLD
I MUST LIVE MY OWN PART.

LIVING FOR THE MOMENT
WITHOUT FEAR OF CONCERN.
COURAGE TO KNOW THE DIFFERENCE
AND SMILE AS I LEARN.
RELEASING THE PAST
EACH MOMENT OF THE DAY.
FOR THEN THE TIME IS REAL
AND TRUE IN EVERY WAY.

LIVE

BRINGS MY DREAMS TO ME AS I
ENDEAVOUR TO LIVE THEM EACH DAY.
ALWAYS PUSHING FORWARD, BELIEVING
TO BRING THEM MY WAY.
LOOKING TO BECOME THE ENERGY
WHICH MAKES THEM REAL.
GLORY IN THE MOMENT, I AM ALIVE,
AT LAST I FEEL.

ANOTHER CHAPTER

FURTHER CHAPTERS IN LIFE
WITH SO MUCH TO ENJOY.
FULL OF INNER BLESSINGS
TO APPRECIATE IT ALL.
FOR EACH DAY IS A GIFT
AS A CHILD WITH A TOY.
ENJOYING THE MOMENT
WITH EVERY THING AS NEW.

THE SUNSHINE AND THE RAIN
BOTH NOURISH THE EARTH.
HAVE TAUGHT ME TO VALUE,
TO ADD TO MY SELF WORTH.
SO FOCUS ON THE BEAUTY TO PUT
AN END TO STRIFE.
THERE IS A PURPOSE FOR EVERYTHING
IN THE PATHWAY OF LIFE.

THE REALIZATION

The realization that my thoughts
Form who I am.
They have accumulated right from birth,
When life began.
Conditioning by positive and negative
Make up my form.
My attitudes bring me sunshine
As well as mighty storms.

The journey is my making
With a choice the road I take.
Changing direction when my heart is
Heavy is the decision for me to make.
Realizing I am a puzzle with a subconscious-ness,
Buried strings.
Gives me the opportunity to cleanse the past, for my
heart to sing.

This little child at my feet
Has dreams to come and share.
When she is free to be her own
True self life will hold no fear.
So look at the story where the
Journey has come so far.
Seek truly what you really want,
Be still, seek out your star.

The wish you have for those you love,
The freedom of the heart.
Is there for you; go on ,
Make a start.
Thoughts of lack need to be let go.
For destiny to come through.
The time has come to love your self
Through thoughts that truly support you.

True worth comes when we accept
That the child within comes first.
When positive thought is in form
We realize our own true worth.
For do unto others as we
Would be done by.
Is receiving the gifts for this child that others benefit
from the energies on high.

So raise your vibrations,
Through inner growth within.
With smiles, laughter, sunshine
Through the seasons as they open.
Make peace with yourself at last.
Let the doubts go.
Life's seeds once planted
Become acknowledged, then they grow.

MEDITATION DAY

Thank you for the hour when
All things come to pass.
Sharing and caring;
It all went by so fast.
The journey individual,
Yet shared by each one there.
May love be with you all
As your hearts become more aware.

Lights are lit along the way
To guide us on our way.
That sunshine shines through
To brighten up our day.
On the path, the love is there.
The support. The quiet time.
When we can go within our self,
The stillness, the end of time.

A guide is there to take our hand
Toward the light of love.
Ever reaching higher to the
Vibrations up above.
The world is one for all to care
And bring their love together.
The prayer is that we search for love
To strengthen it forever.

THE AWAKENING

THE END CAN BE THE BEGINNING.
THE OPENING OF THE HEART.
IT OFTEN MEANS A CHANGE OF LIFE,
A NEW ROAD WE MUST START.

LIFE HAS MANY LESSONS TO UNFOLD
AS WE PASS ALONG THE WAY.
IT DOES NOT MEAN WE CAN BE TOLD.
THERE IS MUCH WE MUST OBEY.

DEEP WITHIN WE FEEL OUR JOY AND GROW
AS WE DISCOVER OUR TRUE WEALTH.
A WARMTH, A JOY COMES IN OUR HEART
AS WE LEARN ABOUT OUR SELF.

THE WAY IS OFTEN LONELY
WITH NO ONE ELSE TO SHARE.
THE MANY LITTLE TREASURES
THAT LIFE HOLDS REALLY DEAR.

EACH MUST FIND THEIR PATHWAY
TO OPENING UP THEIR HEART.
LOVE IS THE BEGINNING.
THE ONLY PLACE TO START.

LOVE IN FOCUS

LOVE IN FOCUS, LOVE EACH DAY.
BUILDS OUR RELATIONSHIPS ALONG THE WAY.
GIVES US CONFIDENCE WITH WHAT WE DO.
ENSURES WE EXPAND TO TRY WHAT IS NEW.
LIFE IS FOR CHALLENGE THAT EACH MAY
LEARN TO RISE ABOVE THE DAILY CONCERN.
TO TAKE IT IN STRIDE AND DEAL WITH
THE SITUATION.
THE PURPOSE OF LIFE, THE REASON
FOR CREATION.

EACH THEIR THOUGHTS WITH MEMORIES
OF THE PAST.
COLOUR TOMORROW SO THAT YESTERDAY LASTS.
STANDING BACK FROM THE PICTURE
LIGHTENS OUR CONCERNS.
THEY COME INTO PERSPECTIVE TO HELP
WITH WHAT WE LEARN.
LOVED ONES WITH SUPPORT
CAN NOT ALWAYS SEE INSIDE.
IT DOESN'T REALLY MATTER IF THEY ALLOW
OUR FOCUS AND DO NOT CRITICISE.

WE ALL MUST DO OUR LEARNING
BY DOING OUR VERY BEST.
SHOWING LOVE THROUGHOUT REMAINS
OUR REAL TEST.
WITH OTHERS LOVE AND POSITIVE FORCE
THE JOURNEY APPEARS LESS HARSH.
WITHOUT THIS LOVE AND TRUST
WE FEEL ALONE AND IN A MARSH
MAY THIS WORLD LEARN TO TRUST
AND FOCUS WHERE WE NEED.
THAT KNOWLEDGE OF THE PATH
CEASES SEARCHING JUST WITH GREED.

WHEN EACH ACHIEVES THEIR PATH
WITH GLADNESS IN THEIR HEART.
THEIR VICTORIES OF PEACE WILL
BRING JOY FROM THE VERY START.
AS THE LESSONS INCREASE THEIR LOVE.
WITH TRUE FRIENDSHIP THERE BESIDE US
AND THE ENERGIES FROM ABOVE.

THE STATE OF GRACE

IF YOU THINK OF PAIN
IT WILL ONLY BRING YOU DOWN.
LOOK AT ALL THE SEASONS AND
HOW THEY ALL COME AROUND.
GOOD TIMES FOLLOW DIFFICULT ONES
IF YOU KEEP ON TO THE END.
THE LEARNING THAT THEY GIVE US
SUPPORTS US AS A FRIEND.

OBSERVE ALL THE GAIN AND
VICTORIES OF THE PAST.
THEY SHOW THE DOWN TIMES
NEVER REALLY LAST.
SO FORTIFY YOURSELF, PUT A
SMILE ON YOUR FACE.
YES INDEED, YOU ALWAYS MOVE TOWARD
THE STATE OF ONENESS WITH GRACE.

A DAY OF LEARNING

EACH DAY GIVES ME LEARNING
WHICH IS HOW LIFE SHOULD REALLY BE.
SO EACH ONE IS A TREASURE,
AN EXTRA ONE FOR ME.
ONLY THE VEHICLE CHANGES
AS IT FINALLY; COMES TO REST.
WHILE THE SOUL IS EVER LASTING
AS IT ACCUMULATES THE BEST.
WHEN WE REALIZE THE JOURNEY IS SPECIAL
FOR LEARNING FOR OUR SELF.
WE FINALLY LET GO OF EXPECTATIONS
OF OTHERS AND OF WEALTH.
FOR THOSE WE TOUCH AS WE PASS BY
GIVE US A CHANCE TO LEARN.
SO WE MUST NOT FILL OUR HEART WITH
LOSS OR SORROW FOR THAT WE YEARN.
IN TIME ALL WILL BE OURS AS WE
BECOME TOTAL LOVE.
FOR THEN WE WILL BE AT ONE
WITH THE HIGHEST DIMENSIONS ABOVE.

BIRTHDAY REFLECTIONS

So what, another birthday.
Here I stand the same today.
But do I look within,
Or into the sky.
Begin to seek to see
If there is more on high.

It is my right to ask questions.
Are there really many more dimensions?
Is there a soul and destination?
Let me look and know the story
Of creation.

Why be in the world,
Why be out of it?
What can there be?
Or must I do without it?
My life is mine as others theirs,
For each our truth over the years.

But let me seek and find
What is mine.
That I may journey each day with
Joy through rain or sunshine.
Is there more to work and play?
Should I be doing more today?

THE SECRET OF THE POEM

WHEN PAIN IS IN THE HEART
AND THE SOUL IS VERY TROUBLED.
WE NEED SOMEONE TO TALK TO.
OUR TROUBLES TO IMPART.
IF WE FEEL ALONE.
OUR PEN WE MUST EMPLOY.
TO WRITE DOWN WHAT IS DEEP WITHIN
AND LET THE PAGES TALK.

IF WE READ BETWEEN THE LINES,
THE ANSWERS WE WILL FIND.
THE PROBLEMS WE FACE UP TO,
HAVE COME FROM DEEP WITHIN OUR MIND.
FOR AT OUR SHOULDER WE HAVE HELP
TO GUIDE US DAY BY DAY.
IF WE DEAL WITH TRUTH AND LOVE,
WE ARE GUIDED ON OUR WAY.

WHICH PATH

PATHS CAME TO MEET ME.
NONE WERE REALLY RIGHT.
SO I WALKED AWAY UNTIL
THE RIGHT ONE CAME INTO SIGHT.

NOW MY HEART IS HAPPY.
EACH DAY GIVES ME THE CHANCE.
TO CREATE THE THINGS WHICH GIVE ME JOY.
THEIR BEAUTY TO ENHANCE.

THE AIRPORT

AMAZING WHAT I SEE,
AS I AM SITTING HERE.
SOME PEOPLE WALK QUICKLY BY,
WHILE OTHERS STAND AND STARE.

PEOPLE BUSY KISSING.
SAYING LAST GOODBYES.
WHILE OTHERS QUIETLY WIPE THE TEARS
WHICH COME INTO THEIR EYES.

CHILDREN ALL EXCITED.
NOT REALLY KNOWING WHY.
WAITING FOR THE TIME,
WHEN THE PLANE WILL FLY.

SUITCASES SLIDING GENTLY PAST,
AS THEY ALL GET WEIGHED.
WHILE EACH PASSENGER HOPES WITHIN
THAT THEY WILL NOT BE DELAYED.

THE CALL WILL SOON COME LOUD AND CLEAR.
FRIENDS, RELATIONS WILL SOON LEAVE HERE
AND SO THE AIRPORT WILL ALWAYS BE.
SOME PEOPLE COME, WHILE OTHERS LEAVE.

SELF GROWTH

ALL MY LIFE I HAVE GIVEN.
SO MANY OUT STRETCHED HANDS.
HOW LONG CAN A BODY GIVE
WITH NO REAL LOVE TO HAND?

A CHILD NEEDS ITS PARENTS LOVE
TO GUIDE IT ON ITS WAY.
IF YOU WATCH A LITTLE CHILD.
THEY LIVE FROM DAY TO DAY.

AS THE CHILD GROWS OLDER.
LIFE BEGINS TO CHANGE.
FOR THE LITTLE ONE IS CHANNELLED,
TO FOLLOW MANS OWN PLAN.

THE EAGER CRIES OF YOUTH
CAN SOON BE LEFT BEHIND.
IF THE PAIN SETS IN TO CONDITION
AND BE A PART OF MIND.

IT DOES NOT HAVE TO BE THIS WAY
IF WE FIND OUT TO OUR JOY
THAT WE CAN CHANGE THE PATHWAYS.
OUR SKILLS WE MUST DEPLOY.

THE TEARS IN YOUTH, THE PAIN WE HAD.
MAY NOT TURN OUT COMPLETELY BAD.
FOR THEY GIVE US WISDOM AND INSIGHT.
WE GLIMPSE A VIEW OF THINGS BEYOND
OUR SIGHT.

WE START TO GROW AS A PLANT
FIRST GIVEN FOOD AND LIGHT.
OUR CONFIDENCE BEGINS TO GROW.
IN THIS WORLD FULL OF THINGS
WE NEED TO KNOW.

THE MORE WE LEARN ABOUT OUR SELF.
WE FEEL WE ARE AGLOW.
SO MUCH TO GIVE AND SHARE.
WE WANT EVERYONE TO KNOW.

EACH DAY BRINGS NEW DISCOVERIES.
WITH LITTLE JOYS TO SHARE.
I WONDER IF WE LEARN IT ALL
IN THE TIME THAT WE ARE HERE.

LIGHTEN UP THE HEART

REFLECTIONS COME TO US
TO LIGHTEN UP THE HEART.
THOSE SUBCONSCIOUS MEMORIES
WHICH CAN HINDER WHERE WE START.
DO NOT LET THEM INFLUENCE,
OR SPOIL THE COLOUR OF YOUR DAY.

JUST OBSERVE AND ALLOW THEM
TO SOFTLY PASS AWAY.
LIVING FOR THE MOMENT
IS THE ONLY PLACE TO BE.
PEACE AND CONTENTMENT.
WHERE YOU KNOW YOU ARE REALLY FREE.

A Christmas prayer from a child's heart

The night was quiet.
The child still
As it leaned
On the window sill.
Tomorrow would be
Christmas Day.
I heard these words
As the child prayed.

It isn't the presents
You wrap I want.
It isn't the money
To buy them.
It is love and laughter for my
Brother and sister, my Mum and Dad.
I try to be good, honest I do.
No one is really bad.

So send the love
Into the world.
That all may be at peace.
Let it grow and grow
Like a little seed
Until it fills the world.
Yes, that's what I want
For Christmas.

MERRY CHRISTMAS

OH CHRISTMAS DAY OF LOVE AND LIGHT.
INCREASE THE FLOW FOR MORE INSIGHT.
THAT SOULS MAY BECOME MORE AWARE
OF THEIR PURPOSE FOR BEING HERE.

CHRISTMAS IS BUT ONE DAY
IN A YEAR OF MANY DAYS.
THE JOY OF GIVING INSTEAD OF GETTING.
A DAY TO REMEMBER INSTEAD OF FORGETTING.

A SMILE, A WORD AS YOU BRIEFLY TOUCH.
MEANS MUCH TO A SOUL WHO HASN'T MUCH.
WE OFTEN MISS THE TREASURES WE HAVE,
WITHOUT REALIZING WHAT WE HAVE HAD.

PEOPLE COME AND PEOPLE GO.
SELDOM DO WE GET TO KNOW.
THEIR INNER THOUGHTS WHICH PAINT
THE PICTURE.
WE ALL PERCEIVE FROM OUR OWN
INNER LECTURE.

IF WE COULD ALL COME TOGETHER
AND TRY TO SEE EACH OTHERS PICTURE.
IT WOULD HELP US TO UNDERSTAND.
INSTEAD OF JUDGING, WE MAY OFFER A HAND.

WE ALL WANT PEACE AROUND OUR SELF.
WE WISH IT FOR THE WORLD.
SO LET US TAKE THIS CHRISTMAS DAY
AND FILL IT FULL OF LOVE.
THAT WE CREATE A BEGINNING,
UNTIL WE MEET THE LOVE ABOVE.

FAITH, GOODNESS, GRACE

FAITH IS MINE TO HONOUR.
TO LIVE WITH TRUST FROM ABOVE.
THAT EVERYTHING WILL TURN OUT RIGHT
WITH FAITH, TRUST AND LOVE.
CHALLENGES COME TO US
WHERE WE CAN IDENTIFY.
THE COURAGE STRONG WITHIN
US TO SUCCEED WITHOUT A CRY.

GOODNESS BRINGS ITS REWARD
IF WE PATIENTLY KEEP ON,
UNTIL THE STRUGGLE ENDS AND OUR
STEP IS LIGHT WITH SONG.
SO FOCUS ON THE MOMENT FORWARD
WITH A SMILE ON YOUR FACE.
FOR ALL THE GOOD OF PAST TIMES
WILL HELP YOU KEEP YOUR GRACE.

LOVE IS POWER

WHEN IT IS HARD TO SMILE
AND THE ROAD SEEMS ALL UP HILL.
LOOK WHERE YOU HAVE COME FROM
BY SITTING VERY STILL.

FOR THERE WITHIN YOUR HEART
THE CHANGES YOU WILL SEE.
THE ONES THAT GAVE YOU VICTORY
THAT YOUR MANY FRIENDS CAN SEE.

YOU ARE NEVER ON YOUR OWN
AS YOU TRAVEL EVER HOME.
YOUR JOURNEY HAS A PURPOSE
WHICH SHOWS YOUR OWN TRUE WORTH.

SO FOCUS ON TODAY, THE MOMENT,
NOT THE HOUR.
FOR SUNSHINE IS AROUND YOU.
YOUR LOVE IS YOUR REAL POWER.

Never give up

Courage isn't easy.
It comes from deep within.
When we glimpse within our heart,
We have the guide of where to start.

Each day gives us the chance to try.
To stop our goal from passing by.
Little victories all add up.
So keep on trying, never give up.

Keep noting the progress along the way.
It sustains us, gives patience along the way.
Courage is yours to keep on going.
You have progressed without really knowing.

Rest if you must to see where you are.
Then re focus on your bright star.
For everything you have ever wanted.
Can be yours in the time allocated.

OPENING NEW DOORS

The end can be the beginning
To open up new doors.
First we must clear our memory
So we can explore.
Deep within our heart
Lies the secret of our dreams.
You are confident, you are strong.
View yourself with high esteem.

Take each day and quietly build.
Everything is yours within this world.
Each step gives you joy
As it opens up your vision.
That you enjoy your journey
For your own sake.
For it no longer matters how
Long the journey takes.

Christmas reflections

It is quiet today sitting here
Looking over the bay.
So many all at home
At the start of Christmas Day.

The waves so dark reflect from
The blue of the sky.
These clouds overhead
Move softly and swiftly by.

My thoughts go with love to those
In Australia and far away.
They care and pass to others in the
World who do not know of Christmas Day.

May the world lift with love
As we remember the birth.
That gave us all hope and the chance
To learn our self worth.

Be still, be quiet;
Let silence enter.
The peace is ours
When we remember.

BIRTHDAYS JOURNEY

HERE IT COMES AGAIN.
THE DAY THEY SAY IS MINE.
THE LOVE IT BRINGS EACH YEAR
SHOWS THE SUN WILL ALWAYS SHINE.
FRIENDS IN THEIR WAY STOP TO SHOW
HOW MUCH THEY TRULY CARE.
SPECIAL THANK YOU FOR THE BIRTHDAY WHERE
EVEN DISTANCE BRINGS THEM NEAR.
EACH DAY IS PRECIOUS, FULL OF
OPPORTUNITIES OF JOY.
FOCUS ON THE SUNSHINE WITH EACH DAY
BRIGHT AND NEW.
GIVES THE CHANCE TO SMILE WITH A
POSITIVE POINT OF VIEW.
SO THANKYOU ONCE AGAIN FOR THIS
SPECIAL TIME TO SHARE.
YES IT IS MY BIRTHDAY. MAY YOU
ALWAYS FEEL YOU ARE NEAR.

OPEN UP YOUR DAY

WHEN TIMES SEEM HARD
WITH A STEEP HILL AROUND.
MAKE A TIME FOR STILLNESS
WHEN THERE IS NOTHING, NOT A SOUND.

LOOK FOR THE LOVE TO
HELP YOU RISE ABOVE.
WHEN OTHERS HAVE SHARED WITH YOU
AND GIVEN YOU THEIR LOVE.

IF THE WORLD APPEARS UNKIND
WITH FEELINGS OF BEING HURT.
TAKE THE TIME TO VIEW SUCCESS.
DUST YOURSELF OFF - GET OUT OF THE DIRT.

FOR RENEWAL IS THE KEY
TO MOVE YOU ON YOUR WAY-
THE KEY TO ADD A SPARKLE,
THAT WILL OPEN UP YOUR DAY.

MUSIC OF THE VOICES

MUSIC OF THE VOICES
THAT RING TO STAY IN TOUCH.

REMINDS YOU TO RECOGNISE THE LOVE
THAT IS THERE; IT IS ENOUGH.

RELEASING OF THE SHADOWS
TO OPEN UP THE DOOR.

FOR TODAY TO BE IN YOUR LIFE
WITHOUT FRICTION ANY MORE.

TIME ETERNAL OPEN TO REFINE
KNOWLEDGE AND EXPLORE.

TO BECOME SERENITY IN THIS
WORLD WHICH OFFERS LIFE AND MORE.

EACH ONE TO THEIR CHALLENGE
FROM LAUGHTER OR FROM PAIN.

OFFERS UP THE EXPERIENCE TO LEARN
AND HAVE FAITH TO TRY AGAIN.

COMPLETE YOUR JOURNEY

IF ENOUGH MONEY IN THE WORLD
CAME MY WAY TODAY.
TO ALLOW ME TO BE SELF-SUFFICIENT
TO SUPPORT ME THROUGH EACH DAY.
THEN I COULD FULFIL THE
DRIVE INSIDE OF ME.
WITH PEOPLE WHO ASK ME TO SHARE
AND LEARN HOW TO BE FREE.
TO EXPLORE THE MANY LESSONS
WE HAVE ALONG THE WAY.
FOR EACH OF US TO DISCUSS
AND HAVE OUR OWN SAY.

THE TIME IS HERE FOR CARING
AND SHARING ALL THINGS NEW.
IN A WORLD THAT'S REALLY NEEDING
A NEW POSITIVE POINT OF VIEW.
TO GIVE PEOPLE THE COURAGE
TO WANT TO KEEP ON GOING.
THAT THEY CAN SEE WHY THEY SHOULD
STAY IN A WORLD DEPRIVED OF KNOWING.
FOR COURAGE IS THE PEOPLE
WHO NEVER DO GIVE UP.
COURAGE ISN'T GIVEN, OR A
PIECE OF LUCK.

COURAGE IS WHEN WE TRY WHEN WE
FEEL WE ARE AT THE END.
COURAGE IS THE EXTRA EFFORT
TO TAKE US AROUND THE BEND.
FOR ONE TO KEEP ON TRYING
THEY MUST FEEL ANOTHER CARES.
FOR ONE TO KEEP ON TRYING
THEY MUST KNOW ANOTHER HEARS.
TO TALK THROUGH WITH OTHERS CAN

LET US SEE WHAT IS ON OUR MIND.
IT CAN BROADEN THE FOCUS;
NOT ALWAYS VERY KIND.

FOR HEALING IN THE PROCESS
MEANS TO SEE WHAT WE MUST CHANGE.
DENYING IT ONLY ENSURES THAT
WE FACE IT ALL AGAIN.
THANK THE ONE WHO LISTENS AND
OFFERS A POINT OF VIEW.
IT IS BEAUTIFUL TO HAVE A FRIEND;
BUT IT IS STILL UP TO YOU.
SO LOOK FOR YOUR VICTORIES
TO BUILD YOUR SELF WORTH.
THAT YOU CAN TAKE YOURSELF ALONG
THIS PATH. THE CHALLENGE WE CALL EARTH.

THE MIRROR OF THE SOUL

WORDS, THE MIRROR OF OUR SOUL
DO WE LISTEN TO WHAT WE SAY?
ARE WE LIVING AN EXPECTED ROLE,
OR FOR THE MOMENT OF EACH DAY?

WORDS COLOUR OUR LIFE.
SO MAKE IT A HAPPY ONE.
FINISH YOUR DAY CONTENTED
KNOWING YOU HAVE WON.

THAT WE SEE THE SUN OR RAIN DROPS.
THE BIRDS IN THE TREES AND THE SKY.
WITH A SMILE AND A SONG IN OUR HEART
TO LIFT US UP ON HIGH.

RECOGNISING THE LOVING FORCE
GIVES IT YOUR SUPPORT.
MAGNIFIES THIS ENERGY FOR THE WORLD
LOVE THAT CANNOT BE BOUGHT.

THE POWER OF THOUGHTS

WRITING ON THE CHALKBOARD
WHERE A DUSTER CAN WIPE IT OUT.
IS THE PERFECT EXAMPLE FOR CLEARING OUR THOUGHTS, FOR
THIS IS WHAT LIFE IS ABOUT.

IF YOU THOUGHT, THAT YOU CREATED
YOUR EXPERIENCES EACH DAY.
BY WHAT YOU SEND OUT AND
RECOGNISE ALONG THE WAY.

YOU WOULD SEND OUT LOVE
THAT IT CAME BACK TO YOU.
IN FACT IT WOULD GIVE HEALING
FOR A DIFFERENT POINT OF VIEW.

WHEN YOUR THOUGHTS ARE NEGATIVE
USE THE DUSTER TO LET THEM GO.
THAT THE LOVING ENERGY SURROUNDS YOU AND OTHERS THAT
YOU KNOW.

ONCE THE WORLD IS WORKING
TOWARDS MAGNIFYING LOVE.
WE WILL ALL EMBRACE THIS LOVING ENERGY.
THE HIGHEST SOURCE ABOVE.

LOVE IS TRUSTING

LOVE IS LOVE WITHOUT FEAR.
COMFORTABLE WITH ALL THAT IS NEAR.

FOR EACH THEIR OWN DESTINY
WITH LIFE'S SPECIAL INNER BLESSING.

THEIR INNER FLOWER HERE TO GROW
FROM EXPERIENCES THAT BLOSSOM FOR THEM TO KNOW.

RELEASING CONTROL FOR OTHERS TO BE FREE.
LETS GO OF FEAR, BRINGS THEM NEAR.

BREATHE SOFTLY

LITTLE PAINS AT THE HEART
REMIND ME JUST TO BE
RELAXED IN LIFE TO ENJOY
WITHOUT ANXIETY.
WITH LOVE THERE TO CONQUER.
BREATHING GENTLY TO EXPERIENCE MORE.
THE WORLD IS OPEN DAILY
WITH MUCH FOR US TO EXPLORE.

LIFE IS CHANGE

WATCH THE MOMENT, YES THE HOUR
FOR ALL THINGS CAN CHANGE.
PATTERNS OF THE PAST DROP
AS YOUR BEHAVIOUR IS RE—ARRANGED.

HOLD YOUR DREAMS, HAVE CLEAR VISION,
THAT THEY CAN UNFOLD.
FOR LIFE THE MOMENT OF CHANGE
IS NOT ALWAYS WHAT YOU HAVE BEEN TOLD.

EACH THEIR LESSONS AHEAD OF THEM
ON THEIR JOURNEY HERE.
FIRST ONE MUST OBSERVE THEM SELVES
THAT THE LESSONS BECOME CLEAR.

THE BEAUTY OF THE MOMENT,
WITH ACCEPTANCE OF THE SELF.
YES THE INNER KNOWLEDGE
THAT THIS IS YOUR TRUE WEALTH.

FOR KNOWLEDGE, MONEY, POWER,
DO NOT GIVE PURPOSE TO LIFE.
IN FACT THEY OFTEN INSTIL UNREST
TO SURROUND YOU WITH STRIFE.

KINDNESS IS THE GIFT,
A TOUCH OR A HUG.
THE AWARENESS OF ENERGY
THAT BUILDS TO TOTAL LOVE.

STARTING WITH THE SELF WITH LOVE,
ACCEPTING WHO YOU ARE.
UNIQUE IN PERSONALITY,
A WONDROUS LITTLE STAR.
SO SMILE ON THIS DAY,

It will never come again.
Yours is the glory
Whether in the sun or rain.

As you love this inner child
Others will receive your love.
God bless this energy.
The purpose from above.

A SHARED WORLD

KNOWING THAT WE SHARE THIS WORLD
MAKES IT A BETTER PLACE.

KNOWING WE ARE THERE FOR EACH OTHER
KEEPS A SMILE ON THE FACE.

FEELING THE SHARED LOVE
AS IT SOFTLY RADIATES AND UNFURLS.

JOY IN THE KNOWLEDGE WE ARE LINKED
THROUGH ALL THE DIMENSIONS OF THIS WORLD.

LETTING GO

Letting go of holding.
Releasing of the past.
Allows a new presence
For peace to flow at last.
Expectations release
With each ones accepted difference.
Observing and learning to be
Still of real significance.

Tolerance, compassion, for each
One on the path.
That they can experience
Wisdom with peace at last.
For stillness is the gift
For true intelligence to flow.
Awareness of the self
That we really come to know.

Seeing our self in different circumstances;
How we really are.
Gives opportunity for growth
For our inner glowing star.
Brings the world together
That the war and greed can cease.
For yes, it is possible
For each to reach their peace.

SUPPORT

WHEN YOU KNOW THAT YOU HAVE DONE
ALL THAT YOU CAN DO.
THAT YOUR HEART WAS FILLED WITH LOVE
AND TO YOUR SELF WAS TRUE.
THEN YOU CAN RELAX
FOR MOVEMENT TO COME IN.
FOR NEW DOORS TO OPEN
AS A NEW LIFE BEGINS.

LET OTHERS SUPPORT YOU
WITH THEIR LOVE AND CARE.
THIS NEW DAY OPENS TO LET THEM
SHARE AND BE RIGHT THERE.
FOR SUNSHINE WILL COME AS
LOVE SURROUNDS YOU SAFE.
YES YOU HAVE FOUND YOUR STRENGTH,
SUPPORT, YOUR TRUE PLACE.

The path of learning

Ours is not to judge,
For each has their own journey.
To go down their path
To realise their own learning.
So cast not judgement or scorn
On others for their action.
Let it pass gently by.
Move on without re-action.

Gather treasures around you
In friends that you can share.
To be there for each other and
Hold each other dear.
Allow them to blossom and have
A garden full of flowers.
A time of joy and triumph
To softly pass the hours.

When each can talk to let
Go of their fear.
Life will give them courage to face
Each day with good cheer.
Happy with the outcomes
Without judgement of self or others.
Calmly moving onward
To the value of their wealth.

MY FUTURE

My future is my thoughts
For all things to be.
Watched over by my guardian angel
With knowledge for me to see.
Living in the moment,
With kindness for all.
Observing all the thoughts
No matter how small.

Refined over and over
To arrive at being whole.
A spirit of love,
Aware to complete its role.
Realisation of the journey
To maximise the moment.
Knowing that eventually the ending
Of reaction in thought is the opponent.

For thinking ever forward or
Backward with the time.
Prevents the newest moment
With space the only line.
Just to be at one
With the moment and the vibration.
Frees the soul to stillness
With no dread or celebration.

UNTIL DEATH DO US PART

PEOPLE COMMIT TO LIFE TOGETHER.
"UNTIL DEATH DO US PART."
WITHOUT REALISING THE INNER KNOWLEDGE
NECESSARY BEFORE THEY START.
TO LIVE THE WORDS AND MAKE THEM REAL.
MEANS KNOWLEDGE SHARED
WITH LIFE THE ZEAL.

FOR MANY THINGS WILL CHANGE
AS YOU WALK THROUGH LIFE TOGETHER.
ONLY WITH TRUE LOVE WILL THIS LAST
FOR EACH FOR EVER.
LIVING FOR THE MOMENT AND SHARING
FROM THE HEART.
DISCUSSING INNER FEELINGS,
EXPRESSED FROM THE VERY START.

FOR VIEWING OF THE TRUTH
OF THE SHADOWS WE COME FROM.
GIVES STRENGTH TO RELATIONSHIPS
TO HELP THEM JOURNEY ON.
LOVE IN CONFIDENCE AND JOY
WITH SOFT MOMENTS TO REMEMBER.
THAT THEY KINDLE UP YOUR LOVE.,
RENEW THAT BRIGHTLY BURNING EMBER.

WHERE THERE IS NO FEAR OR CHALLENGE;
JUST TRAVELLING IN CALM.
FOR LIFE HAS A DESTINY,
A JOURNEY WITHOUT HARM.
FOR THOUGHT IS THE MOMENT
WHEN TIME IS CREATED.

WHEN EMOTIONS PASS THROUGH US
WHICH ARE HIGHLY OVER RATED.

BE ONE WITH THE WAVES AND
THE CRY OF THE GULL.

LOSE THE ESSENCE OF ALL TIME,
LET NATURE PLAY THE ROLL.
FOR BIRDS, TREES, MAN,
HAVE AN ENERGY OF THEIR OWN.
YET SHARE THE DESTINY WHERE ALL JOINS;
THEY ARE NOT ALONE.
SO BE THERE FOR EACH OTHER;
LOVE THE COMMON TOUCH.
GROWING IN INTENSITY IN OUR
WORLD THAT HOLDS SO MUCH.

Hullo my friend

When life becomes hard and
The road seems all up hill.
Your heart feels full of dread.
People are unkind
For reasons of their own.
You wonder if they stay that way
When in their own home.

From observing other people,
We find much to learn.
Even if it is to realise
Their own lessons they must learn.
Life has a purpose
For each and every soul.
For each to seek and follow
To achieve their own goal.

Some will seek out riches
With adornments around their neck.
While others seek out pleasure and
Only look for sex.
Blind to the beauty
The world puts in their way.
No joy in life for them they say,
Unless they drink night and day.

Put aside all these things,
For God has promised more.
The joy, the laughter and the learning
Must be behind another door.
Money cannot buy it,
Not any amount of wealth.
The joy we seek is in our heart,
Deep within our self.
Keep faith as you travel,

Be still and rest a while.
As you glimpse the path once more.
Your face will light up with a smile.
What you do is up to you,
Every moment counts.
Your thoughts, your speech,
What you see, sends energies without.

Our soul takes in the learning
To guide us another day.
No experience is wasted as we learn
More to help us on our way.
For life is a circle
Until our life is whole.
One filled with love and joy
Which has now another note.

To help others as they stumble by,
Shining forth a light.
If they take the time to listen,
They may avoid a nasty plight.
Travel on for self growth my friend,
For you glow for others to see.
Who knows one day where you will
Help to soften misery.

The best is wished for you;
That you get the chance to be
Free in love and beautiful
For all the world to see.
May your heart be free of ties
As it takes on its true song.
That you may serve others now,
With your faith you will be strong.

CLAIMING TODAY

Walk the day as new
From deep inside of you.
Comparing yesterdays memories
Will obscure, change the view.

The newness of the moment
Is there for you to have.
Life has this balance
To be happy, to be glad.

Trust in your faith,
Let go of the fear.
There are many new experiences
Just do it, be aware.

Knowledge from yesterday
Is yours, what you have.
It will colour, change your day
Remove the newness if you compare.

So many opportunities
Are there in our life.
Do we let them happen,
Postpone them once or twice.

For life is a circle.
Our opportunities come around again.
So reach out, enjoy them.
Your life will never be the same.

COMMUNICATIONS GIFT

THE GIFTS OF LIFE ARE MANY,
THEY COME IN DIFFERENT WAYS.
THOSE SPECIAL LITTLE DEW DROPS.
THEY BRIGHTEN UP OUR DAY.
THEY CAN BE BIG OR SMALL.
IN FACT THE GIFT MAY NOT
BE HELD AT ALL.
FOR WHEN THE GIFT IS ONE OF LOVE.
WE CAN GIVE IT AS IT IS ABOVE.

IT CAN BE UNDERSTANDING,
A SPECIAL MOMENT HELD.
THE LOOK, THAT SAYS I LOVE YOU
HAS A VERY SPECIAL SPELL.
KEEP ON SHARING WITH THE LOVE
COMING FROM DEEP WITHIN.
WHEN ALL OF US SEE THIS WAY
THERE IS STRENGTH TO NOT GIVE IN.
PATIENCE IS THE KEY TO LOVE;
THAT AND COMMUNICATION.
HAPPINESS THE JOY TO SHARE,
GIVES STRENGTH TO ALL THE NATION.

BEAUTY IN CREATION

BEAUTY IS CREATION WITH
THE CREATOR THE INDIVIDUAL
BEAUTY IS THE BEHOLDER WHO
PERCEIVES AS AN INDIVIDUAL.
FOR EACH ONE CAN BE FREE
WHERE EVERYTHING IS NEW.
ESPECIALLY WHEN NON CONDITIONED,
TO BE FRESH AS YOU VIEW.

THE SUBCONSCIOUS HOLDS EXPERIENCES
STORED ALONG THE WAY.
THEY BLOCK THE EXPERIENCE OF BEING
FREE WITH NEWNESS FOR THE DAY.
WHEN FEAR, ANGUISH AND OTHER TORMENTS
ALL LEAVE OUR NEST.
WE ARE LEFT BREATHING WELL
TO ENJOY ALL THE REST.

ANXIETY DEPRIVES US OF PEACE AND
STILLNESS IN OUR HEART.
FILLING UP THE MOMENT WHICH
DISTURBS US TO PULL US APART.
SO WHEN YOU FEEL TROUBLED AND
UNCERTAIN WITH THOUGHTS
CASTING DOUBT IN.
TAKE COURAGE AND LET GO
TO FOLLOW THE PATH WITHIN.

WITH YOU

LOVE TAKES OUT THE DISTANCE
WHEN WE REALLY FEEL.
THAT SOMEONE HOLDS US IN THEIR HEART,
THEIR LOVE IS VERY REAL.

IF I COULD MAKE YOUR WISH COME TRUE;
HOLD YOU IN MY ARMS.
IF I COULD TAKE AWAY YOUR PAIN AND
CHASE AWAY ALL HARM.

MAY COURAGE STAY WITH YOU
TO CHASE OUT THE FEAR,
MAY YOUR HEART ALWAYS BE FILLED
WITH THE LOVE THAT IS TRULY THERE.

SURGERY OF JOY

THE BLADE HAS CUT DEEP
MY FEARS HAVE BEEN UNEARTHED.
THE HEALING PROCESS IS IN FORCE.
COURAGE IS ADDED TO MY SELF WORTH.

A NEW ENERGY FOR SHARING
IF OTHERS CHOOSE TO TAKE IT ON.
ANOTHER LITTLE LIGHT TO HELP
OTHERS SOLDIER ON.

FOR ME THE PERSONAL VICTORY
STANDS ABOVE THOSE BEFORE,
IN THIS JOURNEY FOR FREEDOM
AS THE LEARNING GIVES ME MORE.

SOLDIER ON AND USE YOUR TALENTS
FOR YOU HAVE GIVEN MUCH.
THE BATTLE WITH YOUR INNER SELF
IS NOW COMPLETE, ENOUGH.

YOU WON'T KNOW WHO YOU ARE
UNTIL YOU WALK FREE.
THEN YOU WILL BRANCH FORTH WITH LIFE
JUST LIKE A STRONG YOUNG TREE.

YOUR TALENTS LADEN ON THE BRANCHES
AVAILABLE FOR EVERY ONE TO SEE.
MODEST IN THE KNOWLEDGE,
STILL, AT PEACE AND FREE.

TO SERVE

May insight be yours
To be there for others.
May consolidation be yours
For being there for another.
The teacher ever taught
When through the mirror viewed.
Coming from the heart
Gives the colours that are true.

Courage to go forward
Giving an opportunity for growth.
Sharing with another results in
Learning for you both.
So light the light at your heart and
Be still to connect within.
My friend there is no doubt
That you will conquer to win

LOOKING FOR THE BEAUTY

LOOKING FOR THE BEAUTY
IN EVERY THING YOU SEE.
GIVES A LIFT TO YOUR HEART.
ALLOWS IT TO BE FREE.

SMILING IN THE SUNSHINE.
LAUGHING IN THE RAIN.
WATCHING AS NATURE TRAVELS
THROUGH THE CIRCLE ONCE AGAIN.

DESTINY HAS A JOURNEY FOR
EACH AND EVERY ONE.
TO LIVE THE LOVE IN THEIR HEART
SO THEY FEEL THEIR LIFE IS FUN.

MOVING FORWARD

GENTLE ARE THE WAVES
WASHING ON THE SHORE.
THEY SOOTHE ME AND PREPARE ME
FOR THE DAY, THAT IS IN STORE.
WHEN I CAN CEASE THIS WORRY,
LOOK FORWARD TO THE DAY AHEAD.
MY FEARS WILL GO AWAY
WHICH CAUSE THIS FEELING OF DREAD.

SO LOOK AT WHAT YOU HAVE,
WITH FRIENDS THAT REALLY CARE.
THEY HAVE THEIR OWN CONCERNS
YET THEIR THOUGHTS ARE OFTEN NEAR.
WITH A SMILE ON YOUR FACE AND
GRATITUDE IN YOUR HEART.
CONQUER ALL YOUR DOUBT,
GO FORWARD, PLAY YOUR PART.

TREAT ME GENTLE

Treat me gentle, let me feel.
It is all so new to me.
People think I know it all,
That I have given free.
The truth is it has cost a lot
As others abused me cruelly.
Disadvantaged from the age of two
When I was treated poorly.

What is it like to feel me?
Untouched and feeling clean.
What is it like to be in a world
Where one is not demeaned?
To feel so low and unloved
That pain is the accepted form.
Reacting to everyone until it
Has become a regular storm.

The time is here to start again.
Shedding energies of the past.
Knowing that this focus will
Bring gentleness to last.
The starting point is me
To identify within.
For this little child came to a
World where lessons can come from sin.

One does not know where it starts,
The chicken or the egg.
So now is the time to let it go,
The fear and the dread.
Now that I perceive what has been
And why.
I realise that I can dictate
To put my life on high.

COURAGE, PATIENCE, BE GENTLE WITH
YOUR LITTLE CHILD WITHIN.
NEW BEGINNINGS OF EMOTIONS, FEELINGS
NOT KNOWN WILL BEGIN.
I LOVE THIS LITTLE CHILD,
SO BRAVE, GOOD AND TRUE.
I WILL NOURISH HER IN EVERY WAY
IN THIS WORLD THAT IS SO NEW.

SLOWLY, GENTLY DARLING,
LOVE IS ALMOST CRUEL.
YOU HAVE NO MEASUREMENT TO KNOW
EXCEPT TO END THIS HELL.
STILL THE TRAUMA OF THE PAST
FOR NEW LIFE TO FORM.
THE NIGHT IS QUIET, THE CHILD STILL.
NO STRUGGLING; AT LAST NO STORM

INNER SEARCHING

The inner searching has brought
Its own reward.
A special inner knowing has finally
Surfaced to come on board.
For deep within the knowledge
That love is very real.
How wonderful to acknowledge
It is mine for me to feel.

No longer with the feeling
That love is not around.
Within everything we touch there
Is love which can be found.
So look for the sunshine in every
Illusion of cloud.
With love there is the laughter,
So let it ring out loud.

Love will increase now
You acknowledge it is there.
Lightness in your journey
Now you recognise love is here.
Growth for every one as loves
Energy magnifies.
How wonderful to offer it
To put the world on high.

People all around
With sunshine at their heart.
Living in the world,
So glad to be a part.
For joy in the moment
With everything as new.
Gives magic to the moment
With this new point of view.

THROW AWAY THE CAN OF WORMS

ENOUGH, ENOUGH, TO LIVE THIS WAY.
FULL OF FRUSTRATION EVERY DAY.
ANXIETY DICTATING.
CUT IT OUT. GET OPERATING.

SO YOU HAVE A CHALLENGE.
NOTHING NEW TO YOU.
A SPLENDID OPPORTUNITY TO
CREATE A NEW POINT OF VIEW.

THE SMILE IS ON THE FACE
AS THE OBSTACLES DISAPPEAR.
FEELING GOOD INSIDE NOW
YOU HAVE GOT BACK INTO GEAR.

WORKING ON YOUR DREAMS
TO BRING THEM TO REALITY.
DO A GOOD JOB, FOR YOU'RE A MORTAL
WITH IMMORTALITY.

LIFE IS A WONDER

LIFE IS A WONDER.
IT IS ALL AHEAD OF ME.
SO MUCH TO CHOOSE FROM.
MY THOUGHTS CAN LEAVE ME FREE.

BY SELECTING WHAT I WANT TO DO
WITH FEELINGS FROM THE HEART.
I WILL KNOW WHAT I WANT AND
BEGIN TO MAKE A START.

THE ROAD HAS MANY DAYS,
SO TAKE THEM EACH IN TURN.
YOUR DIRECTION CAN BE CHANGED
TO GIVE YOU YOUR RETURN.

FOR FEELINGS JOY INSIDE
WITH A SMILE ON YOUR FACE.
GIVES ONE THE HAPPINESS
TO LIVE IN CONSTANT GRACE.

KIND WISHES

THE THOUGHTS ARE HERE,
THEY STILL LAST
I REMEMBER WHAT YOU
DID TO ASK.
IT IS NOT ALWAYS TO UNDERSTAND
OR REALLY KNOW OUR SELF.
THE PASSING OF THE YEARS HAVE BEEN
TO TRULY REVEAL THE SELF.
MAY TIME HAVE BEEN KIND
TO SHOW YOU YOUR TRUE WEALTH.
THAT YOU HAVE COME TO ACCEPT
AND REALLY LOVE YOUR SELF.

HEALING IN THE PROCESS

WHEN FEAR COMES TO THE SURFACE
JUST LET IT PASS AWAY.
FOR HEALING IN THE PROCESS
HAS BEEN THE RELEASE TODAY.

FOCUS ON THE JOY
OF YOUR TREASURES STILL INSIDE.
IT IS TIME TO BLOSSOM WITH THESE GIFTS
SO SMILE, DO NOT HIDE.

THE TEMPERING OF THE STEEL
IS THERE FOR EVERYONE.
ONCE WE KNOW OUR PURPOSE THERE
IS FREEDOM FOR FOLLOWING GODS SON.

FOR LOVE IS THE WHOLENESS.
THE JOURNEY OF THE HEART.
WHERE EACH ONE RESERVES THE OPPORTUNITY
TO ADD GROWTH; THEIR MISSING PART.

THE EGO

WHAT IS THE EGO THAT
HAS THIS OPINION.
WHO IS THE EGO
TO TRY TO CHANGE MY VISION?
MY HEART SPEAKS OUT WITH JOY
WITH NEW CHAPTERS TO WRITE.
THEN THE LITTLE EGO TRIES
TO BLOCK THEM OUT OF SIGHT.

SENDING THOUGHTS OF DOUBT
BURIED IN THE PAST.
TAKE COURAGE, LET THEM GO
THE SHADOWS NEED NOT LAST.
THERE IS BUT ONE VOICE OF JOY.
IT COMES FROM THE HEART.
LIKE A CHILD WITHOUT MEASUREMENT
IT ALLOWS YOU TO START.

MANY EXPERIENCES ON THE PATH
AS WE TRAVEL ALONG.
THOSE WITHOUT CALCULATION
FILL OUR DAY WITH SONG.
AS DESTINY DIRECTS AND WE
FULFIL OUR PATH.
ENJOYING LIFE TO THE FULL
AS WE STOP DOING THINGS BY HALF.

ATONEMENT

TIME EXISTS FOR MAN
AS A PURPOSE TO AN END.
TO UNDO THOUGHTS NOT OF LOVE
THAT THE UNIVERSE CAN MEND.
THE PURPOSE FOR CREATION
WENT RIGHT OFF THE PATH.
WHEN THE MIRACLE OF LOVE
WAS BROKEN; DID NOT LAST.

EVER WATCHED YOUR THOUGHTS
AS THEY DANCE IN YOUR MIND.
WE HAVE THE MEANS TO CHANGE,
TO ALTER, TO BE KIND.
THOUGHTS OF LOVE
ARE THE MIRACLE OF CREATION.
THE HEALING THOUGHTS OF LOVE AVAILABLE
TO HEAL THE NATION.

SUNSHINE AFTER RAIN

HAPPINESS, THE JOY OF GIVING,
OF NOT NEEDING TO BE RIGHT.
HAPPINESS FROM THE HEART
WHERE EACH ONE PLAYS THEIR PART.
LETTING GO THE DIFFERENCES THAT
STIR UP ALL THE PAIN.
ALLOWING FOR THE SMILES THAT
COME LIKE SUNSHINE AFTER RAIN.

On a Song

The ego is the voice
Seeking out control.
Time has given growth for the ego
To take on a different role.
Instead of seeing what is and
Reporting it intact.
The message is distorted
By thoughts which are not facts.

In living out this role
The heart takes second place.
The focus is on power.
So let the ego's echo
Go back where it belongs.
Your heart will live each moment
As it travels on a song.

SEEING OUR SELF

LESSONS COME IN MANY WAYS
TO TEMPER UP THE STEEL.
GIVE THANKS THAT WE SEE THEM
TO HELP OUR SELF BE WELL.
FOR UNKINDNESS THAT WE THINK
IS SAD FOR US TO SEE.
CAN THAT INDIVIDUAL
REALLY BE ME?

SO TAKE THE LESSON
TO BE A NICER SOUL.
YOUR JOURNEY HAS THIS PURPOSE.
IT IS MANS INNER ROLE.
KEEP ON TRYING FOR EACH
DAY CAN BE NEW.
SO WATCH YOUR THOUGHTS, SHAPE THEM
WITH LOVE YOUR EXPRESSED VIEW.

HEALING —THE RELEASE FROM FEAR

MAN IS ON THE JOURNEY
TO RECLAIM THE POWER.
TIME WILL NOT EXIST
WHEN LOVE IS TOTAL, TO EMPOWER.
FOR MIND WILL SUPPORT
THE INNER VISION FROM CREATION
THAT LOVE IS THE WHOLENESS
WHICH FORMS THE TOTAL MANSION.

WHEN LOVE IS IN ACTION
TIME DOES NOT EXIST.
AT LAST THIS APPEARING MIRACLE
OPENS UP THE MIST.
EYES FINALLY OPEN,
SEE ALL THAT IS GOOD AND TRUE.
AT LAST THE ILLUSION GOES
TO OPEN THE VIEW.

A BETTER WORLD

MY PERFECT WORLD WOULD FILL WITH CARE
AND PEOPLE FULL OF LOVE.
THEIR INNER SOUL WOULD LEARN AND
GROW WITH THE ENERGY ABOVE.
GONE WOULD BE THE GREED
OF EVER WANTING MORE.
THERE WOULDN'T BE THE NEED TO HAVE
THE LOCKS ON EVERY DOOR.
SAFETY IN THE STREETS
WITH GREETINGS FOR EACH OTHER.
TIME TO STOP, LISTEN,
SHOW COMPASSION FOR EACH OTHER.

BALANCES IN NATURE
TO PROTECT AND SHOW WE CARE.
THAT IT WOULD REPLENISH ITS SELF
TO BLOSSOM EVERY YEAR.
BIRDS OUT OF CAGES, NOW FREE
WITH FREEDOM OF FLIGHT TO ENJOY.
THE WORLD THEY BELONG IN,
THE WORLD THEY HAVE BEEN DENIED.
IF EACH ONE HAD A PLAN
FOR LOOKING TO THEIR LAND.
IT COULD BE REALLY BEAUTIFUL,
A JOY FOR EVERY MAN.

CHILDREN SHOULD BE CHILDREN
WITH TIME ENOUGH TO GROW.
TO LIVE WITH JOY AND LAUGHTER
FOR MANY, MANY YEARS.
LIFE WITHIN THE FAMILY
WITH LEARNING IN THE HOME.
SUCH THE JOY OF BEING THERE
WITHOUT THE NEED TO ROAM.
JOY IN THE ARTS WITH SO MUCH

To listen, see and do.
It becomes an appreciation from the
Days of youth and stays our whole life through.

Many are the years
As swiftly they go by.
In this world of love and caring
We would understand why.
Quick would be the learning
As we lived day by day.
To free the soul from constant fear
And remove the pain while we are here.
Love contains no fear or hate,
No greed or envy or desire.
A radiation of care for all with
Each the light of freedom.

America Think Big

America, think big! from the prairies
to the Grand Canyon's size and beauty.
The mighty Sequoia,
the biggest tree in the world.

Yellowstone national park
with the tallest active geyser.
The paddle steamer
on the mighty Missippi river.

Walt Disney's gift to the world
for children, family all.
With the largest theme park
that the world can play and laugh.

My visits to America
have been filled with joy and caring.
The people reached out with interest
with geniune rich sharing.

My taxi driver said "Here in
America we can
achieve anything we want."
It isn't where you come from
but where you want to go.

The thrill of seeing my first tumbleweed
as it was blown across the desert.
Seeing the beauty of the Bryce Canyon
with its colours bright and true.

In the Autumn the leaves change their
shades of green to the brilliant shades of orange.
Finally going red or gold
from Autumn through to winter.

THE STATUE OF LIBERTY REPRESENTING
THE POWER OF FREE CHOICE.
FREEDOM FOR ALL
WITHOUT CONSTRAINT OR VOICE.

A COUNTRY OFFERING SERVICE
TO MAKE THE WORLD A BETTER PLACE.
MAY THE PEOPLE UNITE TO SERVE,
FOR THIS POWERFUL LOVING RACE.

TAKE THE FIRST STEP

CONFIDENCE IS MINE
TO ENJOY THIS WORLD AS MINE.
TO CLIMB THE HIGHEST HILL TO VICTORY
WITH A SMILE ON MY FACE.
THERE ISN'T ANYTHING I CANNOT DO
WHEN MY HEART IS FILLED WITH LOVE.
JUST GO FORWARD AND START IT,
BE ENCOURAGED FROM ABOVE.
EACH DAY GIVES MOVEMENT FORWARD
AS THINGS BEGIN TO HAPPEN.
EACH SMALL THING BECOMES THE TOTAL
AS WE JOYFULLY ARRIVE.
TO SHOW HOW MUCH WE CAN DO
AND REALLY FEEL ALIVE.

GRACE, GRATITUDE AND GLADNESS

THE DAY IS NEW WITH GLADNESS
FOR ALL THAT IS ABUNDANT.
FOR EVERYTHING IS THERE.
SWEET MUSIC, GLORY'S TRUMPET.
OUR GRACE TO GIVE US ACCEPTANCE
FOR EACH AND EVERY DAY.
WITH GRACE TO OBSERVE THE MOMENT,
THEN LET IT PASS AWAY.
GRATITUDE FOR KNOWING
THE ROAD WE WISH TO TREAD.
THE KNOWLEDGE AND THE WISDOM
AS WE WALK THE GOLDEN THREAD.

THE CHILD WITHIN

THE CHILD WITHIN WATCHES EVERYTHING,
SO PEACEFUL AND CALM.
LOOKED OVER BY THEIR GUARDIAN ANGEL,
PROTECTED FROM ALL HARM.
THIS BEAUTY IS AVAILABLE
FOR EACH AND EVERYONE.
NOURISHED FROM WITHIN WHETHER SURROUNDED
BY THE MOON, THE WATER OR THE SUN.

THE JOY OF THE LOVING EXPERIENCE
WHERE DOING BRINGS NO HARM.
BEING THE SPLENDOUR OF THE EARTH,
THE BEAUTY AND THE CHARM.
ENJOYING ALL THE SENSES.
THEY FEEL, SEE AND TOUCH.
TO SHAPE ALL OUR PASSIONS WITH
THIS WORLD TO ENJOY SO MUCH.

A DAY AT A TIME

COURAGE ISN'T EASY.
IT COMES FROM DEEP WITHIN.
WHEN WE GLIMPSE WITHIN OUR HEART,
WE HAVE THE GUIDE OF WHERE TO START.

EACH DAY GIVES US THE CHANCE TO TRY.
TO STOP OUR GOAL FROM PASSING BY.
LITTLE VICTORY'S ALL ADD UP.
SO KEEP ON TRYING, NEVER GIVE UP.

KEEP NOTING THE PROGRESS ALONG THE WAY.
IT SUSTAINS AND GIVES PATIENCE
THROUGHOUT THE NEW DAY.
COURAGE IS YOURS TO KEEP ON GOING. YOU
 HAVE PROGRESSED WITHOUT REALLY KNOWING.

REST IF YOU MUST TO SEE WHERE YOU ARE.
THEN RE FOCUS ON YOUR OWN BRIGHT STAR.
FOR EVERYTHING YOU HAVE EVER WISHED
AND WAITED FOR,
CAN BE YOURS, IF YOU KEEP TRYING AND
OPENING THE DOORS.

QUIET TIMES

THOSE ROCKS GIVE ME COMFORT AS I
SIT AND GAZE OVER THE SEA.
THIS VIEW WITH ITS BEAUTY GIVES ME
THE STILLNESS TO BE FREE.
THOUGHTS DANCE THROUGH MY MIND;
THEY ARE NOT THERE TO STAY.
WATCHING AS WITH SHADOW UNTIL
THEY SOFTLY PASS AWAY.

THE STILLNESS OF THE MOMENT WITH
THIS MIRROR HERE TO SEE.
ALL MY THOUGHTS REFLECTED AS THEY
DANCE IN FRONT OF ME.
LEARNING TO LET GO OF DOUBT AND
LEARNING TO BE CALM.
MY MORNING MEDITATION SETS THE
PATH TO PROTECT FROM HARM.

THIS TIME IS MINE EACH DAY.
THE GIFT TO INNER PEACE.
WHEN ALL THE WORLD IS RUSHING AROUND.
WHEN WILL IT ALL CEASE.
IT ISN'T SURPRISING THAT THEY HAVE NO
TIME FOR THEM SELF.
THAT SPECIAL TIME OF SILENCE WHICH IS OUR OWN REAL
WEALTH.

ALLOW THE STILLNESS TO EXPAND.
YOU WILL DO FAR MORE.
FOR EACH DAY WILL BE FULL OF THINGS
YOU WISH TO EXPLORE.
THE FEAR AND UNCERTAINTIES WILL SLOWLY
LEAVE YOUR LIFE.
AS YOU TRAVEL ON YOUR JOURNEY ON A PATH WITH OUT THE
INNER STRIFE.

STILLNESS IN THE MOMENT

This morning I heard the birds;
It seemed that time stood still.
Then I came to realise it was my mind;
So quiet and still.
Each sang their joyful chorus
As they called in the new day.
Be still and be at peace,
It is the only way.
When our mind is full of thoughts
That chatter day and night.
They do not leave the space
Which allows us our insight.
The very special guidance
Which reaches to our heart.
The message which gives us hope
And shows us how to start.

THE HEART OF THE GARDEN

A GARDEN IS NOT WORK
WHEN YOU LOVE AND ENJOY.
EACH PLANT LIKE A CHILD NEEDS
NOURISHMENT TO GROW.
GROWING IN THE SEASON AND RESTING
IN THE CHILL.
THE LIFE FORCE OF ENERGY. THE CHOICE
OF THE FREE ACT OF WILL.

FLOWERS IN THEIR GLORY. A COLOUR
FOR EVERYONE.
OPENING IN THE MORNING AND CLOSING
WITH THE SETTING OF THE SUN.
A HIVE OF ACTIVITY ABOVE AND BELOW
THE GROUND.
THE WONDERFUL WORLD OF NATURE
WAITING TO BE FOUND.

SO IF YOU HAVE NOT GOT A GARDEN AND
IT IS ALL VERY NEW.
GO TO YOUR GARDEN CENTRE TO SEE AND
LEARN AN EXPERTS POINT OF VIEW.
A SPADE FOR THE PREPARATION.
THEY WILL TELL YOU HOW TO START.
THIS DAY IS REALLY MAGIC FOR THE
GARDEN GIVES YOU HEART.

LAUGHTER FROM THE HEART.

THE MIRACLE OF HEALING IS FREE
FOR EVERYONE.
IT NOURISHES US AND CALMS US LIKE THE
RAYS OF THE SUN.
YOU CAN NOT BOTTLE IT OR BUY IT
OR PUT IT ANYWHERE.
HAVE I GOT YOU WONDERING AND
LOOKING TO COMPARE.

LAUGHTER IS THE MIRACLE WHICH HEALS
THE WOUNDS ACROSS OUR HEART.
THE TIMELESS GIFT OF ENERGY WHICH
GIVES HOPE FOR A NEW START.
SO WHEN TIMES SEEM VERY HARD,
ALL STRUGGLE AND UP HILL.
SHARE THE JOY OF LAUGHTER.
IT IS BETTER THAN A PILL.

LOOKING BACK AT THINGS WE DID
THAT MAY HAVE BEEN A CHORE.
NOW WE TALK OF IT WITH OTHERS AND
LAUGH WHEN THEY LET OUT A MIGHTY ROAR.
SO TAKE EACH DAY AS IT COMES.
LOOK FOR THE JOY AND THE LAUGHTER.
SHARE WITH FRIENDS WITHOUT FEAR AND
LAUGH TODAY AND EVER AFTER.

NEW BEGINNINGS

THE DOOR OPENS WIDE.
OPPORTUNITY AWAITS.
GONE ARE THE PAINS.
THERE IS NOW A PEACEFUL STATE.

THE BEGINNING OF A JOURNEY.
A NEW CHALLENGE AHEAD.
JOYFUL IS THE STEP WITHOUT
THE PAIN AND REGRET.

SO FOCUS ON THE JOB
FOR WHAT YOU HAVE TO DO.
USE YOUR INNER RESOURCES
DEEP INSIDE OF YOU.

SUCCESS WILL COME QUICKLY,
LEARNING AS YOU GO.
GIVING SUPPORT TO ACTION
ALL THE DREAMS YOU KNOW,.

FREEDOM WAITS

EACH MOMENT IS AVAILABLE
TO BE FREE, TO BE TRUE.
TO ENJOY LIFE'S EXPERIENCE
TO OUR SELF WE MUST BE TRUE.

FOR THE UNIVERSAL ENERGY
PULLS US FROM ALL SIDES.
WE OFTEN GO IN ALL DIRECTIONS
LIKE THE CHANGING OF THE TIDES.

OBSERVING OF THE ENERGY
WITHOUT TAKING IT ON.
LEAVES US FREE TO BE OUR SELF
ON THE JOURNEY WE BELONG.

SO LET OTHERS GO THEIR WAY
IT IS NOT RIGHT OR WRONG.
JUST BEING AWARE. TRUE TO SELF.
WILL FILL YOU FULL OF SONG.

NOW THE SKY IS CLEAR
WITH BLUE SO QUIET AND CALM.
THE CLOUDS HAVE GONE AWAY.
NO CAUSE FOR ALARM.

BE STILL, LET GO FOR JOY.
JUST LET IT ALL RELEASE.
SO IT IS INSIDE,
THE BEAUTY, AT LAST THE QUIET PEACE.

LIFE'S JOURNEY

LOOK FOR THE BEAUTY
TO GIVE THANKS EACH DAY.
TO RENEW YOUR INNER GLOW
AS YOU JOURNEY ALONG YOUR WAY.

THE POWER OF YOUR THOUGHTS
CAN OPEN UP NEW DOORS.
LOOK INSIDE YOUR HEART.
OPEN WIDE YOUR HEART FOR MORE.

CONFIDENCE, STRENGTH,
LAUGHTER FROM WITHIN.
THIS IS WHAT I WISH YOU
FOR YOU WILL GROW AND WIN.

YOUR BEAUTY IS LIKE A FLOWER
WHICH HAS SEASONS TO REST.
FROM STILLNESS COMES INSIGHT,
THEN YOU GROW AND DO YOUR BEST.

MAY THIS NEW PERSONAL YEAR
OPEN MANY GOLDEN OPPORTUNITIES FOR YOU.
WHICH WILL START CREATIVE OUTCOMES
FOR YOUR TALENTS TO SHINE THROUGH.

BRIGHTEN UP YOUR DAY

LOOK FOR THE JOYS THAT LIFE HAS BROUGHT YOUR WAY
SO MANY JOYS TO BRIGHTEN
UP YOUR DAY.
BELIEVING IN YOUR SELF
TO KNOW THAT YOU HAVE DONE YOUR BEST.
LIFE HAS A TIME TO BE BUSY AND
A GENTLE TIME FOR REST.

WHEN YOU SEE YOUR VALUE,
REALLY KNOW YOUR WORTH.
THEN THE DOORS OPEN
TO THE JOYS OF THIS WONDERFUL EARTH.

FAITH IN YOUR GROWTH TO BEAUTY

UNDER THE GROUND IN THE FERTILE EARTH ARE THE BULBS
AWAITING THEIR FULL CREATION.
MAYBE FORGOTTEN, MAYBE YOU KNOW.
THEY WAIT FOR SUITABLE CONDITIONS .
NATURE LIFTS THE TEMPERATURE
AS THEY QUIETLY BEGIN TO GROW.
IN THE DARK, UNSEEN,
YOU MAY NOT EVEN KNOW.

THEN THE GREEN SHOOTS APPEAR
AS THEY GROW FROM THE EARTH.
WITH THE PROMISE OF SPRING TIME
TO FULFIL THEIR TRUE WORTH.
THE BUDS THAT FORM
PROMISE BEAUTY TO SEE.
A SCENT SO SOFT TO
PLEASE US NOW FREE.

FOR THE FLOWERS NOW OPEN
IN COLOUR AND FORM.
REMIND US OUR JOURNEY
CAN SUDDENLY TRANSFORM
SO IF YOU APPEAR BLOCKED AND
YOU ARE NOT SURE OF THE WAY.
BE STILL, COUNT YOUR BLESSINGS,
YOUR STRENGTH FOR TODAY.

TOMORROW WILL BE BRIGHTER AND
YOUR HEART WITH A SONG.
FOR FAITH IN ITS BEAUTY
WILL CARRY YOU ALONG.
YOUR THOUGHTS ARE YOUR JOURNEY
THAT YOU CREATE WHILE HERE.
SO BE POSITIVE AND THINK TO SOW
GOOD WILL AND GOOD CHEER.

DIGNITY

Sharing, caring being there
Show support for one another.
Travelling down the road as
You look out for each other.
Each their own point of view
Acknowledged by their friends.
The building of respect,
That the friendship does not end.

When love allows this difference
For growth for each to flower.
To learn from trying each thing new
With grace and sweet surrender.
For courage, faith are the love that
Support our soul onward.
Friendship is the future
To encourage ever forward.

Not to judge or complain
If the other declines with age.
Let the beauty of their inner soul
Give power, strength and courage.
Build their self-esteem that
They feel a good self worth.
What a difference to respect your self
When it is time to leave this earth.

So do unto others
As we would be done by.
Show love and respect
That the energy is on high.
To know that your time here
Has really been worth while.
That you enjoyed the journey and
Still have a lovely smile.

THANKYOU TO MY FRIENDS
WHO ACCEPTED ME FOR ME.
FOR YOU SHOWED TRUE LOVE
ON THIS JOURNEY TO BE FREE.
WITH YOUR LOVE AROUND ME
MY FINAL JOURNEY'S HERE.
GOD BLESS YOU MY FRIENDS WE WILL MEET
AGAIN FOR LOVE IS ALWAYS NEAR.

REACH FOR THE STARS

A YEAR OF TRUST AND BEAUTY
AS YOU LEARN UPON THIS EARTH
THAT THE SIMPLE JOYS EACH DAY
DEVELOP YOUR SELF WORTH

THE COURAGE TO EXPERIENCE
AND TO TRY WHAT IS NEW
WITH CONFIDENCE TO EXPRESS
YOUR UNIQUE POINT OF VIEW

SHARING SPECIAL MOMENTS
WITH DEAR ONES NEAR YOUR HEART
FOR LOVE IS THE PATHWAY
THAT MEANS WE WILL NEVER BE APART

YOUR INSTINCTS WILL SUPPORT YOU
WITH SENSITIVITY AND CARE
FOR COMMUNICATION TO OPEN DOORS
WITH DEAR ONES WHO ARE NEAR

SO SET FORTH WITH TRUE FAITH
AND THE STRENGTH OF INNER LOVE
THAT HAPPINESS IS YOURS TO RADIATE
AS YOU REACH FOR THE STARS ABOVE

THE HIGHEST TOWER

A YEAR OF CHANGE FOR SORTING THROUGH
A YEAR THAT OFFERS A NEW POINT OF VIEW
CLIMBING UP THE HIGHEST TOWER
TO OBSERVE OUR DIRECTION AND REGAIN OUR POWER.
LOVING OURSELF FOR WHERE WE HAVE BEEN
TO USE OUR COURAGE FOR BEAUTY NOT YET SEEN
ALLOWING THIS MOMENT FOR TREASURES NEW
ON THE JOURNEY THAT IS SPECIAL, UNIQUE FOR YOU.
MAY THIS YEAR BE REMEMBERED FOR LEARNING INSIGHT
COMING OUT OF THE DARKNESS TO GIVE GOLDEN LIGHT.
THAT EACH STEP IS FORWARD BROADENING YOUR HORIZON
YES, THIS YEAR OFFERS PROMISE, MAY YOUR FOCUS EVER
WIDEN.

MOTHERS' CARE

MOTHERS FEEL FOR DAUGHTERS WHEN THE STUDY ENDS TO
FOLLOW OUT THEIR PATH.

WHO CAN EXPLAIN THE EMOTIONS
AT THE COMPLETION OF THE TASK.

HOW MOTHERS GO BACK OVER THE YEARS
TO THE SMALL GIFT IN HER ARMS.

ALL THE YEARS OF LOVING, BEING THERE AND PRAYER THAT THIS
LITTLE ONE WOULD COME THROUGH WITH JOY, WITHOUT HARM.

THE FIRST STEPS, THE SMILE, THE CRYING THEN THE VOICE.

QUESTIONS, QUESTIONS, QUESTIONS.
EVER SEEKING, EXPRESSING CHOICE.

FOR MOTHERS FEEL THE JOYS, THE LITTLE SECRET DOUBTS

THE HOPES AND FEARS AS THEIR LOVED ONE LEARNS WHAT THE
WORLD IS ALL ABOUT.

HER HEART IS SOFT AND GENTLE
WHILE HER BREATH IS OFTEN HELD

WATCHING EACH STEP ALONG THE WAY,
PRAYING ALL WILL BE WELL.

BEING THEIR TO ENCOURAGE AND SUPPORT ALONG THE WAY

SO MUCH SHARED THROUGH THE YEARS THAT HAVE SEEMED
LIKE YESTERDAY.

NOW MY CHILD IS A WOMAN
WITH SKILLS OF HER OWN.

MY LOVE WILL ALWAYS BE THERE
WHEREVER SHE CALLS HOME.

MEET THE DAY

YOU LOOK AT OTHERS FOR GIFTS TO SHARE.
TO LET THEM FEEL THAT SOMEONE IS NEAR.
AWARENESS WITHIN MAY BRING FRAGILITY WITHOUT
WHEN THE FOCUS IS ALL OTHERS YOU ARE MISSING OUT.
FOR LOVING OTHERS AS ONE LOVES THEMSELVES
IS TAKING CARE TO NURTURE AND NOURISH YOUR SELF.

YOUR SOUL WITHIN YOUR BODY WHILE HERE
NEEDS LOVE AND ATTENTION THROUGHOUT YOUR YEAR
SO WHEN YOU RISE TO MEET THE DAY
ADD YOUR NAME TO THE LIST FOR GIVING TODAY
YES MY DEAR FRIEND, THIS ONE IS FOR YOU.

YOUR BIRTHDAY IS HERE TO CELEBRATE LIFE
A NEW YEAR AHEAD WITH YOUR CHAPTERS TO WRITE
SO LOOK IN THE MIRROR AND LOVE THAT SWEET SOUL
IT IS NOT ASKING MUCH TO ADD IN TO BECOME WHOLE.

THIS YEAR OPENS FORWARD WITH LOVE FOR YOU
MAY YOU FEEL THIS GIFT AND LET IT RADIATE THROUGH YOU
FOCUS ON LOVE FOR YOURSELF EACH DAY
A WONDERFUL YEAR BEGINS TO COME YOUR WAY.
THE DAYS AHEAD GIVE OPPORTUNITIES FOR YOU
TO EXPERIENCE YOUR DREAMS IF TO YOURSELF YOU ARE
TRUE.

HERE TO LEARN

IF LOVE IS THE REASON
WE COME INTO THE WORLD.
NOT MATERIALISTIC GREED, WEALTH,
OR THE FOCUS ON JUST OUR SELF.
OUR FOCUS MUST BE TO LEARN
TO GIVE OF THAT SPECIAL LOVE.
BY OBSERVING SELF WITH WHAT WE SAY,
ALLOWING STILLNESS FOR GUIDANCE FROM ABOVE

EACH ONE TO SELF OBSERVE,
TO REALLY BE AWARE.
ALLOWS EACH TO MAKE THEIR CHANGES
IN THE TIME THAT WE ARE HERE.
WHEN EACH ONE ALLOWS A MIRROR IMAGE
TO REFLECT WHAT THEY HEAR AND SAY.
THEN EACH ONE CAN SEE THE PICTURE
OF WHERE THEY DECIDE TO CHANGE.

LOVE ISN'T FULL OF SELF
WITH ANGER, PRIDE OR FEAR.
IN FACT THE EMOTIONS OF JEALOUSY,
TOLERANCE OR SELFISHNESS DO NOT APPEAR.
LOVE CONTAINS NOTHING BUT LOVE THAT COMES STRAIGHT
FROM THE HEART.
THE ONE TRUE LOVE OF GOD THAT TELLS US WE WILL NEVER
BE APART.
EACH ONE MUST FOCUS ON THEIR JOURNEY
WHILE THEY ARE HERE WITHOUT CONCERN
EACH DAY GIVES US OPPORTUNITY TO BECOME THAT WE CHOOSE
TO LEARN.

FAMILY TIES

BLOOD IS THICKER THAN WATER
TO HOLD THE FAMILY BOND
WHEN PATIENCE, TOLERANCE, FORGIVENESS
ALLOW THE RELATIONSHIP TO HOLD A SONG.

WE ALL CAUSE HARDSHIPS,
NOT ALWAYS KNOWING WHY
EACH DAY OFFERS LEARNING TO LIFT US UP ON HIGH

FOR JUDGEMENT IS THE MEASUREMENT
FROM OUR OWN SELF
OUR OWN SENSE OF VALUES
WE HOLD THE HIGHEST FOR OUR SELF.

WHEN WE CAN RELEASE THE PAIN,
AND THE JUDGEMENTS' OF THE PAST.
OPPORTUNITY IS OFFERED
FOR RELATIONSHIPS THAT LAST.

FOR EACH INDIVIDUAL IS UNIQUE
AND TO OBSERVE YOUR FAMILY MAY BE THE KEY TO YOUR TRUE
WEALTH WITH ATTITUDES AND LOVE TO BE FREE
TO BE TRUE TO YOURSELF.

WELCOME ABOARD AUSTRALIA

THIS IS OUR COUNTRY, THIS IS OUR LAND
TODAY WITH COMMITMENT
WE STAND HAND IN HAND
A LOVE WITHOUT BARRIERS PRESENTS
ALL THAT IS GRAND, A LOVE IF SINCERE
ALL TIME WILL WITHSTAND

PEOPLE FROM MANY COUNTRIES
PLEDGE ON THIS DAY
YOUR ARE PART OF A NATION
WHICH YOU JOIN HERE TODAY
THE WORDS MUST BE ACTION,
COMMITMENT TO BUILD A NATION
UNITED THROUGH TRUST, LOVE AND SKILL.

GIVE THE WORDS MEANING
THIS IS THE BEGINNING
OUR GOAL TO BECOME AS ONE,
WITHOUT MISGIVING.
BRING THE WORDS TO LIFE
LET THEM BE FROM THE HEART
REMEMBER WHAT WE HAVE PLEDGED TODAY IS THE START.

WE LOOKED AND WE JOINED
THIS HARD NOBLE LAND
WHERE SURVIVAL HAS ALWAYS REQUIRED A STAND TO BATTLE
THE CLIMATE
YOU MUST WORK WITH THE SEASONS.
THE SAME FOR AUSTRALIAN,
SHARE YOUR SKILLS FOR THIS REASON.

THERE IS ONLY DIVISION
IF YOU ALLOW IT TO BE
LET US ALL JOIN NOW FOR AUSTRALIA
LOVE AND UNITY
LOVE AMONGST ALL PEOPLE
WILL ACHIEVE OUR DESTINATION
COME ON, WE CAN DO IT,
LET US CREATE ONE NATION.

THE FIVE CENT COIN

Once upon a time there was a five cent coin that we will call life.

Life was minted with many other five cent coins.

They were all shiny new, Packed in bags ready to go out in the world.

Some became collectors coins in a special box!

While others went to banks to see where they would go.

Life felt excited waiting for the first experience of being in a hand.

Life was taken with other money to make up company wages.

Now in a purse it felt quite snug, made of leather it smelt well too.

Other coins were gathered there as they all rubbed together.

Some were bigger and took up the space

While others with sharp edges could push you in the face.

It was dark inside until there was a ring at a till when the purse opened wide to pay the bill.

Eighteen ninety five and out came life, hardly time to see all the groceries all around before being dropped in with the other five cents without a sound.

We all shared our stories and I said I was new, they said my worth would always be no matter what I did.

As people use me to shop, I would travel everywhere.

Time to watch and learn, not always just the same

Little scratches on my surface show that I am here getting all the experiences.

I've been taken to the airport and off in a plane.

Even on the water while they fished from a boat all day.

AND THEN I REALLY PANICKED, FOR AS HE CAME ASHORE, HE CHANGED HIS SHORTS FOR JEANS AND DROPPED ME ON THE SAND.
LUCK WOULD HAVE A METAL DETECTOR HAPPENED TO PASS BY
AND THERE I WAS LIFTED ON TO CONTINUE ON ONCE MORE.
I'VE BEEN ABROAD WHERE THEY COULDN'T SPEND ME.
TO THINK THEY COULD LEAVE ME IN A COUNTRY WITH NO VALUE ANYMORE.
SAFELY BACK HOME IN AUSTRALIA, I WAS RIGHT
THEN DOWN TO BONDI BEACH FOR AN ICE CREAM I WAS SPENT
IN THE TILL AGAIN WITH OTHERS TO SHARE WITH, WE COULDN'T HELP REFLECT
WE HAD BEEN GIVEN A SPECIAL GIFT
FOR WE HAD EXPERIENCED LIFE
AND REALLY SEEN A LOT.
STILL WORTH FIVE CENTS
LIFE MOVED RIGHT ON.
UNTIL ONE DAY FROM A POCKET LIFE ROLLED, ONTO THE STREET WITH LOTS OF CARS CROSSING,
MANY OF THEM GOING OVER HIS TOP.
UNTIL SUDDENLY ALL WAS QUIET AS THE NIGHT DESCENDED OVERHEAD.
THE SUN ROSE FOR ANOTHER DAY
WHEN A LADY SAW THE FIVE CENTS LYING ON THE ROAD.
AS LIFE WAS GENTLY LIFTED
THE THOUGHT WAS SENT OUT
FOR ALL THAT YOU ARE SCARRED AND BATTERED YOU STILL ARE FIVE CENTS
IN FACT TRUE TO LIFE YOU STILL HAVE YOUR SELF WORTH.

After having a serious accident that stopped my career as a medical representative it was necessary to attend Physio and Doctors 3-4 times a week for months.

Each morning for a week I picked up a 5 cent coin outside the physio door, then finding one near the beach as the sun was rising and noting the coin was battered this poem was written. Expressing that although injured, not working, my self-worth was still there.

To this day a 5 cent coin remains an affirmation to how strong our inner power is.

Healing 15 years later is nearly complete. I do not give up and my faith is trusting that experience is needed to watch what we ask for.

A SONG FOR AUSTRALIA

FOR THIS IS OUR COUNTRY
AND THIS IS OUR LAND.
THE PLACE WE HAVE SEARCHED FOR,
AT LAST WE HAVE FOUND.
A GARDEN OF TREASURES,
OF BEAUTY AND JOY.
AUSTRALIA OUR COUNTRY
OUR HEART AND OUR HOME. (CHORUS)

THE PEOPLE HAVE GATHERED
FROM FAR DISTANT LANDS.
IN SEARCH OF THE PEACE
WHICH AT LAST THEY HAVE FOUND.
THANKYOU AUSTRALIA FOR JUST BEING YOU
AUSTRALIA OUR COUNTRY WE REALLY LOVE YOU.
AUSTRALIA OUR COUNTRY WE REALLY LOVE YOU.

OUR TALENTS FOR SHARING
THAT EACH ONE MAY LEARN.
TO STRENGTHEN THIS NATION
THROUGH TRUST, LOVE AND CARE.
A LAND OF EXTREMES.
A LAND FULL OF DREAMS.
SO LET US UNITE.
ONE NATION OUR DREAM.
SO LET US UNITE
ONE NATION OUR DREAM.

THEIR SHARING AND CARING
GIVES A LOVE THAT IS NOW.
IT IS NOW THAT WE LIVE FOR
IN THIS OUR GREAT LAND.
WE BATTLE THE SEASONS
WHEN THEY ARE EXTREME.
AUSTRALIA WE LOVE YOU.
THIS LAND OF OUR DREAMS.
AUSTRALIA WE LOVE YOU.
THIS LAND OF OUR DREAMS.

SKIPPY

A BORDER COLLIE DOG
BORN IN SCOTLAND.
DIED 17YRS OF AGE.

DOG IS NOT ENOUGH TO SAY
AND TELL YOU OF SKIPPY IN A SPECIAL WAY.
WITH THE KINDEST AND BIGGEST HEART.
HE CHASES STONES SO STRONG AND BOLD.
YOU WOULD NEVER GUESS HE IS VERY OLD.

HIS LIFE DIDN'T GET OFF TO A VERY GOOD START, LOST AND
LONELY HE WAS FOUND.
NOW LOVED, HE IS SAFE AND SOUND.
WHEN THE DAY COMES TO AN END,
HE SETTLES DOWN TO GUARD
FAMILY AND FRIEND.

WANTING LITTLE, BUT GIVING A LOT.
HE EVEN HAS HIS OWN WEE COT.
LYING RELAXED WITH HIS LEGS IN THE AIR.
SKIPPY DOESN'T WORRY WHO IS THERE.

WHEN THE MORNING COMES BRIGHT AND NEW.
SKIPPY IS THERE TO WELCOME YOU.
OUT FOR A WALK IS HIS FIRST WISH.
THEN THE DAY IS YOURS TO PLAN.
LET SKIPPY HELP YOU ALL HE CAN.

THIS SUSTAINS ME

TIMES TO REMEMBER, TIMES TO FORGET.
LIVE EACH DAY NEW WITHOUT REGRET.
FOLLOW YOUR DREAMS TO BRING THEM ALIVE.
KEEP RIGHT ON TRYING,
THERE IS NOTHING TO HIDE.
FOR THAT WHICH WE SEEK,
CAN TRULY BE YOURS.
WITH POSITIVE THOUGHT,
YOU CAN OPEN THE DOOR.

THE LOVE ALL AROUND US
IS THAT WHICH WE GIVE.
THE ENERGY FORCE GIVEN
THAT WE MAY ALL LIVE.
WITH FOCUS ON GIVING AND NOT WHAT WE GET, THE VOID WILL
BE FILLED.
WITH JUST WHAT WE NEED.
MAY YOU NOT THINK WANT, LOSS OR LACK,
BUT SEE WHAT ONE HAS AND SAY.
THIS SUSTAINS ME.

REFLECTIONS

To be old when one is young can be sad.
To be young when you are old is a blessing.
For I confess when I look at your face.
Your age, keeps me guessing.

This poem is dedicated to Aunt Agnes who at 96 years young left this earth.

Her most precious guiding insight to me was:

Self first,
Self second,
If any left self again.

Which says to put your own house
In order first before wanting to change others.

THE BIRTH OF THE MESSENGER

Do we understand the messenger
Named for Christmas day
It isn't words or songs
That we use along the way

When understanding is wholeness
To live in love and light
Then any day is Christmas with the truth always in our
sight

THE BOX OF TOYS

Life is a box of toys
That is wonderful to explore.
With each day to experience
There is so much inside and out of doors.

The journey is ever onward
With so much to see and do!
So many opportunities open before us.
The choice is really up to you!

With many chapters in our destiny
Just like a hand of cards.
How we play is up to us
Where we place each card.

Changing faces in our life
They all have some things to share.
Time gives the understanding to be patient
And to see they care.

Special friends see and love us
For who we really are.
When clouds and storms threaten above
Our friends see us, the little star.

When loneliness tries to beckon
Focus on this love.
True friendship is the love
We will experience when we go above.

For love is the highest
That we can ever go.
Our soul on this journey is forever learning. There is
a need to know.
So give thanks for what you have,
Nothing is so bad.
Look to the birds, trees and the flowers,
Thank you for this life. Be glad!

WHAT IS LOVE

LOVE IS THE ENERGY
THAT ALLOWS ANOTHER TO BE WHOLE
LOVE IS THE ENERGY
THAT SUPPORTS YOU TO MEET YOUR GOAL

FOR LIFE IS THE PURPOSE
TO GROW TO YOUR WEALTH
LIFE THE OPPORTUNITY
THE COURAGE TO UNDERSTAND YOURSELF

ACCEPTANCE IS THE KEY
TO JOY WITHIN YOUR HEART
EVERY MOMENT WITHIN EACH HOUR
GIVES OPPORTUNITY TO PLAY YOUR PART
LIFE'S STAGE IS THE PLAY
YOU WRITE FOR YOURSELF
JUDGE IS THE EFFECT
FROM THE CARDS YOU DEALT YOURSELF

UNDERSTANDING WHO YOU ARE WHERE YOU WANT TO BE
OPENS UP EACH DAY
TO BE HAPPY, TO BE FREE

FOR DEEP INSIDE EACH ONE
THERE IS A LOVELY LITTLE SPARK
THAT GROWS AND GROWS TO LOVE
THE CREATION OF THE HEART

INSIGHT LEADS TO LOVE

THE SORROW OF SEEING ANOTHER SOUL
FEELING ISOLATED, LONELY AND UNLOVED.
OF NOT KNOWING TO ACCEPT
THE LEARNING, THAT INSIGHT LEADS TO LOVE.
LIFE THE EXPERIENCE,
THE JOURNEY TO BE WHOLE.
OPENS MANY DOORS
WHERE WE ARE GIVEN A DIFFERENT ROLE.

BEING TRUE TO SELF
THE MEETING OF OUR INNER NEEDS
BRINGS OUT OUR UNIQUENESS
AS WE PLANT OUR LITTLE SEEDS
SEEDS THAT GIVE CONFIDENCE
THE COURAGE TO WALK THE PATH
WITH ENLIGHTENMENT THEY BLOSSOM
THE INNER GIFT THAT LASTS.

LOVE IS THERE FOR EACH TO CLAIM
IT'S BEAUTY TO UNFOLD.
OUR DESPERATE REACTIONS TO CIRCUMSTANCES
FOR WE OFTEN WILL NOT BE TOLD.
LOOKING TO OTHERS WITH EXPECTATION
TO MEET OUR NEEDS
IS BUILDING LIMITATIONS
FOR YES! WE CAN BE FREE!

FOR TRUE LOVE HAS NO BOUNDARIES,
LACK, FEAR OR DOUBTS.
SUPPORT YOUR INNER CHILD
THAT IS WHAT LIFE IS ABOUT.
WHEN YOU KNOW YOU HAVE TRIED
AND REALLY DONE YOUR BEST
YOU CAN LOVE YOUR SELF
FOR THERE REALLY IS NO TEST.

THE JOURNEY OF THE HEART
SHOULD BE HAPPY, FULL OF JOY.
LIVING IN THE MOMENT
LIKE A CHILD WITH A NEW TOY.
SO WHEN YOUR HEART IS HEAVY
LET GO AND TRUST.
LET YOUR SADNESS PASS AS LAUGHTER, JOY AND SUNSHINE
LIFT YOU OUT OF THE DUST.

My secret garden

What will I plant in my garden
Beginning with a seed.
Perhaps I should prepare the soil
By removing all the weeds.

Others may not see them
The vines that hold tight
Of fears and pains that bind me
Away from others sight.

My heart feels soft and tender
It begins to open wide
The love is there to flower,
I see a seed inside.
The faith of god is mine in love
When I let the voices pass.
That constant negative chattering,
A pattern to end at last.

Looking at your thoughts
That cast seeds of pain to grow.
Pity, anger, greed:
Things we all know.
Identify the weeds
You have sown in your garden.
Decide not to feed them
For all is forgiven, there is a pardon.

For love the perfect energy
Of god and grace above.
Sits ever at your table
To fill it full of love.
Open up your heart
Acknowledge the seed of love within.
For the love of god holds us
As we face this world we are in.

LIFE'S CELEBRATION

WE ARE PART OF EVERYONE WE MEET
ON LIFE'S JOURNEY ALONG THE WAY.
WITH SOME WE SHARE A LIFE TIME.
WHILE WITH OTHERS JUST A DAY.

THE YEARS THEY PASS,
THE JOY THAT HAS BEEN.
LIFE'S VISION APPARENT
WITH THE GREATEST BEAUTY SEEN.

WITH THANKS IN MY HEART
FOR THE JOURNEY TAKEN
EACH DAY GIVES GROWTH
AS I FULLY AWAKEN.

LOVE EVER VITAL
THE EARTH'S GREATEST LIFE FORCE
IS AROUND ME EACH DAY
FOR LIFE TO TAKE IT'S COURSE.

STRENGTH IN THE YEARS
WITH JOY IN MY HEART
THANKYOU FOR LIFE
ONE IS NEVER APART.

THE COURAGE TO TRY

Time to make a start
Decide what you want to do.
Do not look backward
Let your efforts take you through.

For deep within your heart
Is the essence that is you.
Your journey starts from new perspective
With a clear sparkling, a beautiful view.

That love is finally out
With respect for yourself.
All the years of worry
Have deprived you of your wealth.

The little child within
Is excited on the stage.
Come on you can do it,
Write your first page.

It is safe to say goodbye

Others wait for you
They hold you at their heart.
They left this world before you,
But have never been apart.

For each of us will travel
To dimensions still not seen.
Their beauty is the finest,
The best there has ever been.

More exciting than a toy shop
For a little child.
Just picture the colours of creation
You will be there in a while.

Let concerns and fears pass
The problems in your mind.
Open up your heart
Let your beauty unfurl, unwind.

Go to experience on with God
The totality of love.
My heart will always speak
Knowing you are safely up above.

Enjoy the day

Do I want my birthday,
What does it mean to me?
My friend has said celebrate your birthday. Recognise
here comes me!

For today marks my personal journey
When the gift of life began.
There is so much to learn,
With the years I understand.

The beauty of all nature
With the birds, the trees, the sky.
The softness of sweet music
That keeps me on a high.

So much in creation
That is there to see each day.
Yes my birthday is special.
It gave me the world to enjoy today.

THE JOURNEY OF LIFE

LEARNING COMES IN LIFE
BEHIND SO MANY DOORS.
THE JOYS, THE SORROWS
OUR LOVED ONES WE ADORE.

EACH THEIR OWN PATHWAY
FOR THE TIME THAT THEY ARE HERE.
OPPORTUNITIES TO EXPERIENCE LIFE
TO SHOW HOW MUCH WE CARE.

FAITH IS OUR STRENGTH
WHILST ON OUR JOURNEY OF LIFE.
FOR THE INDIVIDUAL HAS THEIR JOURNEY:
ALLOCATED TIME.

WHEN THOSE WE LOVE
PASS THROUGH TO THE ETERNAL LIGHT
KNOWING THAT THE GIFT OF LOVE
WILL JOIN OUR JOURNEY IN GOD'S TIME.

LET YOUR BEST FRIEND BE YOURSELF

LOVE STARTS WITH SELF
WHEN YOUR HEART IS OPEN WIDE.
KNOWING WHAT YOU WANT TO DO
IS YOUR REAL GUIDE.

THE SMALL THINGS THAT MATTER
ADD UP TO THE SPLENDOURS ON THIS EARTH.
SMILING, TALKING, TOUCHING
STRIDING ACROSS THE TURF.

SO LOVE THIS LITTLE CHILD WITHIN
STILL THE TEARS, THE FEARS OR WOES.
SET YOUR PATH OF ACTION
FOLLOW EACH STEP ALONG THE PATH UNTIL IT FLOWS.

FOR BELIEVING IN YOURSELF
WITH ENCOURAGEMENT FROM WITHIN
WILL MANIFEST YOUR DREAM TO FRUITION
GO ON, YOU CAN DO IT, BEGIN.

WHEN YOU SEE A SHADOW OF DOUBT
BETWEEN YOU AND YOUR DREAM.
PUT IN AN ATTITUDE OF CONFIDENCE
TO RAISE YOUR SELF ESTEEM.

BELIEVING IN YOURSELF AS YOU
JOURNEY THROUGH LIFE
WILL BRIGHTEN UP EACH DAY
TO WALK WITHOUT THE CONSTANT STRIFE.

SO NOW YOUR HEART DIRECTS
TO WALK TRUE TO SELF
EACH DAY THE OPPORTUNITY
YOU ARE YOUR GREATEST WEALTH.

RECOGNITION COMES

RECOGNITION COMES
KNOWING JUST WHO I AM
YES THE LORD HAS SPOKEN
FOR HE SAID "I AM THAT I AM"

SO WHAT WE THINK WE CREATE
THE CHOICE IS OURS EACH DAY
WHEN THE JOY BLOSSOMS AS NEW EACH DAY
WE FLOWER IN EVERY WAY

OBSERVING OF OUR JOYS
TO ACKNOWLEDGE THE CONNECTION FROM ABOVE
MAGNIFIES THE BEAUTY
AS WE GROW IN FORM TO LOVE

THIS DAY EACH STEP WILL BE LIGHTER
THERE WILL BE NO LOAD
FOR MY FRIENDS RECOGNITION
HAS RETURNED ME TO THE ROAD

I KNOW AND LOVE MYSELF
THE JOURNEY GIVES INNER GROWTH
RECOGNITION COMES, NOW I FEEL SAFE,
NO DESERT, AT LAST THE COAST.

FOCUS ON THE BEAUTY

FOCUS ON THE BEAUTY IN EVERYTHING YOU DO
EVEN OTHER PEOPLE WITH A DIFFERENT POINT OF VIEW
LISTENING TO OTHERS AS THEIR STORY IS TOLD
SILENCE WITHIN AS THEIR VERBAL PICTURE UNFOLDS

YOU ONLY CREATE WAVES OF RESISTANCE
WHEN YOUR MIND IS DIVIDED IN TWO
HALF LISTENING WHILE THE REPLY
IS ALREADY COMING THROUGH

BE THE BEAUTIFUL PERSON YOU ARE
REACH YOUR FULL POTENTIAL
BY FOCUSING ON THE BEAUTY
YOU WILL HOLD THE JOYS THAT ARE ESSENTIAL

ATTITUDE HAS THE POWER TO CREATE
YOUR TRUE WEALTH
LOVE ON YOUR JOURNEY ALLOWS
THE STRENGTH TO BE YOURSELF

FOR REACTION TAKES US OFF THE PATH
AMONGST THE ROCKS AND WEEDS
SO WHAT DO YOU WANT TO PLANT IN LIFE?
YOU HAVE THE CHOICE OF THE SEEDS

FOR WHEN THE DAY IS ENDED
IT IS THE BIG PICTURE THAT REALLY MATTERS
FEELING LOVE INSIDE AND AROUND YOU
WILL HALT THE CONSTANT CHATTER

LIFE IS A GIFT

OPEN THE DAY WITH YOUR HEART
TO LET THE GIFT OF LIFE BEGIN
FOR IF YOUR HEAD DICTATES
IT WILL OBLITERATE YOUR DAY BEFORE IT BEGINS

DEEP INSIDE YOUR HEART ARE THE DREAMS THAT WILL LIFT
YOU HIGHER
SO OPEN THE DOOR TO BE HAPPY
LET YOUR DREAMS TRULY INSPIRE

IF YOU WERE AT THE BUS STOP
WHERE WOULD YOU WANT TO GO?
TRY A DIFFERENT DIRECTION TO THE BEAUTY,
THERE IS MUCH TO ENJOY, TO KNOW

THE PATTERNS THAT FORM
APPEAR SAFE. THEY ARE ALL WE KNOW
WHAT A BEAUTIFUL FEELING TO EXPERIENCE NEWNESS
FOR YES WE START TO GROW

LIFE IS ABOUT LIVING
GO ON HAVE THIS DAY
EACH DAY SHOULD BE LIVED
TO YOUR POTENTIAL IN EVERY WAY

IF ALL WAS GOING WELL
WHAT WOULD YOU BE DOING?
IT IS NEVER TOO LATE
LET GO OF YOUR FEARS, TIME IS REALLY GOING!

Don't shoot the messenger

Don't shoot the messenger
By being full of doubt
Accept with joy your journey
For that is what life is about
Keep sharing love
With no thought of return
For god has promised if you serve
You will receive in return

For focusing on love to bring
In hope, faith and trust
Sews patience, courage, confidence
To rise from the dust
So dust yourself off
See the sun out today
Decide to smile and enjoy yourself
With each step along the way

Recognise the blessings
They are there every day
A smile, the bird's song
As you pass along the way
This moment doesn't last
It is forever new
With love the constant focus
You will really enjoy the view

For energies of love
Replace all our fears
Those constant companions
That can often cause the tears
Just let it go, change the moment
Let your heart open inside
The flower of love once given light
Will blossom and open wide

DEAREST DREAMS

LOVE IS IN THE AIR
SENDING FEAR OUT THE WINDOW
FOR TRUE LOVE LEAVES NO SPACE
FOR FEAR OF TOMORROW
LAUGHING IN THE SUN
SMILING IN THE RAIN
WATCHING NATURE NOURISH THIS EARTH
TO REFORM IT ALL AGAIN

TAKE EACH OTHER'S HAND
WALK GENTLY FORWARD
SHARING IN THE MOMENT
WITH SO MUCH TO EXPLORE
GROWTH INDIVIDUALLY
FOR EACH ALONG THE WAY
BEING THERE FOR EACH OTHER
TO BRIGHTEN UP THE DAY

ENCOURAGING EACH OTHER
TO TRY THINGS WHICH ARE NEW
OPENS UP THE JOYS
THIS WORLD HAS TO OFFER YOU
SO BREAK THE PATTERN TO EXPLORE
THE TREASURES YOU HAVE NOT SEEN
YOUR LIFE WILL BLOSSOM AS YOU OPEN
TO LIVE YOUR DEAREST DREAMS

Sweet song

The seeds have been sown
With care and love
That they will multiply
Throughout the years with love

Peace comes through giving
Without thought of return
Increasing with experience
As we live and learn

The world is for learning
That we may be free
The purpose for being here
Throughout eternity

There is no end
As the energy goes on
When we serve from the heart
With love our own sweet song

ON LOVES TERMS

We all look for opportunity
To demonstrate our power
Natural as breathing
Every minute throughout each hour

Mutual respect for each other
With co-operation together
Forms relationships that travel
Through rough waters, any weather

There are logical consequences
To each action that we take
Consideration should be made
To the decisions that we make

Good behaviour to belong
To contribute and co-operate
Give freedom to each one to travel
With space the open gate

Equality for the individual
For each one to live free
Gives unity of purpose
That excludes just thoughts of me

We have opportunity to guide and direct
But not to impose our will
Let love be the example to unite
The terms to be fulfilled

With encouragement there is interest
In all things new
We want to learn about them
With new opportunities to create and do
When a team moves together
With inner harmony
The sharing with each other
Will give happiness the sweetest melody

THE FIRST STEP

A JOURNEY BEGINS WITH THE FIRST STEP
NO MATTER HOW MANY MILES
WE TRAVEL THE DISTANCES BEST
WHEN WE PAUSE, REFLECT A WHILE
FOR ENJOYMENT IS THE KEY
INNER BALANCE FROM WITHIN
THAT YOU FOLLOW OUT YOUR PATH
KNOWING NOW THAT YOU WILL WIN

FOR LIFE GIVES US OUR JOURNEY
TO IDENTIFY AND MEET OUR NEEDS
THEY REQUIRE CONFIDENCE AND COURAGE
SO THEY GROW LIKE LITTLE SEEDS
SO IF YOU FEEL CONFUSED
HALT FOR A WHILE
TAKE NOTE OF ALL LIFE'S WONDERFUL JOYS
TO BRING BACK YOUR SMILE

THE NEWNESS OF THE DAY
IS OPEN FOR NEW BEGINNINGS
LIVE FOR THIS MOMENT
WITHOUT FEAR OR MISGIVINGS
ACTION IS THE KEY
FOR LETTING GO OF DOUBT
RELEASING THE THOUGHTS OF WORRY
YES! THAT IS WHAT LIFE IS ABOUT

POETRY IN MOTION

THE ENERGY OF GOD
IS BEAUTIFUL TO FEEL
MANIFESTED THROUGH THE INDIVIDUAL
ALLOWS IT TO BE REAL

FEELING THE LOVE
AS IT RADIATES THE AIR
GIVING OF THIS POSITIVE FORCE
FOR ALL OF US TO SHARE

FOR WE COME FROM GOD
RETURN TO GOD
OUR ETERNAL FLAME GROWS
EXPANDING AS A SPROUT BURSTING FROM A POD

RELEASING OF THE PAST
THAT ISN'T TRULY REAL
FOR NOW OUR EYES ARE OPEN
AT LAST WE LIVE, WE FEEL

FOR THIS LITTLE CHILD
HAS EYES THAT HAVE OPENED
THE PAIN RELEASED AT LAST
FOR THE INNER VOICE HAS SPOKEN

FREE WILL FOR EACH ALONG THE ROAD
WITH MANY PATHS TO CHOOSE
EACH EXPERIENCE FOR OUR GROWTH
ENSURES WE NEVER LOOSE

SO CLEANSE YOURSELF
LET THE PAINFUL MEMORIES GO
THE ENERGY OF LOVE
THIS CALMNESS SUPPORTS YOUR INNER GLOW

GOD BLESS THE CHILD WITHIN

ALL THESE YEARS OF SEARCHING
NOT KNOWING WHAT TO FIND
AT LAST THE FLOWER BLOSSOMS
IT IS NOT INSIDE MY MIND
FOR DEEP WITHIN MY HEART
GOD'S LOVE HAS HELD ME STRONG
THIS BOUNTY HAS ALWAYS BEEN THERE
AND TAKEN ME ALONG

NOW THE VIEW HAS CLEARED
TO LET ME SEE INSIDE
LIFE WILL BE FOR THE MOMENT
WITH A JOYFUL RIDE
RELEASING OF THE BURDENS
THAT SIT INSIDE MY MIND
TO WALK STRONGLY FORWARD
WITH ACTION AT THE TIME

FOR NOW WITHIN THIS CHILD
I SEE THAT I AM LOVED
A CHILD TO FULFIL THE GIFT
THE MAGIC FROM ABOVE
THE LOVE FROM OTHERS AND THE
LOVE OF OBSERVING SELF
HAS GIVEN ME MY FREEDOM
THIS LOVE IS MY REAL WEALTH

OPENING THE HEART

WHAT JOY! WHAT PEACE! WHAT TREASURES
TO SEE THEM FORMULATE
THERE ARE MY INNER DREAMS COMING
THANKYOU IT IS NOT TOO LATE
FOR DESTINY HAS A JOURNEY
FOR EACH AND EVERYONE
DESTINY GIVES THE OPPORTUNITY
FOR RELEASING FEARS TO OVERCOME
WHEN WE STOP AGITATING
OVER SILLY INCONSEQUENTIAL THINGS
THEN THE GATES OPEN
FOR OUR DREAMS TO REALLY SING

ACCEPTING WE CAN HAVE OUR
DREAMS AND SEE THEM BECOME REAL
GIVES MAGIC TO THE MOMENT
WE ARE ALIVE, AT LAST WE FEEL
THIS IS WHAT IT IS ALL ABOUT
HOW WE SHOULD BE
LIFE IS FOR THE LIVING
FOR NOW TO ETERNITY
THANKYOU FOR THE BLESSING
THAT HAS COME MY WAY
AT LAST MY HEART IS HAPPY
I AM LISTENING; NOW MY HEART HAS THE SAY

TURNING HURTS AND PAIN TO GLORY

LESSONS COME IN DIFFERENT FORMS
TO TEST OUR FAITH ON THE WAY
COURAGE IS THE HEART TO TRY
TO DEAL WITH LOVE EVERY DAY
FOR OTHERS MAY APPEAR TO HURT
OR CUT OFF OUR SUPPLY
LOOK CAREFULLY FOR THE NEW DIRECTION
FOR DESTINY IS ON HIGH

STAYING ON THE ROAD
WHEN THE HEART IS FILLED WITH LEAD
GIVES ONE THE FEELING
THEY WOULD BE BETTER TO STAY IN BED
SO NOURISH YOUR BODY AND MIND
WITH LOVE, NOT ADORATION
USE THE TALENTS THAT YOU HAVE
YOU ARE AN INDIVIDUAL, YOUR CREATION

ACKNOWLEDGE THE GIFTS YOU HAVE
RECEIVED ALONG THE WAY
USE THESE STRENGTHS
TO ACCOMPANY YOU EACH DAY
BY BEING TRUE TO YOURSELF
WRITING YOUR OWN STORY
FREE FROM CONDITIONING
WITH LOVE IN ALL ITS GLORY

THE PATH OF THE HEART

The path of the heart sings
As the journey is under taken
No fears or pains are there
For joy is in the heart
The new day has begun
For yonder comes the day
With the rising of the sun

The journey isn't desire
With thoughts of grandeur and recognition
The journey is the joy we feel
While travelling of our own volition
Trusting in our heart
With faith, confidence and trust
Knowing our direction can change
If we decide we must

For life is the experience
To follow out our dreams
It should travel freely
Like the flowing of a stream
So if the journey's painful
And feels all up hill
Take the time to stop;
Be very, very, still

THE JOURNEY EVER ONWARD

WHAT MOTIVATES AND ENCOURAGES US
TO FOLLOW UP THE DAY
KEEPS US TRYING
THOUGH THE ROAD IS TWISTING ALL THE WAY
IT IS WHEN A WINDOW OPENS
THE LIGHT OF FAITH COMES
THAT ENCOURAGES US TO ENJOY
OUR LIFE EXPERIENCE FROM WITHIN

FOR LIFE THE EARTH EXPERIENCE
FOR REFINING OF OUR NEEDS
GIVES OPPORTUNITY FOR GROWTH
FROM ALL THE LITTLE SEEDS
THE SEEDS OF PATIENCE, CARING, COURAGE
THAT WE LEARN ALONG THE WAY
RELEASING OF THE WEEDS OF ANGER,
FEAR AND DOUBT FOR THEY MUST NOT STAY

LIVING THE EXPERIENCE TO FINALLY
LEARN TO BE IN TOUCH
WITH THE REALITIES OF ENERGY
WHICH GIVE US ALL SO MUCH
WHEN WE ARE OUT OF FOCUS
ATTRACTING CLOUDS TO BLOCK OUR VISION
REMEMBER I BELIEVE IN YOU
FOR YOU TRAVEL ON A MISSION

THE COURAGE THAT YOU SHOW
WITH YOUR CARING ATTITUDE
GIVES STRENGTH ON THE JOURNEY
WETHER LOW OR HIGH ALTITUDE
SO RECOGNISE WHERE YOU ARE
AS YOU CONTINUE UPWARD
ENERGIES OF LIGHT YOUR COMPANION
THE JOURNEY EVER ONWARD

THE COURAGE THAT YOU SHOW
WITH YOUR CARING ATTITUDE
GIVES STRENGTH ON THE JOURNEY
WETHER LOW OR HIGH ALTITUDE
SO RECOGNISE WHERE YOU ARE
AS YOU CONTINUE UPWARD
ENERGIES OF LIGHT YOUR COMPANION
THE JOURNEY EVER ONWARD

BIRTHRIGHT

THE RIGHT OF THE INDIVIDUAL
FROM CREATION OF THE SOUL
TO FOLLOW OUT THEIR PATH
FOR COMPLETENESS TO BE WHOLE
FOR DEEP INSIDE THEIR HEART
THEY ARE TOTAL BLISS THAT'S LOVE
REACTIONS TAKE THEM OFF THE PATH
WITHOUT FOCUS ON THE DIMENSIONS ABOVE

LITTLE EXPERIENCES
ADD GROWTH ALONG THE WAY
NO MATTER WHERE WE JOURNEY
OUR GUIDE SAYS THAT'S OK
FOR WE CAN DO NO WRONG
AS WE JOURNEY DOWN OUR PATH
REALISING LIFE'S EXPERIENCES
DO NOT REALLY LAST

FOR LIFE IS FOR THE MOMENT
TO FEEL SEE AND DO
KNOWING THAT EACH PERSON
MAY HAVE A DIFFERENT POINT OF VIEW
SO GENTLY LOVE THE CHILD
THAT IS DEEP INSIDE OF YOU
LOVING EVERY MOMENT
AS GOD STRENGTHENS YOUR FAITH
TO YOURSELF YOU WILL BE TRUE

SO LIGHTEN UP YOUR STEP
CHANGE DIRECTION IF YOU MUST
FOR ALL PATHS LEAD TO GROWTH
WHEN YOUR HEART IS FULL OF TRUST
THE SUN WILL RISE TOMORROW
TO START A WHOLE NEW DAY
GO ON AND ENJOY IT
FOR IT IS THE ONLY WAY

START TO SOW WHAT YOU WANT

DESTINY IS IN THE SEEDS
THAT YOU CHOOSE TO SOW
FREE WILL IS THE DECISION
TO REALISE WHAT YOU KNOW
FOR ACTIONS RETURN TO COME
BACK WHERE THEY START
WOULD YOU WANT THIS THOUGHT
TO COME BACK TO YOUR HEART

SO SEND OUT THE SMILES
ADOPT A POSITIVE POINT OF VIEW
CARING FOR OTHERS
AS IF THEY WERE YOU
SHARING YOUR GIFTS
FOR THEM TO MULTIPLY
THAT YOU FEEL LIGHT IN THE HEART
AS IF YOU ARE IN THE SKY

FOR DESTINY HOLDS THE FUTURE
FOR THE JOYS AND SORROWS THAT WE SOW
SHOULDN'T WE BE FULL OF FAITH
REALLY HAVE A GO!
SUPPORTED BY OUR THOUGHTS AND ACTIONS
TO SHOW WE REALLY CARE
BRINGING IN ALL OUR COLOURS
TO CROWN OUR GLORY WHILE WE ARE HERE

REALISING THAT OTHERS OFFER SEEDS OF WISDOM
FOR US TO EMPLOY
AN ENERGY OF THEIR LOVE
A GIFT INSIDE OF US TO ENJOY

WE ALL SOW IDEAS
THAT OTHERS MAY TAKE ON
HOW WONDERFUL THIS GIFT OF LOVE
WHEN GIVEN ITS HIGHEST SONG

THE FRONT OF THE QUEUE

Toss the key away
Let your heart fly free
Adventure is the key word
For it is a time for me

Giving all to others
With feelings from the heart
At last I see the picture
For joys to really start

For at the end of the line
Is a little child that is me
Thankyou for the strength
To heal that little girl that is me

For deep within her heart
Are the songs that are yet to ring
Little joys and treasures
To make her heart sing

Each day will be a pleasure
As I make her dreams come true
Yes, thankyou for the message
Bring her to the front of the que

Time will open wide
The door of her heart
Releasing fears to focus
On courage is the part

So gently encourage this child
With love, confidence and faith
At last the journey has shown my centre
Yes! My place

ENJOY THE EXPERIENCE

DECIDE TO ENJOY THE EXPERIENCE
THAT WILL LET THE ENERGY GO
THE POWER PERCEIVED WILL RELEASE
TO PUT YOUR LIFE IN FLOW

MOVING WITH THE TIDE
INSTEAD OF FIGHTING AGAINST THE WAVES
WILL OPEN UP YOUR LIFE
FOR HAPPIER CARING DAYS

FOR DEEP WITHIN YOUR ASSUMPTION
THAT LIFE IS VERY CRUEL
IT IS YOUR ACCEPTANCE
THAT YOUR JOYS ARE VERY SMALL

SO FOCUS ON THE MOMENT
THAT NOTHING EVER LASTS
ALREADY THIS MOMENT IS OVER
YES, IT IS THE PAST

RECLAIMING OF THAT TIME
PREVENTS THE JOYS OF NOW
SO SET THE SCENE, IT IS POSSIBLE
COME FORWARD TO TAKE A BOW

FOR YOU ARE OUT THERE ON THE STAGE
ONE OF MANY SCENES
WOULDN'T YOU DO IT A DIFFERENT WAY
TO BRING IN YOUR OWN DREAMS?

SO LOOK TO YOUR DREAMS
AS SOMETHING FRESH AND NEW
NOW YOU CAN SEE IT
FROM A DIFFERENT POINT OF VIEW

GONE IS THE INDECISION
CONNECTED WITH THE PAST
RELEASING OF THE TIME OF DOUBTS
WHEN YOU WONDERED IF IT WOULD LAST

START YOUR DREAM AND LIVE THE MOMENT
FEEL THAT YOU ARE FREE
AT LAST THIS WONDERFUL PEACE
MY ACTIONS ARE REALLY ME

A CHILD OF FREEDOM
WITHOUT CONDITIONING OF THE PAST
FREE IN THE MOMENT
NOT WONDERING IF IT WILL LAST

FOR TIMELESS IS THE MOMENT
THAT'S FILLED ME FULL OF GRACE
FREEDOM JUST IN BEING
WITHOUT A FEEL OF PACE

FEELING ONE WITH THE WORLD
WITH NO BOUNDARIES AROUND
FEELING CONNECTED WITH MY VISION
STILLNESS: YES NO SOUND

Life isn't a risk life is an opportunity

When we try our heart centre opens
We seek for another door
What inner depths of knowledge
Beckon when we start to explore

For nature is the beauty
That softly offers more
The birds, the flowers and the trees
That we do adore

Those little inspirations
That keep our light aglow
As we reap in the bounty
For our inner worth to grow

Where love of life is the key
Softens us within
Listen for the message
That helps us to begin

For faith on the journey
Is our real strength
Confidence in our progress
To handle each event

Ever-stronger forward
For the opportunity is there
Thank you for this day to learn
Acknowledge the learning that is here

It isn't a risk to try
The purpose or our soul
Come on we can do it
The wish to arrive, be whole

EACH POEM IS A MEDITATION FOR YOU TO GROW IN LOVE ON THE JOURNEY TO FREEDOM.
ENJOY THE PROCESS. YOU CHOSE THIS OPPORTUNITY.

MAY YOU CONTINUE TO WALK THE PATH, REALISING THAT NOW YOU UNDERSTAND YOU
WILL NOT GIVE UP AND ENJOY EACH OPPORTUNITY FOR FURTHER GROWTH.

FAREWELL AND LOVE FROM THE AUTHOR TERESA ALEXANDER

FAREWELL AS IN "FARE THEE WELL" AN EXPRESSION FROM SCOTLAND.

DEDICATED

THE AUTHOR DEDICATES THIS GIFT OF LOVE TO WORK TOWARDS THE PEACE IN THE WORLD. TO ALL THAT SHARE AND MEDITATE ON THE WORDS WITHIN EACH POEM. THE MAJORITY WERE COMPLETED IN 1985 FOR MEDITATION AND SENT TO FRIENDS. TERESA, IS A PROFESSIONAL COUNSELLOR AND SAYS EVEN FROM VERY YOUNG SHE COULD FEEL THE NEED IN OTHERS AND TO RESPOND WITH HELP AND SUPPORT. THE POEMS EXPRESSING JOY, LAUGHTER PAIN SHARING AND LOVE ENCOURAGE INDIVIDUALS TO FOLLOW THEIR HEART WITH STRONG ACTION INSTEAD OF LIVING WITH REACTION AND LOW SELF ESTEEM.

THANK YOU FOR SHARING.